Flowers in Salt

D0980611

Sharon L. Sievers

FLOWERS IN SALT

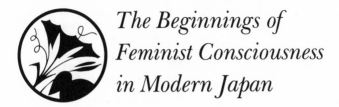

*The Beginnings of
Feminist Consciousness
in Modern Japan*

STANFORD UNIVERSITY PRESS
Stanford, California

Stanford University Press
Stanford, California
© 1983 by the Board of Trustees of the
Leland Stanford Junior University
Printed in the United States of America
Cloth ISBN 0-8047-1165-8
Paper ISBN 0-8047-1382-0

Original printing 1983
Last figure below indicates year of this printing:
95   94   93   92   91   90   89   88   87   86

For MURATA SHIZUKO, GERDA LERNER,
*and all the women whose work has brought us closer
to the realization of a common language*

Acknowledgments

In the early, discouraging days of my research on the history of Meiji women, I began reading Murata Shizuko and Gerda Lerner together. It was a good thing to do, and in the end, I think the one convinced me that I *could* do the work, the other that I *should* do it. Since then I have accumulated a rather large intellectual debt to a number of people, but I continue to be impressed by the perceptions and commitments of these two women, who do women's history so well.

I am also in the debt of a number of people and institutions for their help. The Japan Foundation, through a 1977–78 grant in Tokyo, made it possible for me to do a major part of the research for this book, and the Foundation staff, particularly Nogami Kazuko, was extremely helpful. Morisaki Fuji of the National Diet Library, and the staff members of Tokyo University's Meiji Newspaper and Periodical Library gave me a great deal of assistance and good advice during the course of my research. Murata (Yamaguchi) Shizuko, Tsurumi Kazuko, and the late, remarkable Ichikawa Fusae were generous enough to find time in busy schedules to talk with me about Meiji women, and I learned a great deal in those conversations. In both Japan and the United States, Hanawa Yukiko's assistance with this research and her friendly criticism of my work have been extremely valuable to me.

I would like to thank Tazuko Inui for checking translations and Eiko Fujii Harvey for helping me sort through some of the early translating and research involving the Women's Reform Society. My thanks also to Kondo Magara, Yosano Hikari, and Kishida Yoshikazu for permission to use photographs that appear in this volume and to Hanawa Tomoko, Makino Kikuo of Mainichi Press, Ichijima Toshio of Heibonsha, and Ide Fumiko for assistance in gathering them; to *Signs* for permission to include some of the material in "Feminist Criticism in Japanese Politics in the 1880's: The Experience of Kishida Toshiko," in Chapter Three; and to *Hitotsubashi Journal of Social Studies* for permission to use Tsuzuki Chushichi's translation of an Ōsugi Sakae poem in Chapter Six.

Barbara Mnookin of Stanford University Press has done an unusually perceptive and skillful job of editing this manuscript, and has been good to work with. J. G. Bell was very helpful in shepherding the work through its initial stages.

Though it is impossible to make explicit the enormous debt I owe to women's studies scholars in Japan and the United States, I would like to thank friends and colleagues whose encouragement and criticism has been sustaining— among them Chris Iwanaga, Sondra Hale, Sherna Gluck, Lloyd Inui, Sharlie Ushioda, Laurie Welch, Maylene Wong, and the notorious Tsuchiya-tachi.

Finally, I would like to express my long-standing admiration and appreciation for the work of Emiko Moffitt, Deputy Curator of the East Asian Collection at the Hoover Institution. I am just one of many beneficiaries of Emiko's ability to find a place in the budget for important materials on women, and her constant encouragement of research on Japan.

S.L.S.

Contents

Eight pages of photographs follow p. 66

Introduction

On a rainy evening in 1883, twenty-year-old Kishida Toshiko rose to address a political gathering in a small
town in central Japan. Her message was straightforward
and simple. Daughters, she told the crowd, were like
flowers; they needed rich and unencumbered environ-
ments to develop their full potential. Young women, she
said, were now needed to face challenges too large to be
faced by men alone; old barriers and conventions must no
longer be permitted to stifle women's minds and voices.
Flowers could not grow in salt.

Kishida's vision of a future that included women and
their priorities, a vision shared by many of her contemporaries, was not welcomed by the new Meiji state. Partly as
a consequence of that, Kishida and other women were
forced to struggle not only against the perpetuation of
old barriers, but against their reinforcement in a modernizing Japan.

That Japanese women were oppressed in the Meiji period and after, and share with women elsewhere the difficulty of claiming continuities that carry identity and
power, is indisputable. But it is not enough to recognize
oppression. The stories of many women who refused to be
victimized by that oppression, and who struggled against

it, need to be told. The lives of ordinary, "extraordinary" women, whose priorities were their own, and who saw Japanese society from perspectives that should be important, not just to social but to intellectual and economic historians, need to be described.

Japanese women have begun to reclaim their own past, and in the process have picked up many of the challenges implicit in women's history. The pioneering efforts of historians like Murata Shizuko and Takamure Itsue in the 1950's and 1960's have been followed by an impressive amount of new scholarship in recent years. Japanese women have moved quickly from the "compensatory" and "contributory" stages that seem to mark the progress of women's history everywhere, to new questions and priorities in their research on women.

Western scholarship, however, appears to be only vaguely aware of this important work, and though the number of Western scholars interested in the history of Japanese women is growing, it will take a long time for us to catch up with current research on women. Monographs and general studies of Japanese women and their experience are needed, not simply to round out our picture of Japanese history, but to revise it as well. This work, for example, suggests that, far from being ignored, women as a group were an important focus of state policy throughout the Meiji period; that when young women going to the mills described their work as the counterpart to their brothers' military service, they were telling us more about the reality of Meiji than many volumes have since; and that the state's easy intrusion into the private lives of women should push our estimate of the Meiji government's blurring of public and private back several years. The efforts of women and women's groups to oppose these policies should be included in standard historical treatments of Japan; anything less is the acceptance of a stereotype for women that we rejected for men at the outset.

This book attempts to trace the development of feminist consciousness in the Meiji period. What the women in this volume have in common is a feminist agenda flowing from their life experiences and enunciated in programs developed slowly, sometimes painfully, in the face of great opposition. Many of them were contemporaries, though not all knew each other. They had, for the most part, much more in common than they ever knew.

Whether choosing Meiji's more outspoken critics, as I have done, has simplified the task of separating Japanese feminism from intricate layers of social and cultural context is a question that can only be answered by further research. But it is only fair to note at the outset that the women who were the community and institution builders of the period—Tsuda Umeko, Hatoyama Haruko, Hani Motoko, Shimizu Toyoko, and Yoshioka Yayoi, the great educators of Meiji and Taishō—are barely mentioned here. This is true also of many of the writers and artists identified with Meiji, though some of them were certainly feminists. The choices I have made in this introductory study—to include Kanno Suga, for example, rather than Shimizu, who might be thought more representative— were based on several concerns, not the least of which was a desire to show the unity of Meiji experience for women through its diversity. Occasionally, in the case of a famous (or "infamous") woman like Kanno, the choice was also based on a desire to find new views in old evidence, something women's history is obligated to do.

I think it will be clear to anyone who reads this work that it is introductory—intended not to catalogue the complete history of Meiji women, but to clarify it in outline; not to answer all of the questions raised by their experience, but to suggest important areas for research. It will, I hope, be helpful to students of comparative women's history and encouraging to those interested in pursuing research on Japanese women. I will be gratified if it moves us a little nearer the time when the experience of Japanese women becomes a routine part of the growing international dialogue on women in the modern period.

Flowers in Salt

The central question raised by women's history is: what would history be like if it were seen through the eyes of women and ordered by values they define?

Gerda Lerner

1. *Impressions, 1860*

 In this country women are usually revered. When a man enters the room, he greets women first if there are women present, and men afterward. Also a man takes off his hat when he greets a woman, whereas he does not do so in greeting a man. If a man meets a woman in the street, he steps aside and lets her pass first. The way women are treated here is like the way parents are treated in our country.

Yanagawa Masakiyo,
attendant to the chief envoy, 1860

The deference accorded to American women was obviously inexplicable to the Japanese samurai who traveled with their country's first mission to the United States in 1860. On what grounds would men treat ordinary women, particularly wives and daughters, with the respect reserved for parents in Japan? Could a society whose women danced about in public (as they had when San Francisco's city fathers staged a ball in honor of their Japanese guests) have a sound moral basis?

At home the Japanese aristocracy, to which most of the mission members belonged, applied stern Confucian rules to its women in the interest of preserving "public morality." Husbands and wives were rarely, if ever, seen together in a public setting; women, after the age of seven, rarely associated with males to whom they were not related. All women in Japanese society knew the importance of place, which among other things required that one be outwardly deferential and submissive to men in every social situation. Never could a Japanese woman behave as President Buchanan's niece Lane apparently did when she presided over a White House dinner in honor of the envoys. For the mission's vice-minister, Muragaki Norimasa, she typified the American woman who did not know her place: "Lane was behaving like the head of the house, supervising everything during the dinner. Her power and dignity were so impressive that she might have been taken for the Queen, and her uncle, the President, for her Prime Minister."[1]

Most of the members of the 1860 mission left the United States confused and critical of the place American women seemed to occupy in the society. Though they recognized that American women were less shy and more strong-willed than Japanese women, and that some were in fact "intelligent, high-spirited and faithful,"[2] no Japanese in 1860 suggested that Japan had something to gain by "elevating" the status of women after the American model. Except for extraordinary men like Fukuzawa Yukichi and Nakamura Masanao, who were to make their experiences outside the country in the 1860's a part of a Westernizing reform effort after 1868, there was little interest in explaining the differences between Japanese and American women in terms of larger differences between the two societies.*

To the extent that the men of the 1860 mission thought about it at all, they assumed that the power American women enjoyed was diffuse and of long standing. It took time for Japanese students of American and European home life to appreciate the fact that the power of the women they met there was limited, and based on a relatively new set of virtues assigned to the "true woman"—

* Fukuzawa Yukichi (1835–1901) was a young student who traveled with the mission in 1860 and who was to become one of Japan's great popularizers of Western customs and ideas. His *Seiyō jijō* (Conditions in the West) was one of the best-selling books of the era. Nakamura Masanao (1832–91), a late-Tokugawa Confucian who converted to Christianity after travel and study in Europe, was one of Japan's early thoughtful students of the differences between Japan and the Western world. Both were to express unorthodox views on the status of Japanese women in the Meiji period.

piety, purity, and domesticity—as well as the social values that produced the ladies-first manners of the Victorian era.[3]

The "true woman" in American society, or the "better half" of a European marriage, was a woman who had, at cost, regained some of the power within the family that she had lost when many of the economic functions she had performed moved from home to factory. Her exercise of power in the domestic sphere was therefore based less on economic value than on her supposed moral superiority, balancing the baser nature of the male. In fact, though the "true woman" was often the arbiter of her husband's wealth and social position, her status as a lady depended on the leisure that symbolized the class divisions among Victorian women. As a correspondent pointed out in the letters column of the *Englishwoman's Journal* in 1866, it was impossible to work and be a lady at the same time. "My opinion is that, if a woman is obliged to work (although she may be a Christian and well bred) she loses that peculiar position which the world *lady* conventionally designates."[4]

It is difficult to say precisely when astute Japanese observers began to look beyond the superficialities of nineteenth-century Western social life and the real roles that women played in it. Japanese women showed substantial interest in the implications of the "true woman's" role in the 1880's. But reform-minded male thinkers had concluded by the 1870's that women in the United States and Europe had made an important contribution to general social progress because of the power they exercised within the family. Conversely, drawing on the recent experience of the Tokugawa period,* Japan's lack of progress could

* Tokugawa (1600–1868) refers to that period in Japanese history when the Tokugawa family held the title of shōgun and used it to dominate the country politically. Meiji, or "Enlightened Rule" (1868–1912), Taishō, "Great Righteousness" (1912–26), and Shōwa, "Glorious Peace" (1926–   ) are reign names assigned by the Emperors whose lives they encompass.

be ascribed in part to the low status of women, particularly upper-class women, in their own families.

Samurai women—part of that aristocratic class representing perhaps 8 percent of the population—were considered little more than "borrowed wombs."[5] Not only did they possess less status than aristocratic women of earlier ages in Japanese history (many of whom could inherit property), they were probably more oppressed by custom than women of other social classes who were their Tokugawa contemporaries. Samurai women were obliged in this patrilineal, patrilocal aristocracy to produce a suitable male heir or to accept male heirs produced by concubines resident in the same household (or both).[6] Since the economic status of many samurai households did not match their social status by 1860, women's work in the home was economically important, but its value was not reflected in a share of domestic power. Unlike their Western counterparts, upper-class women in mid-nineteenth-century Japan claimed no "sphere" of their own and enjoyed little authority in their households. A samurai woman, for example, might or might not be the principal nurturer of her young child, but she was never a factor in decisions made about the child's education or general welfare, and she could never become—in any sense—the guardian of her children. All decisions involving children were assumed by a family hierarchy in which power was determined by sex and age. Samurai women, like women in other social classes, could be sent home or divorced for any reason, real or imagined, the husband and his family might claim.[7] Samurai women were nonpersons under Tokugawa law who could be put to death for adultery, or—in practice—any suspicion of adultery.[8]

An eighteenth-century document, *Onna Daigaku* (Greater Learning for Women), is often seen as the quintessential statement on the ideal Tokugawa woman. Though its influence outside the samurai class may have been negligible, and we cannot even be sure how literally its precepts were taken by the aristocracy for whom it was written,[9] it sheds considerable light on the Tokugawa approach to women:

> Woman has the quality of *yin* (passiveness). *Yin* is of the nature of the night and is dark. Hence, because compared to a man, she is foolish, she does not understand her obvious duties. . . . She has five blemishes in her nature. She is disobedient, inclined to anger, slanderous, envious, stupid. Of every ten women, seven or eight will have these failings. . . . In everything she must submit to her husand.[10]

"A woman," a Tokugawa Councillor of State pointed out, "has nothing to do but be obedient."[11] In Japan, as in the West, formal education and participation in public life were denied women on grounds of their inherent irrationality and their capacity for evil. Thus any "education" a Tokugawa woman did get was likely to be limited to learning to read, or to memorize, didactic Confucian literature justifying her low status or dispensing practical information about the primary function of women: childbirth.[12]

Samurai women best match the classic descriptions of what was expected of women in Tokugawa texts; they, more than farmers' or merchants' wives and daughters, were under constant scrutiny, held by their peers to the model roles assigned to them. There was, without question, much more latitude for other women in the society, partly because they were expected to contribute more directly and visibly to production in the household.[13] Women who lived on farms or in merchant households at least worked side by side with men in the family. But their status was still low, and it is unlikely that any of them could have achieved a measure of economic independence in a structure that assumed male superiority at every level, and perpetuated competition among women in each successive

family role they assumed. The family system, whether operating in samurai or peasant households, isolated women
from each other in this competition—making them enemies whose energies were constantly turned toward the
struggle with other women, rather than toward the system
that oppressed them all, irrespective of class and age.[14]

Difficult as it is to measure the effects of a work like
Greater Learning for Women or to measure the status of
ordinary peasant women against their samurai counterparts in Tokugawa society, it is possible to generalize: the
period was very much governed by the principle *danson
johi* (respect the male; despise the female). It is also clear
that this principle was constantly reinforced, particularly
in the samurai class, by the tendency to make women responsible for male sexuality—to define women largely in
terms of male perceptions of their sexuality and to pro-
scribe their legal status accordingly. Tokugawa law and
custom encouraged all classes to treat women as property,
preserving the family line (and its wealth) by insisting on
primogeniture and a system of concubinage to support
it.[15] Consequently, as merchants or peasants acquired sufficient wealth to think seriously of emulating some aspects
of samurai social organization, they paid more attention to
primogeniture, bringing concubines into their homes, and
worrying over the virtue of daughters who could become
legal wives in some prosperous merchant family. Families
might benefit from upward mobility, but the reward for
women was often a closer approximation of the samurai
model: less value attached to their productive efforts and
more control over their sexuality and reproductive roles.

From an institutional standpoint, Tokugawa Japan
could certainly be described as an "early modern" society.
It was, to a significant degree, urban. It possessed a diverse
and prosperous economy, supported by a sophisticated
commercial network of markets and communications. Po-

litical power was in the hands of a huge bureaucracy, which seems to have initiated change in spite of itself. It was, measured against other contemporary societies, a remarkable and self-contained "civilization." But its anachronisms were repressive—and ultimately dangerous to Japan's survival, so much so that it was possible to be anti-Tokugawa after Perry's initial visit in 1853 without even mentioning that repression. When anti-Tokugawa forces merged to bring down the regime that had ruled the country for nearly 250 years, they proclaimed, not a revolution, but a restoration of Imperial rule.

No one could be sure which elements of the old patriarchal system would remain. The Charter Oath, issued on April 6, 1868, called for revolutionary change, promising to "abandon the evil customs of the past." But the priorities of the new government were not clear and would only be understood as policies were enunciated in the first years of the new era. The samurai in power in 1868 were preoccupied with bringing the country under their control, simultaneously using the enormous reservoir of anti-Tokugawa sentiment available to them to bring about rapid change. And they had to begin to justify their rise to power by dealing with the West more effectively than had the Tokugawa regime, which had based its right to rule on its ability to protect the country. Symbolic of their failure were the unequal treaties signed with Western powers, which though they did not technically make Japan a colony, left the Japanese in a subordinate and extremely disadvantageous position, vulnerable to the same pressures that had already negated the past and compromised the future of Asia's great powers, India and China.

From the beginning, the Meiji leaders sought to achieve wealth and power vis-à-vis the West by encouraging social change and diverting resources to a modern military establishment. By their active encouragement of a full-scale program of Westernization, they hoped to undermine one of the arguments supporting the unequal treaty system: the Japanese were not yet sufficiently civilized to join the West on any sort of equal contractual basis. What "civilized" meant to the West could perhaps be spelled out in some quasi-legal fashion appropriate to treaty negotiations, but as some Japanese correctly perceived, the definition Westerners gave the word was often based on extremely parochial attitudes. To the extent that Japan began to look like the nineteenth-century West, it might be considered civilized. Japanese learned that looking like the West could include everything from constructing railroad and telegraph lines to abolishing the heathen practice of mixed bathing. More important, they learned that such apparently disparate issues as telegraph lines and mixed bathing might be of equal weight to Americans or Europeans measuring Japan against their own personal standards of civilization.

Consequently, it is not surprising that the record of the first few years of Meiji is checkered with official proclamations ending mixed bathing, liberating all prostitutes, demanding more fully clothed ricksha men (even in the summer heat), and of course, ending the Tokugawa ban on Christianity. This kind of change could not have been as important to the new government as solving economic problems and establishing a strong military, but it served to distinguish Japan, in the eyes of a growing number of foreigners resident there, as a willing student of Western sensibilities and habits. Discussions of the status of Japan's women in early Meiji took place in much the same context initially. It was no doubt seen as a peripheral issue, the resolution of which could be "proclaimed" and then forgotten. But of course it was never a superficial issue, and it involved a good deal more than deferring to Western sensibilities.

The question went directly to the family, cutting through the tangled web of connections to the larger society. It raised the issue of class differences in a very complicated way. And it asked whether Japan's women were to be participants in a modernizing Japan, defining their own roles and contributing to the society in new ways. Once the debate began, it never ended.

2. The Early Meiji Debate on Women

And now all the writers on Eastern civilization tell us the one insurmountable obstacle to the improvement of society in those countries is the ignorance and superstition of the women. . . . Hence the self-assertion, the antagonism, the rebellion of women, so much deplored in England and the United States, is the hope of our higher civilization.

Susan B. Anthony and Elizabeth Cady Stanton, "The Kansas Campaign, 1867"

As the new government leaders moved to amend any social condition that seemed to justify Western criticism of Japan as uncivilized, they were immediately faced with one of the favored patriarchal myths of the nineteenth-century West: that the status of women was an important measure of any society's progress toward civilization. Though the irony of such a claim was obvious to women in the West who were struggling to improve their status in "civilized" societies, the Japanese were very sensitive to the issue and its potential implications.[1] Consequently, though government leaders, most of whom were samurai, were very comfortable with a continuation of what Takamure Itsue has described as "geisha society," they were forced to enact some policies that could answer Western criticism without actually engaging Japanese women in the sweeping social change of early Meiji.[2] It was not a simple assignment. Government initiatives relating to women in the first few years of the Meiji period were both superficial and contradictory; they reveal the difficulty of proposing even limited kinds of change when image rather than substance is the motivation.

Judged by any standard, the policies that the new government adopted in its first few years were revolutionary. Centralizing the political and economic power of the country, the leaders dismantled the old four-class society and paved the way for a Western-style army by legislating their fellow samurai out of the privileged status they had held for centuries. They imposed unpopular economic burdens on the population in an attempt to maintain the country's economic integrity and independence, and began the long, capital-intensive effort to develop modern industry, in the hope of guaranteeing Japan the wealth and power necessary to survive as an independent nation in an Asia presided over by Western imperialism. Scattered among these priorities were various social policies relating to women. But these initiatives were, for the most part, reactions to outside criticism or advice; there is no indication that they were the product of a central policy envisaging the participation of Japan's women in the processes of modernization.

One of the first tests of the question of the government's intent involved the issue of education. Foreign advisers, among them the American David Murray, encouraged the Meiji leaders to include women in their plans to reform Japan's educational system.[3] In 1872 the government created the Tokyo Girls' School, which offered, for the brief period of its existence (it was closed without explanation in 1877) a demanding curriculum for the young women selected to attend.* This school, with its superior teachers and challenging curriculum, was apparently never intended to be the forerunner of a consistent government

---

* The curriculum included English, history, and biology, as well as the study of Fukuzawa Yukichi's *Conditions in the West* and other recent Japanese works. According to Hatoyama Haruko, who was a student there, everyone was disappointed by the government's decision to close the school, apparently for financial reasons. Hatoyama and others were transferred to another school, where, she reported, there were no foreign teachers, little English, and a "boring" curriculum. (*Takamure Itsue zenshū*, Tokyo, 1977, 5: 535–36.)

policy on education for women. Though the government did include girls in the compulsory education plan it put into effect in 1872—apparently actively encouraging a co-educational system—there were no attempts to promote, at the same time, the requisite changes in attitudes to get parents to pay for the education of daughters, not just sons. And the poverty of many families in early Meiji helped to guarantee much lower attendance for girls than for boys.[4]

In 1871, Kuroda Kiyotaka, then vice-commissioner for colonial affairs, suggested that the new government, which had "already reaped a valuable return" from its policy of sending young men abroad as students of Western institutions, should now educate its women by sending them to the United States.[5] The government agreed, and in the same year selected five girls ranging in age from eight to fifteen to accompany the Iwakura mission sent to renegotiate treaties with the United States and European powers. A number of the young Japanese who traveled with the mission were left behind as students in both the United States and Europe.

Young men sent abroad as students were typically given two-to-three-year assignments specifically related to government needs in such areas as transport, law, finance, trade, and industry; most of these "government students" were expected to enter government service on their return to Japan. By contrast, the girls who accompanied the Iwakura mission were given a vague charge to become "students of American home life" for a ten-year period, and when the two young women who had managed to stay in the United States for the full period returned home, no one in government seemed able to recall precisely what the purpose of their journey had been.[6] Though one of the returnees, Tsuda Umeko, was to become an important voice in higher education for Meiji women, her achievements were certainly not the result of government support or encouragement. In terms of women's education, the decision to send the five girls with the Iwakura mission had little or no impact. But it did produce some benefits in terms of Japan's image in the West, and it continued to be used in later years as a convenient example of Japan's progressive attitude toward women in speeches and articles intended for Western consumption.

Among the other issues affecting the status of Japanese women addressed by the government in the first four years of Meiji, one of the best publicized was the 1872 proclamation freeing prostitutes. Reacting to substantial foreign pressure, which began with the *Maria Luz* incident,* the Japanese government pronounced itself in opposition to slavery in all its forms, including the buying and selling of daughters into prostitution. Though these sentiments were praised by the foreign missionaries in Japan, prostitution remained very much a part of Japanese life. With this proclamation, the government canceled the contracts and outstanding debts of prostitutes to the houses they served, but it did not make prostitution illegal. And, on the issue of concubines, the government's position was already clear; in 1870 the new government had given concubines the same rights as legal wives in the family.

The decision on the legal status of concubines was especially revealing because, unlike other questions directly affecting the status of women, it was "internally generated." A similar example, one demonstrating the government's attitudes toward women and its perceptions of the kinds of roles women should play in a rapidly changing

* The *Maria Luz* was a Peruvian vessel that "recruited" men as laborers and women as prostitutes throughout Asia and then sold them wherever there was a market. Its activities were widely publicized in 1872, after one of its "passengers" escaped while the ship was docked in Yokohama. The government, by then already under pressure from Tsuda Mamichi and other Japanese reformers concerned about prostitution, found itself under even greater pressure from international sources after the incident. (Tanaka Sumiko, ed., *Josei kaihō no shisō to kōdō*, Tokyo, 1975, 1: 83–85.)

Japan, came in an arena government leaders might have been expected to avoid: women's fashions. One of the earliest (and most successful) government efforts to change traditional attitudes involved the pressures it put on the male population, particularly samurai, to forgo long hairstyles in favor of the shorter, more "practical" Western haircut. After the Emperor himself made a public appearance sporting a Western cut, there was an increasing attempt to link short hair with progressive attitudes and individual willingness to embrace drastic change for the sake of the country. In the case of samurai, for example, it signified a willingness to put aside a way of life symbolized by the sword; in its place came a Western-style military uniform and the anonymity of a Western-style conscript army—the machine now charged with defense of the country.

But as more and more Japanese men adopted short hairstyles, indicating their desire to join the country's march to progress, some women decided to join them, by bobbing their hair. An association advocating shorter and more practical hairstyles for women was organized in 1871, in support of the kinds of changes the government was advocating for the male population. The government's response to this uninvited and spontaneous development was immediate. At first it merely called for an end to the new custom of bobbed hair among women, but in 1872 it made short hair for women illegal. Even older women who for reasons of health had to wear a shorter hairstyle were required under the 1872 order to obtain a license from the Meiji government before they could have their hair cut.[7] Informally, the government explained that it favored an end to the blackened teeth and shaved eyebrows married women had adopted from an earlier age, but that hairstyles should not be changed. The Meiji Empress made a public appearance in 1873, demonstrating the correct "look": long hair, with natural-looking eyebrows and teeth. Still, the government's effort to keep Meiji women from abandoning the elaborate hairstyles symbolic of the geisha could not be enforced. Women could always cut their hair at home, and a number of women active in the struggle for women's rights did just that.[8]

The banning of short hair for women—however superficial the issue may seem—is one of the most important and revealing policies on women in the early Meiji period. To the extent that women cutting their hair can be viewed as a real, if spontaneous, attempt to join the progressive forces trying to create a new Japan, the government's denial of their right to do so was also a denial of their right to participate and contribute actively to that change. In fact, it can be seen as a symbolic message to Japan's women to become repositories of the past, rather than pioneers, with men, of some unknown future. It is the clearest example early Meiji provides of an attitude Hanna Papanek has described in societies undergoing rapid development.

In societies that are changing very rapidly, ambiguous signals are presented to women. Fears are often translated into attempts to prevent changes in their roles. They become the repositories of "traditional" values imputed to them by men in order to reduce the stresses men face. Resistance to women's greater participation in economic and political life may be felt especially strongly among groups most exposed to rapid change and ambivalent about it.[9]

Though the government's response to any participation by women in the social change sweeping the country was essentially negative, many of its actions inadvertently contributed to the beginnings of a debate about the status of women in Japan. If women were to be treated differently, where should the difference begin? What limits should there be? One of the slogans of early Meiji was *onna mo hito nari:* women are people too. It might be accepted that women were people and should be treated accordingly, but they were not men, either. What things could women be expected to do, or refuse to do, because they were women? What was the purpose of educating women? How much education was enough, and how should it differ from that of men? Would elevating women's status further Japan's progress toward some universally defined civilization, or was the primary function of such apparent change achieving leverage in treaty negotiations with the West? Since women did not directly contribute to the record we have of these early-Meiji discussions, one can argue their importance. Nonetheless, a beginning was made, and interest in these questions was underscored and reinforced by the translation of relevant sections of Herbert Spencer's *Social Statics* (1877), Sheldon Amos's *Differences of Sex* (1878), and John Stuart Mill's *On the Subjection of Women* (1879).[10]

By 1874 the discussion of women's issues was country wide; arguments were full of contradictions, and the debate itself, carried in growing numbers of newspapers and periodicals, often lapsed into silliness and superficiality. But it is clear from the statements and actions of Japanese women in the following decade that they were reading and listening to the issues in this debate with a great deal of interest.

One of the most important groups involved in the debate was the Meirokusha (Meiji Six Society), named for the year of its founding, the sixth of the Meiji era, or 1873.[11] A self-styled academy whose members represented a wide spectrum of experience and opinion, the Meiji Six thinkers are often described as classic Meiji intellectuals. They interpreted Western ideas and assisted in their adaptation, creating at the same time a new vocabulary to accommodate Western concepts, many of which were implicitly political. Though their watchword was "civilization and enlightenment," their principal concern was the survival of the nation in the face of superior Western strength. Most of the members of the Meiji Six group were influential members of Japanese society who moved in and out of government and academic life. They presented many of their ideas in public lectures, a form of communication totally foreign to Japan but appreciated by some of the Meiji Six group as an important vehicle for sharing information and opinion in the West. Though their journal, *Meiroku zasshi* (The Meiji Six Journal), which began publication in 1873, was of limited circulation and was regularly published for only a short time, it had enormous influence. Its three thousand subscribers included most of the urban press, as well as publications further removed from the cities; consequently, the issues debated in the pages of the journal were often picked up for additional comment or explanation, magnifying their impact throughout the country.[12]

Intellectuals in early Meiji were charged with the responsibility of determining and explaining the reasons for Western success, as well as defining it. It is possible to look at all of the issues raised by the Meiji Six Society from this perspective, and to view the articles presented in the journal not simply as descriptions of Western institutions and achievements, but as heatedly debated proposals that revealed substantial disagreement about which of these institutions and achievements might be appropriate for Japan. Few Meiji Six thinkers saw Western technological superiority as a historical accident, and they tried from the beginning to isolate fundamental differences in American and European societies that could account for their success. Though some intellectuals in the period continued to hope that Western technology might somehow be imported without disturbing an intrinsic Japanese spirit, many of the Meiji Six reformers had decided as early as 1873 that Western wealth and power were the products of a spirit very different from Japan's. The critical question, accordingly, was whether Japan's people could acquire habits of mind that were polar opposites of the passiveness and irrationality fostered under the Tokugawa. Not yet citizens in any real political sense, Japan's people must quickly acquire the ability to think rationally and independently. Japan's survival was contingent on the participation of the people in political and economic life to a degree unprecedented in the country's long history. For whatever reasons, vast numbers of people in the West had made important contributions to the progress of their societies; they had shared in the burdens and the success, identifying their own interests with those of the whole society. Somehow, Japan in 1873 had to find a way to develop and use the same kinds of energies, a process many believed must begin with the family.

Three men who commented often and at length on this question, in the pages of the *Meiji Six Journal* and elsewhere, had traveled and studied extensively in the West before 1873, and had heard Western criticism of the treatment of Japanese women. It was criticism with which they were in fundamental agreement. More important, they believed, as the government did not, that the low regard for women in Japan was a major contributor to its backwardness. Mori Arinori and Nakamura Masanao, both strongly influenced by Christianity, and Fukuzawa Yukichi, who was critical of its irrationality, agreed that the treatment of women in Japanese society was barbaric and inhumane. If there was to be real reform in Japanese society, it must begin with the family—and women must be at the center of change.

In 1874, Mori and Fukuzawa began an attack on that most basic element of the old family system: concubines. Mori's attack, published serially in the *Meiji Six Journal,* argued against the system on grounds that it was inhumane and immoral to continue the system in the modern period—and it invited Western derision of Japanese society. In a commentary on the human dilemma produced by the presence of concubines and legal wives in the same family, one that echoed later attacks on the family by Japanese novelists, Mori said:

> The child of a concubine is commonly made heir to the house.
> . . . The heir treats his real mother like a nurse and looks up to his father's unrelated wife as his mother. . . . To adopt a child from outside the family may not be as shameful for the wife, but for her to be forced to recognize the son of her husband's concubine as her son is indeed cruel and unjust.[13]

For Fukuzawa, the most damaging aspect of the system was its subordination of individuals in the family to an irrational social arrangement permitting the strong to tyrannize the weak. But there was also a strong sense of moral outrage in the remarks he made in his book *Gakumon no susume* (An Encouragement of Learning; 1872): "What a shame to marry a woman and call her unfilial if she does not bear a child! Even if it is only a pretext, is it not terrible? . . . To the parents of the whole country I ask: when your son marries a good wife, do you get angry at her because she does not bear a child, and do you beat your son and wish to disown him?"[14] From Fukuzawa's standpoint, the concubine system was a remnant of Chinese influence that had, in practice, turned the family into an inhumane institution where reciprocity and ethical responsibility were forgotten. Whatever its former justification, Japan should in future advocate monogamy. There was a balance in nature between males and females, and the concubine system could only be supported by men whose self-interest and self-indulgence made them less than human.

> Someone may counter that if a man supports a number of mistresses, there will be no violation of human nature if he treats them properly. This is the opinion of the man himself. . . . If . . . true, a woman should be allowed to support a number of husbands. She should be able to call them male concubines, and give them lower ranking positions in the household. . . .

By nature's decree, the number of male and female births seem about equal. . . . Accordingly, it is clearly against the law of nature when one husband has two or three wives. We should not hesitate to call such men beasts.[15]

Fukuzawa offered no legal solutions to the problems of women in the family, but seemed to feel that attitudes would change if family relationships were reevaluated on the basis of rationality and utility rather than blind obedience to custom. On this basis, he recommended that mothers-in-law, whose harsh treatment of their daughters-in-law was common and apparently customary in all classes, would do well to recall their own younger days, when they themselves were tormented as daughters-in-law.[16]

Mori Arinori was characteristically unwilling to rely on changes in attitude; he wanted men and women to be legally bound to equality in marriage. Self-consciously demonstrating his own commitment to the idea, he married Hirose Otsune in a public ceremony in 1875 that featured the signing of a marriage contract similar to the one he published in the *Meiji Six Journal* in February 1875. Article Seven of that contract provided that

once the marriage is consummated, should either party have intimate relations with a third person or should either suffer unbearable immoral treatment from the other, the [injured party] may bring suit before an official, receive a monetary settlement, and secure a divorce. The amount of the monetary settlement shall not exceed two-thirds of the property of the other party.[17]

Up to this point, Mori and Fukuzawa had done little more than point out what they considered to be the most obvious shortcomings of the family system as it related to women. Neither of them had taken the argument much beyond the suggestion that women be treated more humanely, and the concubine system be replaced by monogamy. Neither had explained what such changes might, or should, imply for Japan's future. In view of the rather limited scope of their arguments, both Mori and Fukuzawa must have been surprised to find themselves described as advocates of equal rights for men and women (*danjo dōken*). To Mori (and perhaps to Fukuzawa as well) it was something of a shock to be identified as the champion of a cause he did not believe in. To clarify the situation, Mori added a postscript to the March 1875 issue of the *Meiji Six Journal*: "I appear in the essay of Katō [Hiroyuki, a critic] and others to be a pioneer in advocating equal rights for men and women. . . . I indeed said that wives and husbands should be honored without distinction because they are on the same level. I absolutely did not touch on equal rights, however."[18]

By 1875 Fukuzawa was becoming tired of diffuse discussions of women's rights in the tenor of Katō Hiroyuki's essays in the *Meiji Six Journal,* which seemed to him to bring the debate to a new low.[19] Fukuzawa did not share Katō's concern about such issues as whether a gentleman should be required to ask permission to smoke in the presence of ladies, and in an article in March 1875 he expressed his growing irritation with the "recent noisy discussion of equal rights for men and women." If anyone found his reasoning on the issue of monogamy "too advanced," Fukuzawa said, "we shall tacitly allow him to keep concubines or take geisha."[20]

Irritated as Mori and Fukuzawa may have been by the apparent misconceptions of their views, they were now merely facing the logical contradictions of their own arguments. It was not as simple as they thought to dissociate the notion of *fūfu dōken* (equality between husbands and wives) from *danjo dōken* (equal rights for men and women). Try as they might to focus attention on the rights of women in the family without mentioning the roles they might play elsewhere, women themselves could always point—as they later did—to the opening lines of Fukuzawa's *Encouragement of Learning*: "It is said that heaven does not create one person above, or below, another."[21] The general discussion of equal rights could not be separated neatly into categories labeled "women in the home" and "women in the larger society." The challenge was to find a plausible (if not logical) argument, carefully drawn to make the distinction clear: Japanese women were not "ready" for significant social roles outside the family, but they were more than capable of assuming greater power in the family to influence and educate Japan's future generations.

Though Mori had touched on the importance of a mother having high ideals in order to "encourage her children to render great services for the promotion of culture," he did not develop the argument fully.[22] Mitsukuri Shūhei, in an interesting essay in the May 1874 issue of the journal, went a step further, not only emphasizing the role of mothers as educators, but also commenting on the need to establish girls' schools to prepare them for this role: "By actively establishing girls' schools and devoting our energies to educating girls, we may train these girls to understand how important it is for them to educate the children to whom they give birth."[23]

But it remained for Nakamura Masanao, writing in one of the last issues of the *Meiji Six Journal,* to coin the phrase that continues to enjoy a certain currency in Japan: *ryōsai kenbo,* "good wife; wise mother." In an essay entitled "Creating Good Mothers," Nakamura, who had spent considerable time in Europe, presented a classic model from the nineteenth-century West. Women, he suggested, should provide the religious and moral foundations of the home, educating their children and acting as the "better half" to their husbands. This was not simply the best thing to do in principle, but would in fact produce a stronger Japan. As Nakamura, who believed the essential ingredient in Western success was Christianity, explained: "We can then have people trained in religious and moral education as well as in the sciences and arts whose intellects are advanced, whose minds are elevated, and whose conduct is high. . . . Envying the enlightenment of Europe and America, I have a deep, irrepressible desire that later generations shall be reared by fine mothers."[24]

Though Nakamura seems to have been willing to entertain the prospect of according men and women the same kind of upbringing, "enabling them to progress equally," the burden of his argument was that women's nature best equipped them to nurture. For women, training in morals and religion must precede education in the arts and sciences. He quoted with approval the formula of the poet Robert Burns, emphasizing the overriding importance of an affectionate disposition in the ideal woman's character.[25]

The ideas Nakamura put forward in this essay did suggest significant social change. For the first time, women were to be recognized as the true guardians and educators of their children; they were now to inherit a "sphere" in which to exercise the powers to which all women seemed best suited. The Tokugawa system had bred servility and submission; Meiji women must be different. They must raise a new generation of Japanese—independent and capable of defending and managing the country. Ultimately, these ideas seemed to imply that Japanese women—after the European model—must now be broadly educated not simply to raise their children, but to be interesting conversationalists for their husbands. Though their significant social roles were limited to the home, they must be able to move outside that sphere if the occasion (as defined by their husbands) demanded it.*

Given the proximity of the Tokugawa experience, the

---

* This was especially true in the 1880's, when the wives of Japanese officials were expected to converse intelligently with foreigners at social gatherings. A number of newspaper and magazine articles written by men in this period were highly critical of the lack of appropriate social graces among Japanese women, prompting Kishida Toshiko, an early feminist, to write an article reminding male critics that "for women, socializing together, in contrast to the past practice of separating the sexes . . . is a new thing." "Women," she said, "have been educated to expect a reprimand for talking too much. . . . Consequently, men

suggestion that women should play major roles in the home, should be educated, and—within limits—should demonstrate their intelligence and competence, was revolutionary. But serious discussion of these ideas was not to be a part of the first decade of Meiji. In 1873 the government faced its first significant political challenge when a group of disgruntled samurai, including Itagaki Taisuke, left the government, contending that the current system of oligarchic rule reneged on an earlier promise to share power more widely. By 1874, a substantial political opposition was forming, calling for more representative government.

The government reacted to this crisis by attempting to curb criticism and modulate the debate over issues of social change. It passed press laws in 1873 and 1875 making editors liable for anything they published. In the fall of 1875, just months after Nakamura's essay appeared, the members of the Meiji Six Society voted to suspend publication of their journal, apparently agreeing with Fukuzawa that they should publish independently and not rely on the journal's reputation for protection from government censors.[26] And in the politically charged atmosphere of the next decade, many of the thinkers who had freely expressed opinions about the place of women in Japanese society fell silent. When Fukuzawa picked up some of Nakamura's arguments in 1885, he conveniently ignored the participation of women in the turbulent politics of the previous decade, insisting instead on the contradictory arguments he had made earlier and was to make again in 1899: women should be used to strengthen the sense of independence and resourcefulness of coming generations of Japanese, but they must not attempt to extend their power outside the home.[27]

should not talk of women's shortcomings, but concentrate instead on their own lack of sensitivity" to the changed situation. ("Danshi no chūi o nozomu," *Jogaku zasshi*, 36, Sept. 25, 1886, p. 22.)

The Meiji Six thinkers, convinced, as the government was not, that women would inevitably be central figures in social change, made a valiant attempt to raise the intellectual level of the debate over the status of women and infuse it with appropriate content. Though Katō and others used the pages of the *Meiji Six Journal* to air their irritation with the increasingly "feminized" manners of the times, Mori and Fukuzawa raised important questions about women in the family, which were expanded, though not fully developed, by Nakamura. The debate was brief, and the arguments often contradictory, but it had a significant impact on Meiji society. It exposed the none too steady foundations of some of Japan's most tenaciously held beliefs about women, and challenged the irrationality and barbarity of Tokugawa custom. Though by 1875 these apparent champions of women among the Meiji Six group were backing away from the implications of their own arguments, hoping to compartmentalize the "spheres" in which women should exercise power, some women, dissatisfied with the limits of the power they were being offered, were already pushing the arguments of the Meiji thinkers to new conclusions. The first real indication of what women thought about all of this came with the development of the popular-rights movement and the creation of Japan's first political parties. For the first time, in this new era, Japanese women began speaking for themselves, claiming public roles and demanding to be included in the struggle for change and the survival of the country.

3. Women in the Popular-Rights Movement

In the summer [of 1884], the Liberal Party decided to hold a gathering to enjoy the cool of the evening on the Asahi River. When they suggested that those of us from the women's group come along, I conferred with Takeuchi and Tsuge, advisers for the group, who agreed, and that evening we were sitting in a boat floating on the Asahi River. Party members, accompanied by musical instruments, sang songs of freedom, and even now, I am left with an indelible memory of overflowing emotion as those sad sounds floated over the water. . . .

Suddenly, a person appeared in the water looking like a sea monster, ordering the gathering suspended and the crowd dispersed. It was inconceivable that some dreadful policeman, suspicious of our entertainment on the river, would hide in the water, listening and checking on us! And now because the interest in the speeches had reached a fever pitch among those on the boats, people shouted, "Kill the *kappa!*" or "Beat him to death!" There was a kind of furious excitement, but at the words of some elderly persons in the crowd, everyone dispersed in an orderly fashion.

Fukuda Hideko, *Half My Life*

Fukuda's experience in the rough and tumble of Meiji politics was shared by other women long before 1884, as they joined a political opposition calling itself Jiyū minken undō (Movement for Freedom and Popular Rights)—a movement that presented them with an opportunity to speak to a range of current issues in their own behalf. By 1878, after having listened for a decade as Japanese men monopolized the debate over women's rights and the pace and style of Japan's modernization,[1] many women were eager to present their own views of the country's future and their potential roles in it. Once a political opposition began to develop on a nationwide basis, women used it to articulate views on issues that went far beyond demands for specific political rights.

Though some of the disgruntled samurai who left the government in 1873 prepared for armed rebellion, Itagaki Taisuke and his colleagues returned to their Shikoku base to organize economic aid societies for struggling former samurai and to establish political alternatives to government by oligarchy then operating in Japan.[2] From the beginning, the popular rights movement they founded borrowed heavily from natural-rights theory and took as its constituency the declassed samurai fighting for survival in the fluid economic situation characteristic of early Meiji. Over time, the movement spilled into small towns and villages, where idealistic former samurai circulated, informing farmers and local merchants that they should not be taxed without being politically represented. Able to combine various criticisms of the new government with the demand that power be more widely shared, popular-rights advocates were the first to put pressure on the government for a constitution and representative political institutions.

Much as they capitalized on the rhetoric of natural rights and liberal politics, the samurai leaders of the early popular-rights movement were no more interested in the political participation of women than the eighteenth-century founders of the European liberal tradition had been.[3] Though they insisted that a lack of precedent should not be a barrier to representative government in Japan, they themselves relied on precedent to deny women access to their movement. Young women who were connected with the early political movement were routinely denied admission to schools, and most leaders were openly hostile to women's rights arguments within the framework of popular rights.[4] At best, the leaders tacitly supported reforms that could indirectly improve women's status; none made a point of supporting the kinds of reforms proposed by Mori Arinori and Fukuzawa Yukichi, elevating the status of women in the family. Indeed, there is little to suggest that the attitudes toward women among these former samurai had been changed at all by their reading of natural-rights theory.[5] They seemed content with Tokugawa custom that had denied women in samurai families significant public *or* private roles.

After 1877, when the last significant military challenge to the new government was put down in Kyushu, all criticism of the oligarchy was increasingly channeled through the only vehicle left: politics. The popular-rights movement was ready to take advantage of this turn of events, though its leaders did so with a wary eye on a government they knew could now turn its full attention to its political critics. By 1878, as a result of the early success of the movement, the samurai leadership began to be supplanted by the growing participation of farmers and merchants, who were eager to expand both the social and the territorial base of the movement.[6] As a part of this initiative, women began to be thought of as a new, and potentially important, constituency. It was not a new issue. Women had demonstrated an interest in the popular-rights movement earlier, and the issue of voting rights for women who held property had been debated in several communities before 1878. Though the issue of gender, rather than property, had prevailed in most of those debates, it was clear to some of the new leaders that, by all logic, their arguments about taxation and political rights should apply to women as well as men. A delegate attending a regional prefectural meeting in Hiroshima in April 1878 made exactly that point, introducing a motion to extend voting rights at the prefectural level to all women who were property owners and taxpayers.[7] The motion failed, but it was symbolic of some of the changes in attitudes about women then occurring in the popular-rights movement.

The turning point for women came in September, only months after the Hiroshima vote, when Kusunose Kita, a forty-five-year-old householder from Shikoku, who had assumed the property and tax liability of her husband after his death in 1872, raised angry questions about the links between property, voting rights, and gender. Her well-publicized complaint to prefectural authorities was picked up by newspapers all over Japan, and she became an overnight celebrity in the nation and in the popular-rights movement. Her letter to the authorities read in part:

We women who are heads of households must respond to the demands of the government just as other ordinary heads of households, but because we are women, we do not enjoy equal rights. We have the right neither to vote for district assembly representatives nor to act as legal guarantors in matters of property, even though we hold legal instruments for that purpose. This is an enormous infringement of our rights! . . .

If it is reasonable to assume that rights and duties go together, then we should make that widely held assumption that they are in fact corresponding responsibilities a reality. . . . I do not have the right to vote. I do not have the right to act as guarantor. My rights, compared with those of male heads of households, are totally ignored. Most reprehensible of all, the only equality I share with men who are heads of their households is the onerous duty of paying taxes. . . .

Officials to whom I complained tell me that men have greater rights than women because they bear the additional burden of military service . . . but my protest stands, since it is well known that men are routinely excused from military service precisely because they are heads of their households![8]

The simple logic of Kusunose's arguments, coupled with the overwhelming sense of injustice she conveyed, had a telling impact on Ueki Emori, a leading theorist and organizer of the popular-rights movement. Her complaint sent him back to what he had read of European liberal theory, most of which, with the notable exception of John Stuart Mill's ideas, denied a public role to women. Ueki had to turn to some of the early ideas of Herbert Spencer for explicit arguments in behalf of sexual equality; he read Spencer's *Social Statics* in 1879. In the meantime, he made a point of discussing the issues with Kusunose and other women, a habit he cultivated the rest of his life.[9] In 1879 Ueki published the first of a long series of articles advocating full equality for women.[10] Though he was well in the minority in arguing for the importance of both women and commoners to the popular-rights movement, he remained a consistent and influential champion of women's rights until his death, and was a good friend of many of the women he encouraged to participate in the movement.

Minken Baasan, as Kusunose came to be known,* may have forced Ueki to deal with the principle of equality in a new way, but she did not have quite the same impact on other movement leaders, who simply saw in her notoriety a valuable drawing card for the lecture circuit—she was an oddity to be exploited. They tried to persuade her to become a public speaker, without success.[11] Though she voiced strong support for the movement and continued to be identified with it after 1878, Kusunose was never as visible a participant as the leaders would have liked. Even so, her influence was not lost on Japanese women; from 1878 to 1881 she was an important symbol of their ability to speak for themselves. Consciously or not, Kusunose had also provided a partial answer to an important question

---

* Minken Baasan can be literally translated Grandmother Popular Rights, but in context it can imply an older, perhaps unyielding woman whose attachment to her convictions is grudgingly respected, though not necessarily understood.

Japanese women would have to answer as their participation in politics grew: whether they would use, or be used by, the movement. It was a question as old as politics and as new as the experience of American women in the abolition movement.

The status of Japanese women in the 1880's was not without parallels elsewhere; those women who thought about it knew that their politics went beyond a simple demand for voting rights. Like women in other parts of the world, they were without basic legal protection in the family. Despite the changes in the divorce laws in 1873, Japanese women were at a severe disadvantage when they tried to initiate divorce proceedings. And those brave enough to try, often found that divorce meant the loss of children and economic support of any kind. The inadequacy of women's education reinforced their low status, and by the 1880's there was growing criticism of the mission schools, which had been an oasis of educational quality for women. Though they worked in and out of the home after 1868, women were always little more than appendages of a family system in which they were undervalued and by extension, underpaid. The concubine system, symbol of male power and privilege, continued—unaffected by the earlier attacks of reformers like Mori and Fukuzawa. In addition, Japanese women could rightfully claim exclusion from important roles in the nation-building effort begun in 1868. Their potential contributions to a modernizing nation eager to retain its independence and integrity had not only been ignored, but rejected by men who wanted them to remain a part of the nostalgic past.

How the changing politics of Meiji could be made to accommodate the priorities of women, and how much success they would have making connections between those priorities and national issues remained a question for the 1880's. The remarkable thing about that decade was the willingness of some Japanese women to assume totally unfamiliar roles, in an increasingly violent political setting, in order to speak to women's issues.

The sea change that was spreading through the popular-rights movement in 1878 was given added impetus by the government's promise in 1881 to institute constitutional government by 1890. That led to the organization of Japan's first recognized political parties, the most powerful of which, the Jiyū tō (Liberal Party), revealed its origins in the popular-rights efforts of the 1870's in calling for a program "to broaden liberty, protect the people's rights, promote their happiness and reform society, and to work for the creation of a sound constitutional system."[12] Public response to the Liberal Party's campaigns at first delighted the leaders as much as it worried the government. Though the oligarchy had hoped that its promise of a constitution would quiet public criticism, it found itself instead faced with increasing anti-government feeling. The demand for political speakers grew, even as the government used greater and greater force to shut down the political lecture, as it had earlier attempted to silence or dilute political journalism. After strengthening press and libel laws in 1877, the government in 1880 handed down a detailed set of regulations dealing with public meetings. Permits were required (three days in advance), and provisions were made for the police to attend such gatherings. No advertising of lectures and debates with political content was permitted, and military personnel, police, and teachers were not allowed to join political associations or attend meetings that featured political discussion. In practice, the interpretation and application of these regulations was left to the discretion of local police, who could arrest speakers, disrupt scheduled meetings, or refuse permits to those they judged disruptive of public order.

The decade of the 1880's, a deflationary period that saw widespread economic hardship, brought large numbers of desperate people into the political movement. Their anger

was a volatile force that fueled the casual violence characteristic of the politics of the 1880's, and contributed to
major "incidents" that the Meiji government viewed as incipient revolution.[13] "Lecture meetings" often ended in
violent confrontations with government authorities, and
many would-be politicians found themselves in jail or paying heavy fines. As surveillance increased, the punishments handed down to offenders became more severe,
and party organizers were hard pressed to escape the vigi-
lance of a police force that seemed to be everywhere. Political activists who spread the word disguised as peddlers
going through the countryside, and political meetings
held on barges in rivers and lakes reflected the political
atmosphere of the early 1880's.[14] To some degree this violence made the political world an even more masculine
arena than it had been; it certainly did not seem an appropriate place for a woman.[15]

And yet it was. In the final months of 1881, a sixteen-
year-old-woman from Kyushu rose to address a political
gathering on the subject of women's rights, and by April
1882, another young woman, Kishida Toshiko, was ready
to publicize the agenda Japanese women brought to the
popular-rights movement.[16] Just twenty when she won
over an Osaka political meeting with a speech entitled
"The Way for Women," Kishida was welcomed by popular-rights leaders, delighted that they had finally found an
attraction for the lecture circuit who was as good looking
as she was respectable. Precisely what kind of crowds they
thought she would draw is not clear, but after speaking on
women's issues in the Osaka area during the month of
April, Kishida began a grueling two-month tour that took
her to various parts of southern Japan, including Kyushu,
during May and June.[17] She drew standing-room only
crowds, made up chiefly of women, everywhere she went,
and attracted a good deal of national attention.

At first glance, Kishida seems an unlikely spokeswoman

for women's rights, since part of the aura of "respectability" surrounding her stemmed from a two-year tenure as a lady-in-waiting and literary tutor to the Meiji Empress. But that experience, coupled with a close relationship with her mother as she grew up in a well-established merchant household in Kyoto, made her an excellent choice to speak to women's issues in 1882. She was bright, well educated, empathetic, articulate, and angry.

Toshiko's mother, Taka, had encouraged her eldest daughter's intellectual growth, filling in the gaps in her daughter's education with reading and discussion of her own.[18] She had also helped Toshiko evade the stifling restrictions common to young women of well-to-do families in the Kyoto-Osaka area, where *hako iri musume* (daughters confined in boxes) was more than just a colorful phrase.* In time Toshiko's reputation for intelligence and good looks brought her to the attention of influential people, who recommended her to the Meiji Court. The first commoner, it is said, who was ever extended such an invitation, she stayed in the Empress's service barely two years, excusing herself from further duties in 1881.[19]

Though Kishida said that she was ill, and may have been, she was clearly not happy at Court. Living in what she described as "an enchanted land, far from the real world, filled with a sense of *ennui* and beautiful women," Kishida felt anguish and outrage when she read newspaper accounts of the outside world, where people were "unable to live peacefully and without suffering."[20] The Court, moreover, was symbolic of the concubine system,

---

* The Osaka-Kyoto area was particularly well known for its custom of protecting marriageable daughters by refusing to allow them out of the house without close supervision and, in some cases, keeping them carefully locked in the house at night. The "boxes" in which daughters were confined could be intellectually as well as physically stifling; Yosano Akiko, later to become one of Japan's leading 20th-century poets, circumvented the intellectual restrictions in her household by reading in her father's library. See Yosano Akiko, *Tangled Hair*, tr. Sanford Goldstein and Seishi Shinoda (Lafayette, Ind., 1971), pp. 6–7.

which Kishida felt was an outrage to women. Her presence there made her vulnerable and, by implication, a part of something she was determined to change. Within months of her resignation, Kishida had made connections with the popular-rights leadership and was on the way to becoming one of the Liberal Party's most celebrated speakers. Her mother left her husband, who had taken a young mistress, and traveled with her daughter. They were to be together until Toshiko's death in 1901.[21]

Kishida was, at twenty, an idealist with an optimistic belief in the possibility of social reform based on enlightened public opinion. Her faith in human rationality was boundless, and she was not restrained in her contempt for "unenlightened" behavior. Interested in the ideas of the French socialist Jean Jaurès, Kishida probably also read translations of the works of Western thinkers (including Spencer) whose ideas figured in the debate over women's status. Her views may have seemed Western to some, but she was strongly committed to universal, rather than Western values; she tended to think of progress as an ethical as well as a technological process. Committed to her country and the women in it, Kishida felt that the exclusion of women from the tasks of nation building was irrational, and to the extent that such exclusion meant a continuation of "respecting men and despising women," unethical as well.

The lecture platform provided by the Liberal Party gave Kishida an unprecedented opportunity to communicate in plain, direct style with women in many different regions, representing the widest spectrum of age, experience, and class. In that setting, the potential for developing a shared consciousness of themselves as women, whose common experiences outweighed their differences, was enormous. The impact of Kishida's tours testified eloquently to that potential. Women who came to hear her speak of generations of inequality now demanding redress were not disappointed. The young Kageyama (later Fukuda, the name by which she is best known, and which I shall use for convenience) Hideko, who was to become one of the most powerful and consistent feminists of her generation, heard Kishida speak of the "overwhelming justice of extending the rights of women" to an overflow audience in Okayama in 1882.[22] The experience was formative for Fukuda, who describes her response to it in her autobiography:

Listening to her speech, delivered in that marvelous oratorical style, I was unable to suppress my resentment and indignation . . . and began immediately to organize women and their daughters . . . to take the initiative in explaining and advocating natural rights, liberty, and equality, . . . summoning those of high purpose to the cause, so that somehow we might muster the passion to smash the corrupt customs of former days relating to women.[23]

In nearly every region Kishida visited, her speeches motivated like-minded women to organize discussion groups and public-speaking societies. Her example encouraged women to think of themselves as important contributors to Japan's future and as political activists who might themselves give public lectures. In October 1883 Kishida helped organize the founding meeting of the Joshi daienzetsu-kai (Kyoto Women's Lecture Society), an event that attracted more than two thousand women.[24] And she found time to honor the requests of women who had never heard her speak but knew about her from the press.*

We do not have a full record of Kishida's speeches, partly because journalists who covered her appearances were more interested in what she wore than what she said. Sōma Kokkō, her only real biographer to date, has left us a

---

* Tomii Oto, a young woman from Hyōgo prefecture, provides one of the better known examples of this. Tomii wrote to Kishida to ask that she be allowed to travel with her and become her student. Tomii later became one of Japan's first female journalists and was able, with Kishida's assistance, to get a job in Tokyo. Tomii's letter to Kishida is reprinted in *Nihon fujin mondai shiryō shūsei*, 10 vols. (Tokyo, 1976–80), 8: 114–15.

record of Kishida's itinerary and the titles of most of her speeches, suggesting that virtually all of her time was spent addressing women's issues. But she also made some interesting connections between women's rights and popular rights as she spoke to the educational and economic needs of women. This is clear enough from the title of a speech she made in Okayama: "The Government Lords It Over the People; Men Lord It Over Women."[25] We have two documents that together provide a reasonably complete picture of Kishida's approach to women's issues in the context of popular rights. One is an article, "To My Brothers and Sisters," published serially in a Tokyo newspaper in 1884 and based on many of her speeches. The other is the text of a speech she delivered in Ōtsu, on October 12, 1883, "Daughters Confined in Boxes," which seems to have been carefully preserved by the press because it led to her arrest by local officials.[26]

The issues Kishida raised spoke to the universality of the problems they shared with other nineteenth-century women. Aware of Millicent Fawcett's campaign for women's suffrage in England, Kishida understood that the "advantages of Japan's backwardness" did not readily apply to women's rights, since there were so few precedents anywhere.[27] Still, she seems to have been optimistic in her assessment of the ability of Japanese women to capitalize on an era of very rapid social change. Convinced that social progress relative to women's issues in the nineteenth century was universally uneven, Kishida emphasized that equality between men and women was the hallmark of civilization. Japan could begin to achieve the recognition it sought as a civilized nation only when it accorded women the rightful place a rational examination of the record showed they deserved. And since, by her definition, no society in the world had achieved a civilized state, Japan's opportunity to move ahead was obvious.

The agenda Kishida addressed on behalf of women was

similar to that raised by women in the United States and Europe. She argued for equal opportunity in education and the training in practical subjects that would enable women to become adequate managers of their own resources; for a single sexual standard; and for laws to protect women in matters of property and civil law. But before any of this could begin, and before women could take up roles as partners in a nation-building process, men must begin to change their attitudes about the value of women in society.

In ancient times there were various evil teachings and customs in our country, things that would make the people of any free, civilized nation terribly ashamed. Of these, the most reprehensible was the practice of "respecting men and despising women." . . . We are trying, through a cooperative effort, to build a new society. That is why I speak of equality and equal rights. Yet in this country, as in the past, men continue to be respected as masters and husbands while women are held in contempt as maids or serving women. There can be no equality in such an environment.[28]

Sharply critical of the ladies-first manners of the Rokumeikan era,* Kishida pointed out that men who went from the old custom of despising women to the new habit of opening doors for them "without considering the meaning of such a change at any profound level" would never produce the revolution in attitudes that the society needed. "Equality, independence, respect, and a monogamous relationship are the hallmarks of relationships between men and women in a civilized society," Kishida said, and cosmetic changes demonstrating that Japanese men were, like their Western counterparts, capable of putting women on a pedestal, should not be taken as meaningful change.

* The Rokumeikan (literally, the Crying Deer Pavilion) was an expensive building designed by a British architect to provide the Japanese government with an appropriate place to entertain Western diplomats and their guests. Completed in 1883, the Rokumeikan gave its name to an era of Western-style dancing and socializing that symbolized one of the government's most superficial Westernization programs, and one that met with substantial public criticism.

"Ah, you men of the world," she lamented, "you talk of reform, but not of revolution. When it comes to equality, you yearn for the old ways, and follow, unchanged, the customs of the past."[29]

Kishida, the speaker, was fond of a debating style that first named the arguments of the opposition, then demolished them one by one. She considered all of the arguments against women's equality irrational and assumed that minds pushed to an objective examination of Japan's experience could be changed. To the garbled Social Darwinist argument that Japanese women were destined to inferior roles because of their lack of physical strength, Kishida replied that was an argument for barbarity, not civilization. Status was not determined on the basis of physical strength in any but the most primitive societies, she said, and if Japan wanted now to follow that example, perhaps sumo wrestlers should become councillors of state. Never, she said, should a society condone the behavior of a man who used "the strength of his arm" to control a woman. Accepting the right of those with superior force to dominate those who were weaker, whether man over woman, or Western nation over Asian nation, was an argument for savagery, not civilization.[30]

And what of the argument that the inferior status of women was a natural corollary of her intellectual deficiencies? Kishida pointed to the past accomplishments of Japanese women, from early Empresses to writers like Murasaki Shikibu, to counter the argument, but she also noted the achievements of women in the West, including Madame de Staël, Catherine the Great, and Elizabeth Barrett Browning. If it seemed that Japanese women in the Meiji period were intellectually less accomplished than men, Kishida said, it was certainly not the natural consequence of gender, but the result of the old patriarchal system that had denied women access to education.[31]

Kishida clearly believed that education was critical to

raising women's status in Japan, and felt that the failures of Meiji education for women had less to do with state policy than with family attitudes toward women. Speaking at a time when fewer than 50 percent of the nation's eligible young women were attending school, though compulsory education had been instituted in 1872,[32] Kishida condemned, as "an enormous error," the common attitude of women that too much education was a hindrance to marriage, an attitude that originated in the family. Kishida both chided and appealed to parents, declaring that they were compromising the future of their daughters by clinging to traditional attitudes about them:

I hope in the future there will be some recognition of the fact that the first requirement for marriage is education. Today, we have come to feel that we have "managed" if eight out of ten daughters who are married do not return home in divorce. Actually, no one should make such a claim. One of the first requirements ought to be learning what it is to manage after marriage. . . . Daughters must be taught basic economics and the skills that would permit them to manage on their own. Even a woman who expects to be protected during her husband's lifetime must be able to manage on her own, armed with the necessary skills, if he should die.[33]

To those who feared that more education and, by implication, greater rights and opportunities for women in and out of the home would lead to increased family strife, Kishida replied that initially such changes would lead neither to greater problems nor to a utopian state of affairs in which disagreements would vanish. But, she insisted, in the long term, the relationship would be improved, since the root of strife lay in the inequality woman experienced in the family, where relationships between men and women continued to be based, "not on love and respect, but on power."[34] Real parents, she said, "are people who open the doors of knowledge to their daughters and give them appropriate tools for managing their lives. Heaven has given freedom to daughters; this is an age that demands that they develop a thorough knowledge of the world around them."[35]

In her critique of the family's handling of women, Kishida reserved her greatest anger for parents who perpetuated the old system of "protecting" them by putting them in boxes and "educating" them by teaching them tea ceremony, flower arranging, singing, and dancing. Such training, in place of intellectual challenge, was not, as some people suggested, an "expression of parental tenderness." It was time for parents to see the suffering they were inflicting on their children; time they recognized the contradiction between protecting and developing their daughters' "womanly virtues" while educating them in a way that made them little more than apprentice geisha. Putting daughters in boxes, Kishida implied, was like growing flowers in salt. There was simply no way for a "child of any brilliance to be noticed in such an educational setting"; no way for a young woman to develop her potential with the family system ranged against her. The only appropriate box for daughters was "as large and free as the world itself." Ultimately, Kishida believed, parents with a "real appreciation of the feelings of their daughters" would see such customs for what they were: creations of the past totally out of place in Meiji Japan.[36]

Kishida's Ōtsu speech, one of the earliest attacks on Japan's family system by a woman, was stopped by police, who arrested her and dispersed the crowd. Police harassment and intimidation were not new to her; she had been followed by police since June 1882, and had had her speeches interrupted before. But the eight days she now spent in jail were a new experience and an ominous reminder of what women could expect as they attempted to expand their activities in an increasingly violent political arena.[37]

As Kishida reflected on the dangers inherent in the new roles women had assigned themselves, the movement she had helped create moved forward, rippling out from several centers simultaneously. From 1881 to Kishida's arrest in the fall of 1883, newspaper records show a very high level of political activity among women, who organized associations, lecture and study groups, "freedom houses," and cooperative societies "to promote women" in Fukuoka, Shikoku, Okayama, Sendai, Kagoshima, Kyoto, and Hamamatsu. They organized private schools to provide compensatory education for women; they petitioned prefectural authorities, demanding that women's normal school curricula be improved; they collected dues for the Liberal Party; and they attended party rallies and participated in political "events" such as the mock burial services held in Shikoku for Liberal Party newspapers shut down by the government.[38]

Kishida, aware that she was a symbol of many of these changes, not only in the eyes of women but in the eyes of the government as well, had managed to live with the pressures of her new role. She seemed untouched by continuous newspaper gossip linking her with most of the (married) leaders of the popular-rights movement; and she had become very accomplished in handling awkward incidents and the slights of male politicians that occurred from time to time.*

But in November 1883, as she traveled by boat from Ōtsu to Tokyo with Nakajima Nobuyuki, a Liberal Party leader (and her future husband), she must have heard firsthand what many women in the movement did not yet

---

* In late 1883, for example, a man who was supposed to speak to a political gathering scheduled as part of Kishida's Kyushu tour refused to share the speaker's platform with a woman. He asked local officials to make excuses for him, saying that he had a toothache. When Kishida rose to speak, she told the crowd of nearly 800 that, "as thinking people," they ought to reconsider the merits of "a man who could get such a terrible toothache at the mere sight of a woman." (*Chōya shimbun*, Dec. 6, 1883, cited in Showa joshidai kindai bungaku kenkyū-shitsu, *Kindai bungaku kenkyū sōsho*, Tokyo, 1957, 6: 40–41.)

suspect: the Liberal Party was on the verge of collapse, the victim of divided leadership and government oppression. Itagaki, the titular head of the party, had been stabbed in April 1882, as he left a speaking engagement in Gifu, and after his recovery, had left Japan for Europe. The impact of this departure at a critical moment in the party's struggle for survival was made worse by the growing realization that the money for the trip had come from Mitsui business interests, transmitted by the same Meiji government responsible for the repression they had experienced in the political movement. The lack of a leader of the same stature, and the difficulty of maintaining organization and structure in the face of new regulations prohibiting "corresponding or joining together with other similar societies," meant the rapid dissipation of the movement's recently organized national strength.[39] Without central leadership and organization, increasing burdens fell on local Liberal Party leaders, burdens they found overwhelming in the face of government oppression.

Whether they resorted to legal tactics or violence, local leaders found it difficult to prevent the government from destroying the Liberal Party and achieving full political control over local and regional governments. The oligarchy not only imprisoned party leaders in prefectural assemblies for their efforts to use legal means to combat its will, but also demonstrated its own taste for violence in clashes with protesters in the countryside.[40] By the time Kishida was sent to jail, death at the hands of police carrying out their duties under various "regulations" endorsed by the state, or death in prison, was an increasingly common fate of those who challenged the government. "State criminals," whose crime was political opposition to the oligarchy, began to swell the prison population as the Movement for Freedom and Popular Rights, a powerful political alternative to the failure of armed rebellion after 1877, was treated by the government as an incipient revolution.

Unfortunately for the Liberal Party, some of its own leaders seemed equally fearful of the developments in the countryside. Those who wanted to take advantage of the new situation were forced to admit the frailty of that hope in the face of Itagaki's steady retreat from the movement after his return from Europe in 1883. Itagaki, whose commitment to the ideology of the popular-rights movement was always suspect, was not interested in continuing the Meiji revolution or in supporting challenges to the government by groups he could not control—particularly the peasantry. By October 1884 the Liberal Party was dead. The leaders announced its dissolution on the eve of what was later described as a "miniature civil war"—the Chichibu revolt.[41]

To say that the collapse of the Liberal Party came too soon for Japanese women is something more than understatement. They had continued, through the summer of 1884, to organize and to speak out, calling on women (as one of them put it) "with even a little patriotic spirit" to "move forward, involving themselves in world affairs, sharing with men the responsibility of building the foundation of a strong and wealthy country."[42] But the exuberance and power Japanese women had so recently discovered was already fading. Kishida returned to the political platform in January and February 1884, but she was aware of the changed circumstances in which women were operating, and had begun thinking seriously about her own future and the future of other women now involved in politics. How could they express themselves politically and survive?

Generally speaking, historians have not interested themselves in the impact women had in the popular-rights movement; they have not asked whether the ability of women to use the movement to raise feminist issues precipitated a self-conscious response on the part of the Meiji government. In part, this failure is the result of the inherent difficulty in separating a government response to women's demands from a government response to the popular-rights movement as a whole. But it also stems from an inability or unwillingness to see the participation of women in this movement in a feminist context. Feminist criticism is subsumed under the general heading of popular-rights theory, which was both humanist and universal. Kishida's harassment and arrest in the middle of a speech attacking the family system is therefore interpreted as another familiar episode in popular-rights history. The titles of Kishida's speeches suggest feminist content; but according to this view, such topics were meant to be metaphors for popular-rights issues that could not be announced in advance.[43] There may be some basis for such an interpretation, but from the standpoint of women's history it seems a convenient, if not naïve, approach to the problem, given what we know of Kishida's arguments and those of other women as well.

In the mid-1880's, the government's position on public roles for women differed only slightly, in a qualitative sense, from the effort in the previous decade to make women the repositories of tradition. The authorities approved women's participation in the charity bazaars and volunteer work of the Rokumeikan era, but they were not happy with the emergence of "public" women who encouraged others to acquaint themselves with "political ideas and cultivate freedom."[44] And they were increasingly harsh with teachers who seemed to be filling their students' heads with political theory and feminist issues.[45] The woman worthy of praise in the eyes of the Teiseitō (Imperial Government Party) was an accomplished seamstress who joined women's associations for charitable, not political, purposes.[46] Immediately after the Liberal Party announced its dissolution in 1884, the Imperial Party in Shikoku announced the formation of the Joshi konshinkai (Women's Friendship Society), patterned after the Fujin jizenkai (Women's Charity Society) then sponsoring bazaars and benefits in Tokyo's Rokumeikan. Though the attempt to organize Shikoku women in associations encouraging "womanly virtues" and "womanly warmth and gentleness" (presided over, at a distance, by the wives of a new Tokyo-based aristocracy) does not seem to have been successful, there is little question that the government's ultimate intent was to get women out of politics.* These efforts to set up government-encouraged organizations for women were reinforced in local areas by government newspaper criticism of women's education, which, it was said, neglected traditional womanly pastimes in favor of discussions of equality and other women's issues.[47]

These activities on the part of government should perhaps have been seen as warnings of impending disaster, but women in 1884 were preoccupied with the negative impact of the Liberal Party's dissolution. It was a crippling blow to women who had just begun to organize around issues raised after 1881 by Kishida and others. The Liberal Party had given women platforms and organizational ties that they had been able to use very effectively from 1881 to 1884. They had demonstrated they were capable of speaking articulately in their own behalf, and they had used the political arena to raise the consciousness of other women, who in turn had begun to forge the networks so vital to the continuity of women's movements everywhere. But a few years was scarcely time enough to develop the structure and resilience needed to survive the division and isolation they now faced. Armed with newly discovered visions, whose power lay in the fact that they were shared by other women, the leaders of the women's movement now were forced to struggle alone.

* This overture on the part of the only government-sponsored party in Meiji politics is extremely significant, since it was such an accurate preview of policies the government would later implement in education and civil law. That these policies were clearly related to women's activities in the 1880's is demonstrated by the way they were developed in Shikoku and other areas.

Kishida's political future was compromised by the dissolution of the Liberal Party as surely as it denied other women opportunities they had only begun to imagine. It is at this point, when she began thinking seriously about a journalistic career, that she published her multipart article, "To My Brothers and Sisters."[48] Shortly after this initial attempt to reach women through the press rather than lectures, Kishida married the Liberal Nakajima Nobuyuki, whom she had known since her first speech in Osaka in 1881.[49] Though her decision to marry Nakajima has often been described as an opportunity to flee from the turbulent politics of the period to the comfort and security of life as an "ordinary housewife," her life with Nakajima was never very comfortable or ordinary. Responsible for rearing the three children he brought to this, his third marriage, Toshiko also managed the often difficult financial problems of the family. She was an effective household manager who avoided the kitchen with a tenacity her contemporary, the American feminist Charlotte Perkins Gilman, would have appreciated. A woman who insisted on equality in marriage as well as a life for herself, Toshiko taught at Ferris's School for women in Yokohama for a time, and wrote for the influential *Jogaku zasshi* (Women's Education Magazine).*

Many women turned to the growing numbers of newspapers and "women's magazines" (which were to become a permanent part of the publishing world in Meiji), to express their views after the Liberal Party's collapse. But the transition from public speaking to writing for journals and newspapers was a costly one for the early women's movement. By definition, women writing in the Meiji period

* Sōma Kokkō, *Meiji shoki no san josei*, Tokyo, 1940, pp. 58–115. *Women's Education Magazine*, edited by Iwamato Zenji, a well-known Christian educator, was central to efforts to elevate the status of Meiji women from a Christian standpoint in the 1880's. After 1884 it became the voice of several important social reformers, including Kitamura Tōkoku. Its audience was urban and middle to upper class. (See Nishida Taketoshi, *Meiji jidai no shimbun to zasshi*, Tokyo, 1961, pp. 219–20.)

were unable to reach the diverse audiences they might have addressed from a public platform. The journals and newspapers for which they wrote had increasingly well-defined constituencies strongly informed by interests of both region and class. And many women who might have been impressed by the arguments of a women speaking in an angry, straightforward style would easily have been frustrated by the indirection of the literary style that characterized much of the writing of the period. Kishida's articles for *Women's Education Magazine* echoed many of her earlier political views, but they did not have the impact of her speeches. The power to move women to act in their own behalf, power that Kishida the public speaker had, slipped through the grasp of Kishida the writer. Living in Yokohama and Tokyo, writing for the middle- and upper-class women who read *Women's Education Magazine*, Kishida, like many of her feminist contemporaries, found herself more isolated, narrowing the focus of her concerns about women and increasingly unable to maintain the intensity of an earlier day.

Fukuda Hideko also found herself alone in the fall of 1884. Only the year before, she and her mother, lamenting the "lack of basic education among Japan's women" and the inacessibility of most public education to working mothers and daughters, had opened a private school for girls and women ages six to sixty, and boys of six to ten. Intended to provide a place where (in Fukuda's words) "women can study at their discretion, and where we will attempt to provide curriculum for primary-school students," the school offered classes in reading, writing, mathematics, and, on Saturdays, debate. In keeping with its emphasis on working mothers, the school's hours were 3:00 P.M.–6:00 P.M. and 6:00 P.M.–9:00 P.M.[50]

The day after the episode she recounts in the epigraph to this chapter, the prefectural authorities closed down her school. Stung by this decision to punish her for her political activities, Fukuda had borrowed money to travel to Tokyo where, she felt sure, she would find Itagaki and other Liberal Party leaders ready to intervene to get the school reopened.[51] She arrived just in time to witness the dissolution of the party she had dreamed might offer her, and women like her, a different future—one emphasizing the public, political roles women should assume. Disillusioned and embittered by the readiness of the Liberal Party leaders to dissolve their organization, this eighteen-year-old feminist from Okayama decided to remain in Tokyo while she sorted out her future; working, as she always had, she also attended a mission school near Tsukiji. In Tokyo she met and became a friend of Tomii Oto, Kishida's former student who was now working as a reporter for *Jiyū no tomoshibi* (The Light of Freedom).[52] Fukuda and Tomii dreamed of financing an academy for women, but in fact most of Tomii's extra cash went to women friends who were struggling to achieve independence, and as Fukuda became increasingly involved with the left wing of the former Liberal Party, most of her money went to finance their plans for reform.[53]

In 1885, disgusted with the quality of leadership in the old Liberal Party, and convinced that she had the "will to struggle for the country, even to the point of death," Fukuda involved herself in a plan to challenge the Meiji government by setting up a reform government in exile—in Korea. When the plan failed she was picked up by the police in November 1885—the only woman involved in what has come to be called the Osaka Incident.[54] Later sentenced to a ten-month prison term as a state criminal, Fukuda's heroics and her self-proclaimed struggle for freedom made her the idol of young women throughout the country, who became avid readers of newspaper stories characterizing her as "Japan's Joan of Arc."[55]

While Fukuda was in prison, teaching her fellow women prisoners how to read and write, and lamenting the hopelessness of the economic situation most women faced, women in Kōfu's textile mills staged Japan's first strike.[56] That spring and summer of strike activity in Kōfu was followed, in December, by the expansion into a national organization of Tokyo fujin kyōfūkai (Tokyo Women's Reform Society), a group of middle-class women interested in raising the status of women.[57] These seemingly disparate developments in the women's movement, one involving the daughters of impoverished farmers, the other seemingly comfortable urban women whose Christianity pushed them to social reform, had a good deal in common. They both had benefited indirectly from the public participation of women in the popular-rights movement, and their protests, as well as their willingness to voice them in a hostile public arena, were linked by concerns common to many Japanese women. The strikers in Kōfu, for example, demanded not only higher wages, but an end to working conditions in which male supervisors had unlimited power over the hiring, firing, and general treatment of all women workers—a condition linked to many of the later proposals of the Reform Society.[58]

The Kōfu strike was particularly distasteful to the Meiji government, since it cast the first large shadow over an industry considered critical to national development. Women constituted more than 60 percent of the entire industrial work force in 1876; most worked in the competitive textile industry, which earned foreign exchange needed to carry out capital-intensive modernization programs in heavy industry.

The diverse group of women who joined the Reform Society were not economically important to the government, but their refusal to fill the roles the government wished to assign to women must have come as something of a shock—particularly since these "highly respectable" women looked so much the part. At the same time as they insisted on improvements in opportunities for women, including better education, Reform Society members focused on the continuation of concubinage and prostitution in Japan as central to the question of women's status. They attacked "exported prostitution," involving the exploitation of women on the lowest rung of the economic ladder, and were the first to demand an end to the export of Ame-yuki and Kara-yuki-san—young women sent to the United States and other parts of Asia as prostitutes.[59]

As they waited for the initiation of constitutional government at the end of the decade, Japanese women had already demonstrated a remarkable resistance to government definition and redefinition of their roles. They had insisted on public, political tasks for themselves; had refused to work under intolerable conditions for the "good of the country"; had challenged social institutions that were perennial barriers to the elevation of women's status. Though women seemed to share an interest in bettering their status that might have bridged the natural (and unnatural) divisions of the larger society they increasingly reflected, the differences that now existed between various groups of women were enormous. Thus, when Fukuda plunged back into her activities after her release from prison in 1889, eager to work for "women's rights and equality,"[60] she drew the fire of *Women's Education Magazine*, which despite similar goals was prompted to describe her activities in these acid terms: "A party of women headed by one Ei Kageyama is to come together in Osaka, to deliberate on the subject of Women's Rights. Some of them are said to be of very vulgar origin and others to be of very rude and masculine manners."[61]

Women could have had little hope in 1889 that they could operate through traditional party structures. They had been written out of the new constitution announced that year.* But, as if to demonstrate the viability of the

---

* Not only were women excluded from any serious consideration in all but two of the constitutional drafts (including Ueki Emori's); the final version contained a clause that, for the first time in Japanese history, formally excluded women from access to the Japanese throne, matching the Salic tradition of the West, which excluded women from succession to monarchical power.

ongoing struggle, women in 1889, in textile mills and in their own political gatherings, continued to lash out at the injustice around them.[62] At the very least, women expected the constitution to usher in a new and less threatening political climate. The excesses of a government that had pulled out all the stops to defeat its political critics would surely, after 1890, be a thing of the past. After elections in the summer of 1890, women would be free, as they were in Europe and the United States, to engage the political system. What was needed in 1890 were new opportunities and goals around which networks could develop; associations and connections could break down the divisions and remind women of their shared experiences—as they had on other occasions.

But by 1890 some members of the Japanese government had decided that women were not going to be given further opportunities to develop their power. After the summer elections produced a majority for the resurgent Liberal Party in the Lower House, the outgoing cabinet, as one of its last acts in office, revised regulations on public meetings—adding women to the list of those denied the right to participate in politics on any level under Article 5 of the Police Security Regulations.[63] After 1890 Japanese women who tried to organize a political association, join a political group, or attend a meeting defined by authorities as political were subject to fine or imprisonment. And to emphasize the exclusion of women from politics, organizers of the new Diet included a rule prohibiting the attendance of women as observers at future legislative sessions.[64]

Shimizu Toyoko's protest of Article 5 of the revised regulations was typical of the reaction:

The revised regulations on public meetings has dealt all of us who are women a rude shock. . . . With the inclusion of the two characters "*jo shi*" [women] in the revision, we have all, 20 million of us, been rendered incompetent. . . . This law represents an expedient use of politics; if individual rights are to be protected, and the peace and order of society secured, laws should not be discriminatory, granting advantage to men only, and misfortune only to women.*

Thanks to an effective protest organized by Yajima Kajiko and others, the legislators failed in their effort to bar women from the observer's gallery of the Diet.[65] But for women this victory was little more than a hand emerging from the debris of a political avalanche. Japanese women, after a decade of valuable political experience, were now unable to mount a campaign against the regulations without violating them. Their ability to bring about social and political change had been compromised by the short-circuiting of connections they would have to make in the next decade if their efforts were to have any continuity. How could they now regenerate that common sense of past and future that had brought them this far?

---

* Shimizu Toyoko (Shikin), "Naniyue ni joshi wa seiden shūkai ni sanchō suru to o yurusarezaruka?" *Jogaku zasshi,* 228 (Aug. 30, 1890). Shimizu (1868–1933) was born in Kyoto and was influenced by the appearance there of Kishida Toshiko. She was a frequent contributor to *Women's Education Magazine* and became an important Meiji writer and educator. See Yamaguchi Reiko, *Naite aisuru shimai ni tsugu* (Tokyo, 1977), for an account of her life.

4. The Textile Workers

Some were children, only eleven or twelve. Just out of the fourth grade. . . . They would leave at three in the morning . . . and by the time they reached Yamaguchi village the February snow would be so deep they would have to walk single file. . . . From the front of the line where someone would be carrying a company flag a cheerful voice could be heard singing.

> We don't cross Nomugi Pass
>   just for show.
> For ourselves, for our parents.
> For men, the army.
> For women, the mills.
> Spinning thread is for the
>   country too.

Too few of the demands women made in the popular-rights movement reached the ears of working women who, in the 1880's, were caught up in an increasingly ruthless cycle of obligation, poverty, and exploitation. The dramatic story, now well known in Japan, of young women textile workers who year after year braved the winter snows of Nomugi Pass to work in the mills of neighboring Nagano prefecture illustrates both the courage and the desperation that characterized their lives. Wearing only straw sandals, or walking barefoot through the snow and ice, long processions of factory workers made their way across the mountains, leaving a trail tinged reddish-pink from the cuts on their feet and the dye of their red under-skirts. They clung to each other in the blowing snow, and when someone fell, tied their obi together and tried to pull her back up to the path.[1]

At the end of what was for some a 100-mile journey was the mill and the knowledge that, if they could survive the work and its hardships, they could go home again at the end of the summer. For some who crossed over in the early days, bringing home a small wage was a luxury; the real point of a year's work in the mill was to be fed by someone else. Shimokawa Aki, who was eleven when she traveled over the pass in 1884, remembered: "In those days, because we went to reduce the number of mouths to feed, money was not the issue. It was better than being at home, because we could eat rice."[2] Later, when wages were paid, they were not for the young women themselves, but for parents, whose gratitude could sometimes erase the memory of intolerable working conditions.

I don't know how many times I thought I would rather jump into Lake Suwa and drown. Even so, when I went home with a year's earnings and handed the money to my mother, she clasped it in her hands and said, "With this, we can manage through the end of the year." And my father, who was ill, sat up in his bed and bowed to me over and over. "Sue," he said, "it must have been difficult. Thank you. Thank you."
Then we put the money in a wooden box, and put the box up on the altar and prayed. . . . Whenever I thought of my mother's face then, I could endure any hardship.[3]

These "excess" daughters of Japan's countryside, born in a predominantly patrilineal, patrilocal society, where their value was always tempered by the expectation that they would eventually marry and become workers in someone else's household, soon became the backbone of the country's economy. Though a daughter's potential value as a bride required careful family management, daughters were, in the best to the worst case, commodities to be managed, and if necessary sold, to keep the family going.[4] Their domination of the Meiji work force, where they constituted an average of 60 percent of Japan's industrial labor from 1894 to 1912,[5] probably did not come as much of a surprise to a government that had encouraged young women to join the labor force in the 1870's "for the good of the country." Working in a textile mill was patriotic; short hair and involvement in politics were not.

The Meiji government stood ready to act as entrepreneur in the development of capital-intensive heavy industries as it began an accelerated program to strengthen the country. But the importance of light industry, where less capital had to be invested and where exportable goods might, over time, earn the foreign exchange the resource-poor nation needed to import material and equipment, was obvious to many from the beginning.[6] Reports from government officials and visits by observers to spinning mills in England reinforced what the government already knew: that spinning and weaving industries, with little or no government encouragement, might become competitive in world markets by using at least one resource the country already had in abundance.[7] Japan, like Europe and the United States, had a reserve labor force of young women who were used to hard work and whose low wages were easily justified.

In fact, this "resource" came to dominate factory labor in Japan down to 1930, not just in sheer numbers, but in the value of exports produced. Silk was one of the nation's few exportable commodities in 1868, accounting for nearly two-thirds of all export volume in that year; by the end of the Meiji period (1912), Japanese women had made their country the world's leading exporter of silk.[8] The growth of cotton spinning and weaving, hampered at first by low tariffs and severe competition from imports, came into its own after 1900. By 1914 Japan was dominating world cotton manufacturing, and it managed to maintain that position until just before the Pacific War. What these exports meant to the country's ability to build both heavy industry and military strength without extensive borrowing is clear enough. Without the work of Japan's women, the apparent miracle of Japan's economic growth might not have been possible; it is as difficult to underestimate their contribution as it is to deny the social costs that were a part of it.[9] Given the chance, Meiji working women might well have been among the first to ask for a redefinition of Japan's economic success.

By ignoring or discounting the experience of women workers economic historians have managed to emphasize the success of Japanese industrialization to the virtual exclusion of its social costs.[10] This is all the more remarkable given the volumes of description of conditions in the textile mills published since the late nineteenth century.[11] Those sources make clear not only that women bore the brunt of Japan's industrial revolution in its early stages, but that the Japanese experience matched, if it did not surpass, the worst conditions of both Europe and the United States.

The expectation that their lives would be occupied with work of various kinds was not new to Meiji women; in fact, Confucian arguments about the "inner" roles of women seem to have had little effect in a Japan where women were accustomed to working outside with men—even to working away from home for someone else.[12] But the patterns they found replicated everywhere were family patterns; hierarchies of sex and age were preserved in the workplace, and women found it correspondingly difficult to achieve any measure of upward social mobility, much less economic independence, through their work. Young women who left home to become apprenticed to weavers during the Tokugawa period were never referred to as apprentices or workers, for example; they were "servants of the weaver" because of the housework they were required to do in addition to learning a trade.[13] Samurai women quietly did weaving and piecework to help their families survive; peasant women hired out as day laborers on neighboring farms. Divorced and widowed women worked on farms, did piecework at home, or worked as servants in order to survive. But the fact that work for women was defined by the family and justified by the importance of its continued existence reinforced the notion that economic independence was irrelevant, particularly for women. Women would always be protected by the families into which they were born or were married. This comforting myth of woman, protected throughout her life by a benevolent family structure, conveniently denied the reality of divorce, death, and other economic hardships so common to women in Japanese society.

The transition from Tokugawa to Meiji for working women was outwardly less dramatic than it should have been, partly because of the ability of the government and managers to keep this myth alive, and to maintain the connection between family and work in spite of significant economic change. As a consequence, though the settings in which women worked changed, as Meiji women (single, married, divorced, and widowed) left home to work in coal mines, match factories, and textile mills, the apparent connections to family and family-like structures remained. Nowhere was the cultivation of this relationship easier than in the case of the young, predominantly unmarried young women who, as textile workers, came to dominate the industrial work force. Their ties to their families who remained in the countryside were readily exploited, and their consciousness of themselves as workers with a significant contribution to make to Japan's industrial revolution was thus diluted.

More than any other group, young women in the textile mills were models of government and management attitudes toward women workers. They were not workers, but "daughters" or "students" spending a few years before marriage working for their families, the nation, and the mills. Lack of commitment and lack of skill justified both the low wages paid to this work force and its characterization as part-time or temporary.[14] Unlike their brothers (second and third sons) who had gone off to the city, young textile workers were expected to return home to pick up their lives again and marry. Their futures remained with their families; work in the mill was simply an interlude, designed to bring in a little extra money. For them there was to be no alienation, no conflict with management, and no sense of themselves or the value of their work. The Meiji government accelerated this process by building model textile mills in various parts of the country, designed to show private investors the latest technology as well as methods for managing the work force.

When the government proudly opened the first of these mills in Tomioka, Gumma prefecture, in 1873, it had the most up-to-date equipment and best foreign supervision available. Recruiting a work force to match, planners used government and quasi-governmental agencies to make an argument appealing both to patriotic sentiment and to status. Local governments were asked to provide "student workers" who would come to Tomioka to become teachers, then take their skills back to other newly developing factories.[15] Not surprisingly, a large number of samurai families responded to this early government request, although it required that parents overcome a good deal of initial reluctance, since exposure to such a different life so far from home, working with male supervisors, might damage their daughter's marriage chances. A few government officials saw to it that relatives, socially visible young women whose connections to the Meiji leadership were well publicized, went to work in the model Tomioka mill to prove that factories were "safe" places for young women.*

* Wada Ei, *Tomioka nikki* (Tokyo, 1976), pp. 9–13. Wada, whose father was a council elder at the time, recalls that the government asked various districts to provide 16 women from 13 to 25 years old for Tomioka. Officials were asked to send their own daughters to encourage others and diminish superstition about the plant. Before she left for the mill, her parents talked to her. "Father told me not to fail for the honor of the country and the family; mother told me my body was most important, and I should be especially careful with so many men around . . . not to do anything to disgrace either my father or mother" (pp. 12–13).

Within the year, Tomioka had put 556 women to work, a good percentage of whom came from former samurai families.[16] In the early days of Tomioka, workers were treated well, and though there was more than enough supervision, there was little of the exploitation that later masqueraded as paternalism. Off duty, young women lived in adequate dormitory housing, where they had a chance to get to know other young women from all parts of the country.[17] Parents often visited their daughters at the factory, and the company advanced salary to workers who needed travel money in a family emergency. Workers who tired of the work or became ill were apparently free to leave and return home, if their families approved.[18]

Conditions at Tomioka were better than those developing elsewhere in privately owned mills, but the hours were still long, and the work physically demanding. Supervisors, both French and Japanese, enforced a harsh discipline on the factory floor that bordered on harassment. Workers who made mistakes were berated, particularly those who let the thread break. There were few rest periods of more than fifteen minutes in a long day that lasted from dawn until sundown; conversations on the factory floor were not permitted. And the Tomioka women were especially sensitive to the criticism of their foreign supervisors. "Japan has a lot of lazy daughters!" Wada Ei's supervisor Justin Perrin would shout, and all the women would work with renewed energy, to prove that what he had said was not true.[19]

By the 1880's privately owned textile mills were being developed throughout the country; few were modeled on Tomioka in any but a technological sense, and the lessons essentially involved adapting expensive, large-scale operations to a smaller, less costly enterprise.[20] A plentiful labor supply was taken for granted. The economic policies of the 1880's, the same policies that produced so much support for the popular-rights movement in the countryside, forced more and more families to adopt desperate measures. They held meetings to try to find solutions, and delegated respected members of the community to speak to government officials and moneylenders on their behalf.[21] If negotiations failed, there was often violence, reminiscent of the peasant uprisings in the years preceding the Meiji Restoration.

Daughters in these impoverished families were obvious recruits for the textile mills, just as Irish immigrant women were logical replacements for the "well bred" and "literate" first generation of Lowell workers.* Their poverty forced them to accept whatever mill owners, engaged in competition for survival and profit, chose to make the conditions of their work. Mori Arinori, writing as a representative of Japan and an observer of American life in 1872, had noted this change in conditions in the American textile industry:

Although a few years ago, much the larger proportion were native Americans, so great a change has taken place . . . that the majority are now foreigners, and chiefly Irish. . . . Widows are there, toiling for the education of their children; and daughters are there, hoarding up wages to pay the debts of improvident fathers. The labor of the women is essentially on an equality with that of the men; but whereas the former receive from two to three dollars per week in addition to their board, the latter receive from four to six dollars for the same period. . . . A brief time only is allowed for meals; and the only opportunities the

* It was as if the Japanese government, by its harsh economic policies in the countryside, had created its own Irish potato famine. There are interesting parallels, not only between daughters of farm families and Irish immigrants in American textile mills, but between the Yankee farm girls who left Lowell in the face of worsening labor conditions and the daughters of former samurai who, after working at Tomioka, seem to disappear in the 1880's. The change in the American textile worker is clear and well documented, but the disappearance of former samurai daughters is less certain. In the 1880's and later, many former samurai families were little better off than farmers in the countryside, and were in fact sliding into the commoner class that fed the mills. The industrial revolution in Japan was producing a new aristocracy as surely as it produced a new working class that very likely included daughters of former samurai.

operatives have for recreation or study are at night, when worn out with the jar and whir of the machinery in the mills.[22]

After both silk and cotton textile mills were mechanized and organized around the modern factory system in Japan, few traces of the kind of paternalism that had sometimes characterized earlier handicraft and wage-earning patterns remained. But maintaining the illusion of that paternalism was still important to mill owners looking for workers to run their imported equipment.

As demand for labor increased in the 1880's, mill owners looked for a system that would bring them long-term commitment from their workers without the costs that this could entail. The answer was the contract system. Companies hired labor recruiters, who went through the countryside encouraging parents to sign their daughters to a one- to five-year contract with a distant mill. The contract itself was simply a legal document protecting the employer; it obligated the worker and her family to accept whatever conditions employers offered, for the time specified. The following example, taken from a government study done at the turn of the century, is typical:[23]

1. The period of work covered by this contract is five years.
2. The worker must give evidence that there is no employment relationship with another company at the present time.
3. There is to be no betraying of company secrets.
4. Factory employers' and supervisors' orders and regulations will be observed now and in the future.
5. Except in extreme cases, no one will be allowed to leave work before the contract expires.
6. The company may dismiss workers at any time at its own convenience.
7. Wages are paid at company convenience.
8. The company may decrease or confiscate the wages of employees for a violation of company regulations or of the contract.

The contract system, a one-sided and very unusual way of enforcing obligation in Japanese society, could not have worked without the accompanying façade of traditional paternalism erected by the mill owners and their recruiters. The illusory relationship created between daughters, parents, and factory management was based almost exclusively on the verbal promises of recruiters and the willingness of mill owners to loan badly needed cash to the families that signed the contracts on their daughters' behalf. Promises and needed cash made the relationship seem more reciprocal than it was, and that in turn made it seem more traditional than it was.

Having to guarantee nothing on paper, recruiters promised everything. Most offered free room and board, easy access to medical facilities, frequent days off, and time for recreation, which the company would provide. The factory, as in earlier days, would be a family away from home for workers. Owners and managers would stand in for parents, and would keep them informed of their daughter's progress. The dormitory system, with adequate supervision provided by the company, would ensure that the futures of these young unmarried women would not be compromised by their work in the mills. And when they returned home, their marriage prospects would be even brighter than before, since the mills not only would broaden their horizons in a general sense, but would also teach them new skills.[24] The claims were endless, and always tailored to meet the specific concerns of an individual family. For young women who had not completed four years of elementary and supposedly compulsory education because their parents lacked either the money or the inclination to send them to school, the mills promised to provide an equivalent course.* For those who had completed the fourth grade, contractors offered a

---

* This was one of the few promises the mills made good, but usually only in the case of very young children. And since a 10- or 11-year-old was offered a 2-hour class after a regular shift of 12 or more hours day or night, attendance at these classes was predictably very low. (Yasue Aoki Kidd, "Women Workers in the Japanese Cotton Mills," Cornell University East Asia Papers No. 20, 1978, pp. 21–22.)

finishing-school course in flower arrangement, tea ceremony, and dance, designed to increase any daughter's value in the marriage market.

But it was the loan, the most immediate and tangible part of the contact between family and the mill, that was binding. Companies often paid half of the worker's projected wage as a loan after the contract was signed and promised the other half after its successful completion. Acceptance of badly needed cash in advance obligated both parents and daughter in what seemed a traditional relationship with the employer. It established special conditions, obligating those who received the kindness to extend themselves to the limit for the person who had extended it. Not a few parents who received earnest money, which could range from as little as one yen to one hundred, must have felt that they were selling their daughters to the mills.[25] In any case, they often sent their daughters off with apologies for having to do it, and pleas that they put up with even the most difficult circumstances. "Please," they would say, "be careful!" Or: "Though this hardship comes to you because your father isn't resourceful enough, we ask you to endure it."[26] Stories circulated among the young women who crossed Nomugi Pass about two mothers who set out to accompany their daughters up through the way stations and, unable to let them go, went to the mills with them and worked the whole year of their contracts.[27]

As conditions in the mills became better known, villages would occasionally refuse labor recruiters access to the area, but poverty continued to force most families to sell their daughters to the textile mills, long after the promises of owners and recruiters were recognized for what they were: a parody on traditional worker-employer relationships. Families that thought better of it and tried to free their daughters from mill contracts by paying off loans, discovered that interest rates and other conditions arbitrarily set by the companies (on almost a case-by-case basis) made repayment virtually impossible.[28]

The lack of any sense of reciprocity in the relationship between owners and workers, and the attitudes of mill owners who made no effort to provide conditions of work that were even marginally acceptable, meant that even the contract system would bring mixed results to the textile industry.* Poverty, the place of daughters in the family system, and the cash advances on contracts continued to bring in large numbers of new recruits for an expanding number of mills. But in the absence of other incentives, the contract system failed to persuade workers that they were bound to the terms they had agreed to. Labor turn-over was extremely high in the textile industry throughout the Meiji period. Few workers lasted more than a year on the job, irrespective of what the contract stipulated; most stayed only six months or slightly longer. The runaway or "escaped" worker became a symbol of the industry's pref-erence for recruiting new labor and using it up, rather than investing in improved working conditions and higher wages. An annual turnover rate of 50 percent was typical of Meiji textile mills, and some owners seem to have gotten into the habit of replacing virtually their entire female work force each year. Turnover was also used as a mecha-nism for dealing with periodic business downturns in the industry, obviating the need for layoffs.[29] High rates of turnover and escape continued well into the twentieth cen-tury, long after industry leaders had come to recognize that a stable work force promoted productivity. Mill own-ers made few attempts to increase worker productivity by

* In fact, once families in the countryside understood the lack of reciprocity in the contract system, they were free to manipulate the process as cynically as the owners. One can well imagine that some families took the cash advance and encouraged their daughters to leave mill work "without permission" at the earli-est opportunity. As long as the daughter remained healthy, she could work for someone closer to home after a short time at the mill for at least the same wages, and the family would have both the advance and a daughter bringing in a wage through work less damaging to her health.

making long-term employment more attractive; the few efforts that were made seem to have been carried out with little enthusiasm, and they had equally little effect.[30]

The rate of escape, even taking into account the possibility that some employers looked the other way (thus avoiding any possibility of severance payments), was remarkable. In most cases, there was considerable risk involved, and often very harsh punishment for those who were caught. The typical mill dormitory was designed for security—that is, to keep workers in. Doors were locked at night; barbed wire was strung around walled factory compounds; supervisors patrolled the dormitories and watchmen patrolled the grounds. The workers themselves clearly knew the dormitory for what it was: "The dormitory windows had heavy metal screens to prevent [escape], but if a woman did escape, the watchmen would jump on their horses and ride in all directions, closing the passes and the roads. Eventually the railway station would be closed. Usually the woman was brought right back. It was literally a prison."[31]

Yokoyama Gennosuke interviewed a number of escapees around the turn of the century, who gave the following reasons for their willingness to risk running away from the mills: (1) they were constantly watched and at most places were never allowed to leave the company grounds; (2) meals in the dormitories never varied; (3) the work, particularly on the night shift, was intolerable, and the slightest delay was interpreted as negligence, for which workers were severely punished; and (4) wages were so low that workers ruined their health trying to earn a bonus for a little spending money.[32]

Working conditions began to deteriorate badly in the 1880's, the result of growing numbers of mills in competition, the organization of owners into spinning and weaving associations that tended to standardize the worst conditions in the industry, and the initiation of night-shift

Kishida Toshiko, ca. 1890, an early political speaker who took to the lecture platform to press for improvements in women's social and economic status

The short hairstyles of these young women of the early 1870's mark them as "progressives"

From left to right, Ishida Taka and Tominaga Raku, two members of the women's rights movement; Ueki Emori, a political theorist and one of the few male champions of women's rights in the Meiji period; and the young Shimizu Toyoko, who was later to write extensively on the subject of women's political rights, ca. 1884

This woman activist is leading a workers' protest against the Fuji Spinning Mills in Kawasaki, ca. 1915

Biology students at Japan Women's University in Tokyo. Founded in 1901, the university was attended primarily by the daughters of the city's upper-middle-class families

Yajima Kajiko, ca. 1920, founder of the Women's Reform Society and the force behind the unrelenting campaigns against prostitution conducted through much of the Meiji period

Hatoyama Haruko, ca. 1920, an advocate of increased power for women within the family and an important Meiji educator

Okumura Ioko, ca. 1905, founder of the Japan Women's Patriotic Association

Members of the Commoner's Society at Tokyo's Hibiya Park, February 28, 1905. The group has gathered to see two of their number, Kōtoku Shūsui and Nishikawa Kōjiro (standing, left to right, behind their luggage), off to prison. Among those pictured are Fukuda

Fukuda Hideko, ca. 1905, founder of the journal *Women of the World* and a lifelong feminist

Hideko (sixth from left), Kōtoku Chiyōko (standing next to her hus-band), and (from left to right, at the far right) Sakai Toshiko, Kawa-mura Haruko, Matsuoka Fumiko, and Imai Utako.

Itō Noe, one of the
editors of the *Bluestocking Journal.* Itō was
jailed and murdered
in her cell by a Tokyo
police captain in 1923.
Killed along with her
were her common-law
husband, the anarchist
Ōsugi Sakae, and Ōsu-
gi's young nephew.
This picture was taken
ca. 1911, when Ito was
16 or 17 years old.

Itō Noe and Ōsugi
Sakae two years before
their deaths at the
hands of the police in
1923

Kanno Suga, ca. 1908, a journalist and avowed anarchist who was hanged in 1911 for plotting the assassination of the Meiji Emperor in what came to be known as the Great Treason Incident

A newspaper artist's sketch of some of the defendants in the Great Treason trial. Kōtoku Shusui is on the left and Kanno Suga in the center. Like Kanno, Kōtoku was found guilty and hanged.

Yosano Akiko (right), a poet and writer on women's issues, with her friend and fellow poet Yamakawa Tomiko, ca. 1900. The young Yamakawa died of tuberculosis a few years after this photograph was taken.

Hiratsuka Raichō (left), founder of the Bluestockings, and Yamada Waka, an Ameyuki-san who returned to Japan to become a strong advocate of women's rights, ca. 1919

work, enabling owners to run their equipment nonstop. Of all of the changes in conditions, night work probably had the most immediate and profound effect on the lives of Meiji textile workers.

The average workday in Japan's textile industry from the 1880's to 1900 was 12 to 13 hours, broken only by two 15-minute meal periods. But night work effectively increased the number of total hours for many workers because they were required to stay on the job until replacements arrived. As the Meiji government's own research revealed, night work was usually "very disagreeable" to the factory worker, and so "there is a lot of absenteeism on that shift. In many cases, workers who are about to leave are ordered to remain on the job for a total of 24 hours. Occasionally they are told to work until noon the next day, remaining at work for a total of 36 hours."[33]

What was "disagreeable" about night work was not only the increased physical strain, but the fact that women found they were much more subject to sexual harassment during that shift than at other times. These facts were well known to employers, whose own studies indicated as much.[34]

The importance of the night shift and the difficulty of getting workers to show up for it made the dormitory system important to owners in new ways. The dormitories now became a preserve of captive labor, always ready to assume night work when "commuters" failed to appear; this made supervision and security all the more important. And it made any function the dormitory might have performed in some paternal context a very bad joke. With night work, many owners put twice as many women in the dormitories as they were built to hold. Women worked and slept in shifts, and shared bedding and sleeping space. There was a new urgency in "protecting" workers by locking dormitory facilities, and young women, sleeping in large rooms in groups of 30 or 40, were checked in and out of the rooms by supervisors, who also censored outgoing mail and reported uncooperative workers to their factory supervisors.[35] The reality of their lives is reflected in a song textile workers sang: "Working in the factory is like being in jail. / The only thing missing is the chains."[36]

Low pay for work that women do has a universal history.[37] Wages in the Japanese textile mills were low to begin with and were made lower still by a number of devices owners used to discourage escape and encourage productivity. Everything was deducted from a worker's wage, often including the recruiter's fees and the worker's transportation to the mill. Room and board were deducted on a daily basis. Interest payments on loans made to parents and the savings deposits that most mills required were often automatically deducted too. The savings accounts workers were forced to keep might or might not accrue interest, depending on company policy, but it was understood that if the worker defaulted on her contract the company could confiscate all the money, total savings as well as any interest.[38]

Workers often found, in the first months of the contract, that they owed their employers money, rather than the other way around. The net result was to ensure that workers never had sufficient savings to encourage an attempt to escape, and to force them to work for bonus money by increasing their productivity if they wanted any spending money at all. The calculation and payment of wages varied slightly from mill to mill, and there were significant differences in the wage scales of various regions, but most companies paid a basic daily wage plus a bonus for exceeding quotas. Women who made above-average wages were women whose productivity and stamina were unusual; "100 yen" workers (those whose output earned them a year-end bonus) were used as models for others, who were encouraged to take advantage of the same incentives. Companies also sponsored contests between competing teams of workers to increase productivity, with flags and candy given to the winners. Women who participated in more or less constant contests between occupants of various rooms in the dormitories, or between women from various prefectures working in the mill, no doubt found it relieved the monotony of their work. But it also undermined their health.[39]

The most dramatic commentary on conditions in the textile industry during the Meiji period was that most workers showed the wear and tear of mill life after only a few months on the job. Young women who left their villages may have been undernourished and overworked, but they often looked a good deal healthier than when they returned from the mills. Lung disease was an industry-wide problem, the result of long hours, inadequate nutrition, and a working environment conducive to the development of tuberculosis. High humidity in silk-reeling rooms was thought to decrease the chances of thread breaking; in cotton-weaving industries (often attached to cotton-spinning mills), high humidity was considered important for a quality product. In both industries, steam rose from various artificial sources and quickly condensed into moisture on the ceiling, to fall like rain on the workers below. In the winter, workers who came into the mill after walking through bitter cold, were immediately confronted with drenching steam and 70- to 90-degree heat. In the hot days of summer, the humidity increased the effects of working in the heat. In cotton spinning and related industries, fine particles of dust from both fiber and machinery produced chronic lung irritation.[40]

In general, what health-care facilities the mills provided were minimal at best, but the greater problem was that workers were under so much pressure from supervisory personnel to stay on the job they rarely got medical attention in the early stages of an illness. Tuberculosis, endemic to the industry by 1900, was easily spread via crowded sleeping rooms and shared bedding in the dormitories. Death rates among textile workers were much higher than for the general public during the Meiji period, and nearly 25 percent of those workers fell victim to tuberculosis.[41] Workers died of other killing diseases they acquired in the mills, but tuberculosis was a nineteenth- and early-twentieth-century "social disease" with particularly tragic circumstances. Parents whose daughters became ill on the job were notified that they must come to the mill to pick them up. In such cases the company often failed to provide any severance payment or other assistance to the worker or her family; the principal concern was to get the affected worker off the premises as quickly as possible. Since the disease was often in an advanced stage by the time parents were notified, they were simply taking their daughters home to die.

Some women, despairing of their ability to endure or overcome the conditions of their lives in the mills, committed suicide. Suicide in Japan, as elsewhere, can be seen from several perspectives. It was, for some women, an acceptable way out of what they saw as an impossible situation. But it can also be seen as an implied protest against both the mill owners who exploited them and the parents who had put them there. Though textile associations do not seem to have kept a statistical record of suicides among workers, many firsthand accounts indicate that it was a common occurrence.[42] (Common enough, anyway, to lead workers in silk-reeling mills around Lake Suwa to claim that the water level of the lake changed because of the frequent suicides, and that local fishermen performing for the Imperial family on one occasion were chagrined to find a woman's body in one of their nets.)[43]

Escape and suicide, costly individual acts of protest, were relatively passive ways of dealing with conditions in the mills, and as the 1880's moved on, women workers learned to use more effective, collective action. In an effort to better their situation and force owners to take responsibility for the conditions they had created, women organized boycotts, walkouts, and strikes—actions that were to be commonplace in the textile industry from 1885. Textile workers, who until as late as the 1950's were described by Japanese labor historians as "ignorant farm girls," uninterested in or incapable of protest, were in fact the pioneers of Japan's modern labor movement.[44] When, in 1897, socialists and returned students organized the Association for the Promotion of Labor Unions, they billed it as the beginning of unionism in Japan.[45] But by then Japanese women had been confronting management for more than a decade with demands for better working conditions and higher wages, and had backed those demands up by refusing to return to work until they had won concessions. Without benefit of organizers or well-developed ideology, Meiji textile workers demonstrated that they understood the importance of unity, of consensus around demands, and of the need to take risks to force a response from management.[46]

Yet these workers, like women workers elsewhere, were largely ignored by Japanese labor organizers once the unionizing effort began in Japan. Except for women who worked in the printing trades, coal mining, or other predominantly male industries, would-be unionists discounted the potential of a group whose numbers dominated the work force: women were "unorganizable"; they were too attached to the family, too young, too filial, and too impermanent a part of the work force to undertake the historic mission of workers in a labor movement. Since women had to struggle against this sort of discrimination in the union movement until well into the twentieth century, hearing continual objections from male unionists when they did make any inroads, one suspects that, from the beginning, the problem was less that they were unorganizable than that they were women.[47]

Not only have women textile workers traditionally been made to bear major responsibility for the failures of the early labor movement in Japan,[48] but labor historians have not been interested enough in the record of labor conflict involving women in early Meiji to study it in its own right, making it difficult, if not impossible, for Japanese women to claim their own history as workers. There are few detailed, accessible records of the many walkouts, boycotts, and strikes women used to protest nineteenth-century working conditions. Until further research is done, all we have are newspaper accounts of a few early strikes and a slowly growing collection of items from local histories, the bulk of which document actions taken in the larger mills in heavily populated areas. Even these incomplete descriptions, however, suggest strongly that Meiji working women knew how to organize and make effective use of the few weapons they had. Their advantage was the ability to hurt owners by shutting down their equipment for even a day or two. Since many mills ran 24 hours a day, day in and day out, the loss of even a few hours was seen as expensive, compromising an owner's ability to compete.

Shutting down the equipment, from the workers' standpoint, required substantial organization, unanimity, and risk. The typical pattern of the early-Meiji strike involved an initial stage of discussion aimed at achieving unity, so that when the second stage came, sufficient numbers of workers would leave the factory to close it down. Workers would then gather somewhere in the community near the factory, and wait for management to listen and act on their demands.[49] None of these early strikes lasted much more than four days; longer strikes would have made the workers vulnerable to replacement, and could even have finished off some of the smaller mills. But a brief strike, resulting in a shutdown of mill equipment, was a successful tactic for those who had the organizational skills and discipline to pursue it. Such workers were typically rewarded by management's agreement to one or two of their demands. It enabled them to exploit the only vulnerability owners had, without exposing their own.

One can argue, as some labor historians have done, that these early strikes were not effective,[50] but this seems an arbitrary judgment, one that ignores the context Meiji women faced. Japan's first strike, on June 12, 1886, at the Amamiya silk mill in Kōfu, illustrates the strengths of Meiji workers organized in their own behalf. The women at Amamiya had confronted managment over working conditions the previous year, but now 100 of them walked out of the mill in a direct challenge to the owner's effort to increase working hours and at the same time lower wages. The strike seems to have been the result of long and careful planning, backed by many hours of discussion over attempts on the part of owners to get better control of their workers by forming a spinning association. When the 100 Amamiya workers walked off the job, they gathered in a local temple to discuss more fully issues they already understood in some detail. Chief among these were wages, hours of work, and a general worsening of conditions that would result from the regulations adopted by the new spinning association. For four days the strike force, which had grown to 196 workers, kept the factory closed. Finally, mediators hired by the mill discussed the issues with the strikers' elected representatives, and the strike was settled.

Though the Amamiya workers did not win on the issue of the spinning association's new regulations, they did get the owner to back down from adding 30 minutes to each shift, thus making the normal work schedule 15 hours, and to retract his promise to punish women who arrived late, or left early, by deducting the lost time from their wages. The Amamiya management agreed to relax the reporting time for workers by one hour in the morning, and to study ways to improve general conditions of work in the mill. They said nothing, and agreed to nothing, on the subject of wages, a major issue in the strike.

The apparent success of the Amamiya strike, coupled with the efforts of owners to enforce their new regulations throughout the Kōfu area, produced at least four more strikes in the summer of 1886. Most were settled in less than four days, with workers winning some, though not all (and not always the most important), of their demands. But precedents for strike actions were being set, and in the Kōfu area at least, the idea of women workers confronting owners seemed less and less unexpected. On one occasion, bemused townspeople in Kōfu city watched as 70 young women from a nearby mill filed through city streets in the late afternoon heat, looking for a vacant temple in which to meet and wait for management to address their complaints. Since all the temples seemed too filled with travelers to accommodate one entire shift of workers from the local mill, the marchers just proceeded on, continuing the search for a meeting place, now closely followed by flustered management representatives from the mill. Almost as soon as the workers found a place to sit down, nervous managers agreed to mediation, and the strike was settled within hours.

The summer of 1886 was not to be the end of strikes in the Kōfu area; the following year 150 workers in a local mill walked out to protest working conditions and later staged a full-scale strike. And on the eve of the government's celebration of its new constitution in 1889, strikes and walkouts seemed to be gathering force throughout the country, sending spinning-association members to meetings called specifically to work out countermeasures to strike actions. The failure of these measures was demonstrated effectively in September–October 1889, in a strike involving 300 workers in a newly established cotton spinning mill in Osaka. The strike centered on workers' demands for higher wages and more control over their bonus pay. Both of these economic issues were central to management's control over labor, particularly the bonus payment, which was often turned into involuntary savings. Since most of the Osaka workers had signed a five-year contract, the company routinely retained the bulk of the savings by default, for few workers completed the full five-year term to the satisfaction of the owners.

The Osaka strike produced noisy, if not violent, confrontations between management and workers. At one point, management officials burst into a meeting and fired the strike leaders, warning the other women that they too would be fired if they did not go back to work. The company then advertised 300 jobs available for qualified applicants. The workers persisted and were joined, unexpectedly, by male machinists in the mill. Finally, on October 5, the sixth day of the strike, management agreed to the demands of the workers for higher wages and some control over their savings, making it the most successful strike in early Meiji. In fact, it may have been one of the most successful strikes staged by women anywhere in the world before 1890.[51]

Unfortunately, scattered successes like these, remarkable as they were in the Meiji context, did not do much to alleviate the general condition of women in the mills, or those working in match and tobacco factories, coal mines, and printing shops. There were labor disputes outside the textile industry in the 1880's and later, and the issues women raised in these confrontations were very similar.* But there were few connections outside the local arena. The 1880's demonstrated that Meiji working women had a rising consciousness of themselves as workers and the abil-

---

* An example is the strike at the Ōmori match factory in August 1888, in which workers protested labor regulations and working conditions similar to those in the textile industry (*Nihon fujin mondai shiryō shūsei*, 10 vols., Tokyo, 1976–80, 10: 37).

ity to organize locally. But extending these strengths beyond a single factory to include workers in the entire industry or in other industries required resources they simply did not have. The creation of a genuine labor movement would have meant overcoming barriers of illiteracy, strong regional and local loyalties that often interfered with organizing (even on the local level), and widespread skepticism among women workers that factory work, even with substantial improvement, could be made tolerable.[52] In the textile industry, moreover, because of the dormitory system, companies that could not prevent their workers from striking could at least make it difficult for them to communicate with other workers. Thus, though there were five major labor-management clashes in the Kōfu area in the summer of 1886, and though the successes of the first strikes no doubt encouraged the others, there is little evidence of direct communication between the groups of workers involved, all of whom were protesting the same conditions. The dormitory system probably made communication among would-be strikers easier in a single plant, but it made communication with other workers outside difficult, if not impossible.

Japan may or may not be a good test of the theory that when women enter the industrial work force, it not only accelerates social change, but also gives those women greater power. The participation of women in Japan's industrial labor force from 1870 to 1930 is unparalleled; in no society has the proportion of women workers reached the 60 percent that Japan averaged in this critical period.[53] But numbers alone certainly did not produce changes beneficial to Japanese women; in fact, it can easily be argued that Japan's industrial revolution, the social costs of which have been underplayed until quite recently, was more damaging to women than to any other single group. To acknowledge the price women paid in Japan's effort to catch up and survive in a world dominated by Western imperialism requires trying to measure the immeasurable: death, despair, hopelessness, unrecovered lives.* At the same time, an attempt needs to be made to recognize and measure the complexities and contradictions of the Meiji working women's experience. They were "filial daughters" of Japan's countryside, some of whom were genuinely convinced of their parents' worth and not their own. They were capable of enormous endurance, a virtue still highly regarded among Japanese women. But they also showed, in well-planned and executed struggles with management, a strong and eminently organizable working-class consciousness.

That potential was never exploited, but neither did the feminist activists of the 1880's make connections with the working women whose experience was central to their critique of Japanese society. The record is incomplete, but with the apparent death of the Liberal Party in 1884, there were fewer and fewer connections of this kind between women in large cities and women in the countryside, even on an occasional basis. It is possible that only one woman's-rights advocate, Shimizu Toyoko, ever spoke to a group of women factory workers about problems they shared.[54] This failure of political women to make contact with working women is of course not unique to Japan, and is partially explained by the timing of popular-rights activity and protests by workers, as well as by the government's ability to frustrate political communication in the period.[55] But it was a costly omission, and yet another instance of the failure of women's movements everywhere to overcome social

* Certainly factory work was not something to occupy their time for two or three years before coming home and marrying. A survey of 28 prefectures in 1910 revealed that of 200,000 female factory workers from villages around the country, 120,000 did not return home. Some married, but most, according to Ishihara, simply drifted from one job to another until they were compelled, by failing health and economic need, to take up prostitution or other kinds of unsavory work. Of the 80,000 who returned home, 13,000 were seriously ill. (Ishihara Osamu, *Jokō no genkyō*, pp. 187–89; Ishihara Osamu, "Jokō no eiseigakuteki kansatsu," in *Nihon fujin mondai shiryō shūsei*, 3: 244–76.)

divisions that diluted their potential strength, separating them into mutually exclusive constituencies that could relate only along class lines.

Those divisions, clouding a shared perception of powerlessness among women of all classes, may have lapsed for a time in early Meiji, but in the 1880's they were being recreated in new forms, by a new aristocracy composed of business leaders, bureaucrats, and intellectuals, as well as the old Court aristocracy.[56] By the turn of the century, there were compelling distinctions not only between the "lady" and the "mill girl," but between the mill girl and other working women who occupied new, more respectable jobs.[57] Young women forced to go into mill work were by definition of the lowest class; they could never make up the distance between their own experience and the requirements of work as a nurse, telephone operator, teacher, or department store clerk.*

Still more important, after 1887, the "lady" was coming into her own in Japanese society. With her came all those definitions that served men so well and had so little to do with the realities of women's lives. Though many of those ladies did work, and many championed the economic independence of women, they sometimes had difficulty relating to textile workers—except as objects of ladylike social reform programs.

---

* Mitsukoshi was the first major department store to hire women clerks for its clothing shop in 1901. By that time women were working in some numbers as nurses, telephone and telegraph operators, office workers, and teachers. There were a few women physicians. (*Nihon fujin mondai shiryō shūsei*, 3: 18–19.) Office work, however, did not become a major source of employment for Japanese women until well after the Pacific War, in contrast to the early demand for female office workers in the United States.

5. The Women's Reform Society

The purpose of the society is to develop the dignity of women by reforming corrupt social practices, cultivating morality, and prohibiting drinking and smoking.   Bylaws of the
Tokyo Women's Reform Society, 1886

The work of reform is extremely difficult, but . . . the opportunity is at hand, and we will not give up hope until all of us together, brothers and sisters, have spent the last ounce of strength to bring it about.

Tokyo Women's Reform Magazine, 1888

The last decade of the nineteenth century was a difficult and sobering time for idealists and advocates of change in Japan. Though basic political and economic issues had still not been settled in the 1890's, the country was much less amenable to social change than it had been in the previous two decades. Equality with the West remained elusive, but as Japan joined the ranks of the colonizers, revision of the unequal treaties began. The social costs of Japan's transformation were temporarily forgotten in mid-decade, the result of a popular war with China in 1894–95 that made patriots of the most unlikely people.[1]

Success in that war, as well as the beginning of treaty revision talks, gave the government something to show for the efforts the citizenry had been asked to make. But it did not inhibit demands for continuing sacrifice or, in the wake of the Triple Intervention that followed the war,[2] the pretense that the country was still engaged in a desperate struggle to survive. The indemnity won from the Chinese thus brought an infusion of cash for heavy industry and arms without, at the same time, relieving the burdens of tenant farmers or their daughters. The constitution and the operation of new political forms did little to redress the inequality of social life or the authoritarian character of government; and as a result, an oligarchy operating both through the constitution and through extra-constitutional mechanisms was still forced to weave a façade of stability from a social fabric torn by political and economic distress. Though the language of the decade seemed more traditional, often Confucian, the institutions that permitted increasing control over the population were borrowed from authoritarian models in the West. As the government continued to restrain political protest and assume more and more control over the pace and content of social change, women found themselves more frequent targets of direct government policy. Women, in the last decade of the century, became a test of the government's ability to initiate and define acceptable change; to undo unwanted change and institute in its place a government vision of social stability based in large measure on women's acceptance of male-defined, "proper" roles in society.

Once it was clear that the political arena would be closed to them, women made the decade one of social reform. This development can be seen either as a natural corollary of earlier experience, including the influence of missionary schools or as a response to the futility of direct involvement in politics. For some women it may have been both. It is clear that both Kishida Toshiko and Fukuda Hideko would not have chosen social reform over politics if they had been given a choice. And in fact, neither of these important women played major roles in the decade. They contributed to the legacy that came down to women as reform in 1890, and were directly affected by the activities of reformers.* But it was not a time for public appearances

---

* The comments in Kishida's diary indicate her frustration with vicarious involvement in politics through her husband, the president of the new Lower House. Fukuda, who sent a petition to the government protesting the exclusion

in the political arena; not a time for heroic female figures to move across the turbulent stage of Japanese politics. It was a time for chiding, persuasive, ladylike understatement that assumed, great as the political differences might be, a common social ground from which to work. The striking thing about the reformers of 1890–1900 was the similarity of their experience: they were teachers or former teachers, often very heavily influenced by Christian educators; journalists concerned about women's education; intellectuals whose personal experience and superior education had made them critical of women's roles in Japan; women with an international consciousness of women's issues.

More than other women in the period, Yajima Kajiko symbolized the reforming zeal of the decade. In 1886, when Kōfu's textile workers were striking, Mary Leavitt, an American representative of the Woman's Christian Temperance Union, was touring Japan, attracting large audiences.[3] Yajima heard her and was particularly impressed by words that spoke directly to her own experience. "Drinking," Leavitt said, was

not an individual, but a social problem; an abuse from which no benefit is derived. Drinking contributes to the break up of the family, assists the decline of morals, and contributes to crime. The women of this world are the people most affected by it. It may bring pleasure to men, but it is the old enemy of women. Therefore the struggle to liberate women must begin with the liberation of men from the evils of drinking.

---

of women from politics in 1890, had become the common-law wife of Ōi Kentarō in 1889 and bore his child in 1891. She attended a Women's Reform Society meeting in the Kansai area and described it as a "high point"; there is some evidence that her decision to move to Tokyo, ultimately settling her Okayama family there, was related to the growth of the society's activities in the area. However, once she arrived in Tokyo, she was preoccupied with the struggle to survive. The private school she founded in 1891 with the help of her family was not much of an economic success. Kishida's diary indicates that she was one of the women who donated cash to Fukuda's school. (Murata Shizuko *Fukuda Hideko,* Tokyo, 1965, pp. 59–61; *Nihon fujin mondai shiryō shūsei,* 10 vols., Tokyo, 1976–80, 2: 88–95.)

Yajima talked with Leavitt the next day, and soon after, with a number of other women, including Ushioda Chieko, Sasaki Toyosu, Asai Saku, Honda Sadako, Ebina Miyako, and Yuasa Hatsuko, founded the Tokyo Women's Reform Society.[4] It was December 1886. Yajima Kajiko, then fifty-one, became its first president.*

Kajiko was a symbolic name she had given herself when she left Kyushu for Tokyo in 1872. She gave up Katsuko, a name that had served her for almost 40 years, as she stood on the deck of a ship watching the small oars that propelled and guided great ships in Nagasaki's harbor. She became Kajiko, for *kaji*, the oar. The family's excuse for her departure was that her brother in Tokyo was in need of care. In truth, she was leaving to begin her life again; she left behind three children, lost in a divorce action for which she was criticized all her life.[5] Even after her death, one of her famous nephews, the editor Tokutomi Sohō, remarked that he understood she had probably become a prime mover in the Japanese version of the WCTU because her husband drank; but he also implied that had she been more like her sisters, she would have stayed with her husband and persuaded him to mend his ways, rather than cutting all ties and going out on her own. A number of male relatives criticized Yajima on various occasions for her failure to stay in the marriage, as a good Kyushu woman should have done.[6]

Actually, the bitterness and anguish Yajima felt about marriage as an insitution began even before she was married. An observer as her older sisters were married off one by one, Yajima was especially upset by the situation of the family's fifth daughter, Setsuko. Setsuko was married to the well-known political leader Yokoi Shōnan after his

---

* In the next months the society circulated its prospectus to encourage the development of local groups elsewhere; it began publishing its own journal in 1888, expanded into a national organization in 1893, and eventually affiliated with the international WCTU. For details on the society's organizational history, see Kubushiro Ochimi, ed. *Yajima Kajiko den* (Tokyo, 1935), pp. 198–200.

wife died, but she was never considered anything but a concubine, a status that she shared with several other women in the household, who doubled as servants. When it was Yajima's turn to marry, the family decided on Hayashi Shiichirō, a widower with three children, who was a student and drinking crony of Yokoi's. He was well known in the area as *shuran,* a man who became violent when he drank. Yajima's obvious efforts to be a dutiful wife, and the fact that she bore him three children, did not prevent violent episodes in a stormy marriage that sent her back to her family's home from time to time. She left Hayashi only after a particularly upsetting episode involving her infant daughter. According to later accounts, Hayashi returned home one night after a drinking bout and threw a knife at the child; Yajima managed to shield her daughter from further attack, but only at the cost of having both of her own arms slashed; she swept the baby up and ran barefoot from the house, never to return. When the Hayashis' servant went to the Yajima household the next day to offer the usual apologies and escort Kajiko and her daughter back, he was met by a servant, who handed him a tray. On it lay the long black hair of Yajima Kajiko. It was 1868, the beginning of a new era; Yajima was preparing for divorce, taking her own name back. By 1872, her hair almost grown long again, she was on her way to Tokyo, ready to make a new life for herself.[7]

She became both student and teacher in Tokyo, living at her brother's house. She also made connections with Christian women educators, and became a teacher and administrator at a Christian school in the Tsukiji area of Tokyo in 1878; the following year she was baptized. Sometime during this period she also had an affair with a married man from northern Japan who was in Tokyo studying with her brother; Yajima had a daughter as a result of this relationship, and though she never publicly acknowledged the girl as her natural daughter, she provided for, and eventually adopted her, giving her the name Yajima Taeko.[8]

By the time she heard Leavitt speak, Yajima had lived a very full life, one of contradictions and of anguish, but also one of no small triumph. She had escaped the tyranny of a violent marriage—but had to give up three children to do it. She had a child by a married man—but was able to care for her and live with the innuendos. Now, at fifty, her tenacity had made her economically independent, able to use her skills as manager and teacher to carve out a niche for herself. But the anger and the sense of outrage that filled her life were still with her, and as head of the Tokyo Women's Reform Society, she could begin to vent some of it in constructive social criticism. That anger, as it turned out, had much less to do with drinking than with the fact of male privilege and patriarchal institutions in Japanese society.

The issues the Reform Society raised were not unfamiliar to Japanese society by 1886; men and women had been discussing them in print since the beginning of Meiji. The principal issues for Yajima and her colleagues were the concubine system and prostitution—these were the "corrupt social practices" the society wanted to reform. Drinking, a major target of the international WCTU, initially got little more than a passing nod from the Reform Society.[9] The extraordinary success of the organization was certainly related to a widespread response to these issues among women throughout the country, coupled with the rather genteel image of the society itself. And yet the society's "genteel" leaders did not shrink from the wider implications of the issues they raised. Then, as now, any discussion of the "traffic in women" led inevitably to much wider criticism of the place of women in the society as a whole. What began as an apparent critique of Japanese society, voiced by women whose Christian morality was offended, easily became a feminist argument about the exercise of male privilege and the repression of women in the society. The concubine system and prostitution (domestic and exported) were simply two aspects of a huge problem involving the sexual abuse of women in and out of the family structure.[10]

Their incipient feminism was a very sharp line dividing them from the wives of the new elite, who graced the costume balls and charity bazaars of the Rokumeikan era. From 1883 to 1887 Itō Umeko, the wife of the prominent government leader Itō Hirobumi, reigned supreme as the paragon of *kifujin shakō,* or ladylike social life: ordering gowns from Europe, learning English with a tutor, and setting the standard for unfamiliar kinds of social intercourse between men and women. It was Umeko who led the way in the establishment of women's "improvement" groups—places where women gathered to improve their etiquette and conversational skills so that if they were asked to attend some social function in the company of their husbands, they would not embarrass them.[11] For the most part, these women ventured little further in the development of new social roles than their husbands dictated; and, not surprisingly, when the Rokumeikan era faded, so did their intense interest in English and Western etiquette. The period did have some unintended consequences, in raising, for example, the thought that men and women might be able to socialize in an atmosphere of apparent equality; or that women's conversations, let alone opinions, might be expressed and appreciated in the company of men. But though improvement groups continued to meet, there was little experience of such social contact for most women once the Rokumeikan era had ended.*

---

* These groups, we may note, prompted heated debate in newspapers and magazines; the subject of male-female communication in new social contexts was one nearly everyone tried to speak to in the period, including Kishida and Fukuzawa. It is interesting that, after the Rokumeikan era, many of the women's improvement societies continued to meet as a part of a separate women's culture, trying out their English and eating together at Western-style restaurants. It is a practice one still occasionally sees among older Japanese women.

Though Reform Society women and Itō Umeko's followers often encountered each other at Rokumeikan bazaars and improvement society meetings, they were distinctly different groups. They may have enjoyed similar status, but Reform Society women, motivated by Christian convictions and a desire to better the conditions of women, tried consistently to determine their own priorities.* They often couched their views in ladylike language, which may have made them more acceptable to a society unaccustomed to women who controlled their own lives, but they made unpopular choices. In the process, they reversed the emphasis on improvement for women, implicitly insisting that men, not women, were the proper focus of improvement and reform in Japanese society.

The membership of the various branches of the Reform Society before 1900 is uncertain, but it is safe to say that the movement touched the lives of a very large number of women before the turn of the century. The reformers' methods included solid local organization, the wide dissemination of programs and goals through their own journal and through others friendly to their cause, and an ability to raise sufficient funds to keep several different campaigns running simultaneously.[12] They used the lecture platform effectively before 1890, but they also confronted the government directly with memorials and petitions, often signed by hundreds of women from around the country. These tactics gave them, among other things, a high degree of public visibility through newspaper coverage, and made them a political force to be dealt with in the period. Their tenacity in placing petitions before a government that tried to ignore them went unheralded in

* Some confusion is understandable, especially in the case of a woman like Hatoyama Haruko (1861–1938), who was a translator for Itō Umeko and sometimes sat in with her improvement group. But the two groups' notions of "improvement" and "reform" were as different in 1885 as were their definitions of what constituted a "good wife; wise mother" in 1900. On Itō and her group, see Takamure Itsue, *Takamure Itsue zenshū* (Tokyo, 1977), 5: 538–44.

the Meiji period, but it was a tactic that deepened many women's understanding of the issues that affected them, and that ultimately won the Reform Society a good deal of support.

In the first decade of the Reform Society's existence, the issues of monogamy and prostitution were so closely linked that one was rarely raised without the other. They were the principal problems the society named in the 1887 prospectus it sent to women's groups all over the country, and they continued, after the political shocks of 1890, to absorb the attention of women who hoped to improve their status in Japanese society. The reformers' long campaign against prostitution can be faulted by feminists for its occasional lapses of consciousness about how the system really worked, producing a tendency to castigate the "fallen woman."[13] But the burden of the society's attack was on male institutions, at local, national, and international levels. The Reform Society was the first group to attack the problem of overseas prostitution, pointing to the link between the concubine system, domestic prostitution, and the sexual requirements of trade and Empire.[14] Stressing the "national shame" of overseas prostitution, the society submitted a petition bearing hundreds of signatures to the genro as early as 1887, following it up with a campaign to educate the public through lectures and newspaper articles. The government was thus indicted for the plight of women who, with tacit approval, were exported to various parts of the world, from Shanghai to San Francisco; they were the predecessors of the *karayuki san,* who were later sent all over Asia to service Japanese troops.[15]

Society members in various parts of the world reported their unsuccessful attempts to deal with the problem. In August 1890, for example, the Reform Society magazine printed this account, submitted by a member in Sausalito, California:

When I arrived here three years ago, in 1887, there were only about 10 other Japanese women in the area, most of whom I met in church. But now I have learned about the increasing number of women arriving, as well as of their unsavory business. A charitable organization has been set up . . . to help these arriving women and keep them from falling into sin. . . . We have met every ship coming in and interviewed the women. . . . We are able to persuade some to come to our church and talk things over, but . . . they disappear into thin air the next day.[16]

There followed, in a later article, the interesting argument that the export of prostitutes to North America was adding to discrimination against Orientals, an attitude that was already "bursting the seams" of society there. The Chinese, the writer said, had been excluded because "they were skilled and had more stamina than Americans . . . and eventually took work away from them." But if Japanese were deported because of something as shameful as prostitution, there would be no defense. "The rebuff of the Chinese may be something to be proud of, but not a single word of excuse is possible in the case of the expulsion of Japanese women."[17]

Still, for most Reform Society members, the important links were those between prostitution and the way husbands and wives behaved at home. Government policy, influencing one, must influence the other.

In Europe and America . . . there are strict laws and religious beliefs that severely condemn prostitution and therefore make possible proper relationships between men and women. . . . This presents a good impression . . . and is indicative of internal order and happiness. . . .

People traveling through Singapore, Hong Kong, and Shanghai report many Japanese prostitutes in those cities. . . . In fact, our own government's sanction of this business encourages them. . . .

For the government to officially approve prostitution on the one hand, then claim on the other to be interested in maintaining purity in the relationship between men and women at home, is hopeless.[18]

No matter how polite the language, the women of the Reform Society were saying that any household where the concubine system was still in place was (irrespective of the social status of its inhabitants) not just a household that fostered prostitution; it was a center of prostitution. Concubines and prostitutes were not merely symbols of uncivilized society; to the women of the Reform Society, concubines by any other name were still prostitutes, and their children were illegitimate, even when fathered by the head of the household.[19] Their failure to equivocate on the issue did not endear them to the country's leaders. Still less appreciated, not surprisingly, was their insistence that men who wanted to lead the country should be willing to submit to certain tests of moral character, a position strengthened by a thinly veiled attack on Itō Hirobumi in *Women's Education Magazine.**

Such public criticism of the male aristocracy by well-bred and respected women had no precedents in Japanese history, and it carried significant political implications. To insist that Japan's leaders be morally upright men was quite consistent with the positions taken by both *Women's Education Magazine* and the Reform Society. There may have been equal parts of Christianity and Confucianism in the belief that bad men forfeited the right to rule; but there was also feminist content in the notion that immoral men would impede the country's march to civilization for women, since the root of civilization was sexual fidelity in

---

* Itō, one of the most prominent men in the government, reportedly seduced or attacked a young married woman in the spring of 1887 during a masked ball held at the Rokumeikan. He later arranged for a cash settlement to the family involved, and the incident was hushed up. Kishida Toshiko tried to see the woman to discuss the series of events, but was unsuccessful. Though she said she would pursue the story even if her husband divorced her for it, she finally agreed to let Iwamoto Zenji write it up for an article in *Women's Education Magazine,* published that year. Kishida revived the issue in 1889, on the eve of the inauguration of constitutional government, suggesting that women should make every effort to keep men of dubious moral character out of politics. See Iwamoto, "Kan'in no kūki," *Jogaku zasshi,* 65 (May 21, 1887): 81–83; and Nakajima Toshiko, "Nihon shakai no kūki," *ibid.,* 153 (March 16, 1889): 10.

relationships between men and women. What Kishida outlined in her 1889 article was in fact a political position suggesting unequivocally that women, even without the vote, could and should ruin a politician's ability to run for or hold office.[20] Asai Saku later expanded on the theme of the potential political power of women in an article for *Tokyo Women's Reform Magazine:*

Since we women do not have the vote, we have had to rely on men to make choices. . . . But we are very concerned that when questions arise involving the welfare of women, men will make those decisions alone, and the archaic system of "respecting men and despising women" still prevails in the country. . . . Since the success or failure of issues related to women's rights is to be left in the hands of the Diet, we feel a great deal of apprehension. . . . But perhaps encouraging men from behind the scenes will bring us a step closer to our goals. . . . If, for example, someone running for office were totally unscrupulous in his attempts to control the voters, wouldn't it be a wife's place to point out the unsuitability of that person?[21]

At the time Asai wrote these words (July 1890) the Reform Society was the closest thing to becoming a political arm of the women's movement since the popular-rights days. The reformers had generated local groups throughout Japan and were on their way to establishing a national organization; they were able to communicate with relatively little interference, arranging lecture tours throughout the country and using local journals to good advantage. They had a number of allies, men and women, all over Japan, many of whom were highly respected educators. And they seemed to know how to raise enough money to keep the organization actively engaged in several struggles at once, in several different localities. The Reform Society also had international links, formalized after the Tokyo group became a national organization in 1893. This connection may have been less important as a source of ideology than as an outlet for news about Japan's women to the rest of the world, but if nothing else, the Reform Society's disclosures at international meetings meant potential embarrassment for the Japanese government in the world press.

The anti-prostitution campaign was a forceful demonstration of the society's ability to mobilize public opinion. Not only did the reformers' activities encourage the development of independent anti-prostitution groups around the country, but local governments were pushed to propose and pass regulations dealing with the problem. The Reform Society's ability to influence local politics and to increase the visibility of "women's issues" through well-publicized memorials and petitions to the national government made it something very close to a Woman's Party. The leadership, and most of the financial support, came from women; the society spoke to and for a female constituency about very broad issues directly related to the status of women in the society. And it knew how to mobilize support for those issues.

But the political potential of the Reform Society and its national network was never fully developed. Like all other women's groups after 1890, it had to be cautious about what officials might construe as the political content of its efforts. That summer in 1890, just weeks after Asai had published her article about women and the vote, activists all over the country were caught totally off guard by the government's bringing women under Article 5 of the Police Security Regulations. By the time they had begun to mobilize against this action, they were struck by the news that organizers of the new Diet intended to exclude them, even as observers, from Diet meetings.

The first action, in which the outgoing cabinet added women to the list of persons denied access to the political process under regulations drawn up earlier, prompted a flood of articles and editorials of protest throughout the country, but the government was changing over to new constitutional forms and, conveniently, no one seemed accountable. Tactically, the action put women back on the defensive, trying to make sense out of irrationality, and in the process resurrecting all the old arguments about women and their intelligence, their physical strength, and their capacity for public life.[22] The issue of excluding women from the observer's gallery was easier to deal with directly, in part because it was less important, but also because it was clear who was accountable, and they (the Diet organizers) could be reached by members of the Reform Society.

The society's memorial on the issue, written by Yajima Kajiko, is an interesting political document, made up in equal parts of polite gesture and blunt outrage, praise and ridicule. After discussing, with tongue in cheek, the apparent grounds on which women had been denied all political rights, Yajima pointed out the differences in the more recent decision to exclude women from Diet sessions.

But, when it comes to attending Diet sessions, we think it exceedingly strange to say that women, simply by virtue of the fact that they are women, may not attend sessions open to everyone with the possible exception of people carrying weapons—sessions open to boys chasing horses, old men selling candy, or farmers fresh from their fields. . . . It is insupportable to think that women can be excluded in such circumstances.[23]

What most struck Yajima and others, including Shimizu, about the events in the summer of 1890 was the ease with which the authorities managed to shut women out of the political process, without any explanation or justification for their actions. It was possible to make educated guesses about the outgoing cabinet's decision to restrict the political activities of women, given the government's previous record. Depending on one's point of view, that action could be interpreted as yet another resurrection of traditional attitudes about women or as an important denial of potential membership and support to the antigovernment parties that had just won the election—parties with roots in the popular-rights movement.* But the second decision came from the leaders of the parties women had supported—from the very men who had been expected to push for women's rights in the new Diet. And that decision too went unexplained. The politicians who proposed it did not bother to present their views on the necessity of barring women from the observer's gallery, and women like Shimizu Toyoko were left to speculate. She remembered having read the argument in a newspaper, she said in an article entitled "To My Beloved Sisters in Tears," that women might be a distraction to the lawmakers if they were allowed to observe Diet sessions, but she had thought the argument so preposterous at the time that she had simply laughed about it.[24]

After the fact, she and other women like her were not laughing. In the same article Shimizu asked an angry but logical question: were there no limits to attempts on the part of men to exclude women from politics? How much more injustice would women have to suffer at their hands? What would the impact on the country be if the Diet were organized this way, after women had already been denied the right to engage in the political process?

If, in dealing with the functions of the Diet and the reasons it was inaugurated, we speak to the question of individual and collective human rights, rather than simply the irrationality of one part of humanity arbitrarily controlling the other part, it is clear that this is not the best way to manage affairs of state. . . .

Still, as the Diet is about to be inaugurated, women, who cannot send their own representatives to the Diet, who will not participate in general discussions about the welfare of the country but must conceal their opinions, are told they may not attend Diet sessions as observers. As Yajima Kajiko says, it is not ethical

---

* When Shimizu Toyoko interviewed Itagaki Taisuke, the former popular-rights leader, he made the interesting observation that, though he did not know why the government had denied all political rights to women, he thought one reason might be their support of the antigovernment parties. ("Naite aisuru shimai ni tsugu," *Jogaku zasshi*, 234, supplement, Oct. 11, 1890, pp. 2–4.)

for one part of the human race to oppress the other part of the human race who happen to be women. Is there anyone who can agree to making decisions relating to affairs of state and conducting this wonderful constitutional government in this way? . . .

As I look at these regulations, the sadness I feel for my sisters is surpassed only by my sense that, for our Imperial Diet, it is even more tragic.[25]

When the Diet opened a few weeks later, the offending regulation had been deleted, but whether the protest by Reform Society members and others can be termed a successful political action is open to question: Article 165 in the bylaws on attendance was removed as silently as it had been added by Diet organizers. The right of women to be in the observer's gallery was symbolically important, but while Kishida Toshiko sat there, quietly frustrated by the low standard of political discussion she saw, women in other parts of Japan were being arrested and fined for violating regulations barring them from politics.[26]

After the Reform Society became a national organization in 1893, it was one of the best hopes women had for expressing themselves politically. Its reformist image could be used to cover the political content that was now illegal, and the respectability of its leaders kept male critics, in and out of government, at bay. But the Reform Society was affected by the anti-feminism intrinsic to the conservative mood of the decade; it was especially vulnerable to the growing attack on Christianity for its supposed subversion of Japanese culture. Reform Society women were among those charged with an excessively literal reading of Christianity and an insufficient appreciation of the virtues of Japanese tradition. Some of their deficiencies as Japanese women were explained, in the eyes of critics, by the connections that many of these women had with mission schools.

The society's response to all of this was ambivalent. It continued to campaign against the concubine system and prostitution much as it had before 1890, except that now bazaars were often substituted for lecture meetings as a place to educate the public. But it also turned in another direction, becoming more and more involved in the area of public philanthropy and disaster relief. Thus, as the decade wore on, the Reform Society was increasingly seen as an organization of upper-class Christian women who divided their time between campaigning against prostitution and organizing relief for earthquake victims.[27] The society's creation of the Jiaikan in 1893, the first of several shelters it established for young women who could not support themselves except by prostitution, was also seen as part of a broad, philanthropic enterprise, though it had obvious political content. Indeed, the society's own description of its purposes made clear the connections between women's lack of economic independence, life in the mills, and prostitution.[28]

This activity, coupled with increasingly sympathetic articles on the plight of working women in the society's various journals, provided a climate in which a political alliance between these two important groups of women might have been made. But the alliance never materialized. Within a year the country was at war with China, and the Reform Society, like all other large organizations, was under growing pressure to praise the country, not criticize it.[29]

The 1894–95 conflict with China had a telling impact on the nation—and on women. It accelerated a number of conservative tendencies that were by definition anti-feminist, and created a greater appreciation among government leaders of the roles women could play as child bearers and supporters of national policy. Above all, the war and its aftermath sharpened the already sharp conflict between conservatives who wanted to reinstate the past and modernizers who wanted to use the most politically conservative ideas from the West to consolidate authoritarian control over social institutions.[30] What emerged from this dialectic by the end of the century was, in fact, an amalgam of Tokugawa style and rhetoric couched in Prussian institutions. For women, it was a deadly combination, the effects of which were most compelling in education and family law. In both arenas, the stakes for women were very high. As they found themselves a focus of resurgent conservatism, the question was whether women would be able to maintain and consolidate the gains they had made in the family and education—both keys to any future improvement in their status.

The last decade of the nineteenth century had begun with the ominous language of the Imperial Rescript on Education, issued in October 1890. Designed to counter the liberality of the new constitution, the rescript tied education to the patriarchal family, celebrating both home and classroom as foundations of filial piety and national virtue.[31] The backward-looking atmosphere that led to the rescript encouraged increasing attacks on various educational institutions for women, but it was on higher schools for women that the debate centered after 1890. In both the Diet and prefectural assemblies, higher education for young women was the subject of critical speeches and proposals to cut off funds. A speech given in the Shimane prefectural assembly was typical of the widespread disapproval: students "failed to appreciate local custom," and women teachers were both "insufficiently motivated," and "generally inadequate" for the jobs they were supposed to perform.[32]

By the time Japan went to war with China in 1894, there were fewer than ten public higher schools for women in the entire country, and the criticism of all higher education for women was focused largely on the much more numerous mission schools.[33] The mission school, critically important in offering intellectual challenges and a humanistic view of women to their Japanese students since early

Meiji, was now criticized for failing to pay attention to the "special characteristics" of Japanese women and for being "insufficiently protective" of traditional Japanese virtues. The education they offered young women was "frivolous" and "impractical."[34]

These criticisms went directly to vital issues that had emerged in the early-Meiji debate but had not been pursued to any consensus. Were women being educated to play roles in the home or outside it? Was the function of women's education to prepare women to be good wives and mothers, or to become economically independent? Should the equality of men and women be stressed in education, along with the notion that men and women could play similar roles in society if they were properly prepared? Or should the stress be instead on the differences between men and women, including the "special characteristics" of Japanese women, with a curriculum training women to play "women's roles" in society?

To many of the people who, in mid-Meiji, were in a mood to reinstate Japanese values and virtues, girls' higher schools, particularly mission schools, were centers of unwanted social change, where young women learned to dress differently, to value themselves too highly, and to ignore decorum and propriety. The mission school, according to its critics, was a place where foreign women, in addition to making every effort to convert paying students to Christianity, filled their heads with subjects totally inappropriate to the reality of women's lives. What good were English, world geography, world history, biology, and mathematics to a woman who was going to marry into a traditional Japanese family and perform ordinary household and childrearing tasks?

From time to time critics added the separate-spheres arguments of the West to their attacks on women's education, arguments that women had themselves used, though to very different ends. In 1885, some years before the return to the purported Confucian traditions in the 1890's, the young Meiji Emperor, who had made education a special interest, remarked on the importance of differentiating between education for men and education for women. Criticizing the appointment of Tani Kanjō as president of the newly created Peeresses' School, the Emperor commented:

Though it would be premature to pass judgment on the appointment of Tani as President, women's education is not the same as men's. The position of President of the Girls' School would have been more appropriately filled by a person of calm, rather than active, disposition. Women's education has heretofore been conducted in a vigorous manner, but this has had numerous bad effects. Therefore, a person of greater composure should have been selected to direct the education of girls.[35]

In 1888 Tani was replaced by Nishimura Shigeki, a Confucian with extensive Western experience and a former member of the Meiji Six group, who favored gradual and highly selective borrowing from the West. One of the things that led to his appointment was his obvious interest in women's education, as evidenced in his book *Fujo kagami* (A Model for Women), published the year before. The book, later recommended by the Empress for use in all women's educational institutions, was not a straightforward Confucian document. Its attraction lay in the fact that Nishimura used examples from the West, as well as from Chinese and Japanese classics, to provide a guide to the education of his ideal young woman. But though it seemed to be a synthesis of Japanese and Western experience, it was very long on Confucian moral tales and very short on an understanding of the experience of women in the West.* Most damaging was its easy confu-

---

* As an example of a model American woman, Nishimura told the story of a mother and daughter who were on board Henry Clay's steamship when it sank in the Hudson River in 1852. Only one of the women could be saved, and the daughter immediately "joyously" jumped into the river so that her mother could live. (*Fujo kagami* in *Nihon fujin mondai shiryō shūsei,* 5: 355–68.)

sion of Christian and Confucian morality. It is possible that Nishimura's book, widely circulated because of its Imperial favor long before the government monopolized and standardized the content and printing of public school textbooks (1903), was the first significant misinterpretation of the content of "true womanhood" embodied in the Japanese phrase *ryōsai kenbo* ("good wife; wise mother").

The "cult of true womanhood" in the United States, developed to counteract what some women saw as the declining power of women in the home, was concerned with morality and "virtue." Virtue was a compelling argument for woman's superiority in the home; she was the counterweight to the unrestrained male. And she did have special characteristics, womanly characteristics, that made her the best educator, as well as nurturer, of her children. But Christian virtue and Confucian virtue were, after all, not really the same thing, despite the importance that sexual propriety assumed in both, especially for women. In the West filial sentiment never informed the "true woman's" ethics in the ways that Nishimura thought it did. Even more important, Nishimura's model woman did not exercise power in the home, including power over the education of her children, as the true woman in the West did. Though Nishimura may have grudgingly assumed that women gradually would assume more power in the home, he preferred a refined submissiveness in women, based on an assumed reciprocity in the family. On basic questions relating to the education of women and their roles in the family, Nishimura and Catherine Beecher, a champion of domesticity in the United States, would not have had much in common.[36]

The unselfishness and self-sacrifice of Nishimura's model women were qualities the state was increasingly interested in developing after 1887. The family, as all good Confucianists knew, was the pillar of the state; and women were crucially important because they could do much to shape the family's character. As Mori Arinori, then Minister of Education, pointed out in speeches in 1887 and 1888, education was the basis of national wealth and power. "We must not forget," he said, "that the flourishing of women's education is crucial to the wellbeing of our country."[37] These views, though often interpreted as more conservative than Mori's early statements on women, were entirely consistent with his advocacy of marriage contracts and increased power for women in the home in the 1870's. After his death in 1888, however, the Education Ministry was dominated by men who had never agreed that women should exercise more power in the family. Their initiatives in the area of women's education would produce separate schools for men and women, with separate curricula, including the equivalent of "domestic science" for women's schools.

Ranged against this growing effort to control women's education and use it as a vehicle for state social policy were the women reformers and Christian educators, who continued to insist that women's education should not be used to train Japanese women in the "traditional" virtues. Unfortunately, Iwamoto Zenji and other influential Christians were on the defensive in the 1890's, attacked by those who saw in Christian higher schools for women a source of encouragement of sexual license. The debate over the value of Christian morality and Confucian morality for women was never resolved in Meiji, and the romanticism that pervaded the atmosphere of some Christian higher schools for women, a romanticism stemming from a commitment to new kinds of relationships between men and women, as well as from a love of nineteenth-century Western literature, made those schools and their supporters easy targets of Confucian critics in the last decade of the century. Romanticism and sentiment were equivalent to sexual license; young women who attended schools like

Iwamoto's Meiji Women's High School were criticized for their presumed promiscuity and for their selfish commitment to love, rather than arranged marriages.[38]

Even the strongest feminists were pushed, in the 1890's, to make conservative or critical statements about women's education, though some of them tried to turn that criticism to the advantage of women by insisting on more, not less, opportunity for women to prepare themselves for important social tasks.[39] Some women, for example, agreed with critics who described women's education as impractical, in order to ask for more courses preparing women for economic survival, if not independence. Shimizu took young women high school students to task for thinking, as she put it, that "education was only a prelude to a marriage that would make them completely secure": marriage was the "real" world; women were not secure in it, and young, well-educated women would serve themselves and the long-range interests of their sisters best by using their education to improve the status of women in the society as a whole.[40]

A number of women in the period took what they probably saw as a middle ground between warring factions. They accepted the notion that women's primary role was in the home, but insisted that quality education was the best preparation for it. They tried to reinstate an important part of the definition of "good wife; wise mother" that had already been eroded by opinions and events, namely, the responsibility and power of women in the home. Nishimura's refined submissiveness did not impress women who considered themselves the first and most important educators of their children, helpmates to their husbands, and general managers of their households. The home for them was woman's proper sphere, and her power there represented an enormous improvement in status over the Tokugawa era. For these women, the reverse of the Tokugawa maxim was true: women were light; men dark.

The woman who became the principal ideologist for these views was Hatoyama Haruko, a well-educated woman who lived on the periphery of an elite whose educational views she did not really share.[41] Best remembered now as an important Meiji educator and the mother of a Prime Minister, Hatoyama was an advocate of some important role reversals in the Japanese family. The mother, she said, should be educator and taskmaster; the father should be the source of love and play. The wife should be an efficient manager, who was also well educated and intelligent enough to be a true companion to her husband. The home was, in turn, a haven for the husband; a place to refresh and renew himself for his struggles in the outside world.

This view of the home and the place of women in it, so familiar in the nineteenth-century West, was met with some ambivalence by Meiji feminists, who rightly guessed that the assumption of power in the home would be balanced by relinquishing power in the outside world.[42] But it was extremely appealing to many Meiji women, particularly those who recognized the possibility of substantially improved status for some women should Hatoyama's views gain public acceptance.

But the last decade of the century was not to be a time when Japanese women could contribute to socially accepted definitions of their roles; it was, instead, a time for patriarchy to reject the feminism that had been a part of Meiji down to 1900 by adding to the repressive regulations governing women's lives enacted in 1890. In 1898, after nearly a decade of debate in which a "liberal" civil code had been rejected because of the threat it was said to pose to "traditional Japanese concepts of loyalty and filal piety," a new code was announced—one that strengthened the concept of the *ie* (house/family) and tied it to a patriarchal Emperor system.[43]

Women who had hoped it would contain language redressing their lowly status in the family were stunned to find instead that it sanctioned that status. As Takamure Itsue later described it, the Meiji civil code attempted to convert all of Japan into a single Tokugawa samurai model, one of the most repressive, from the standpoint of women, in Japanese history.[44] Resurrecting the *ie*, the patriarchal family of earlier days, the civil code based competence and legitimacy on the family line. Only men could claim posterity; only men were legally recognized persons. Married women were not able to bring legal action independently; they were classified in the same category as the "deformed and the mentally incompetent" in the code. Husbands were totally free to dispose of their wives' property as they liked, and free to operate under the same kind of sexual double standard that prevailed in Tokugawa. Adultery, as before, was a punishable offense only in the case of wives. The stipulation that all property would be inherited by the oldest son not only did away with the diversity of custom practiced since Tokugawa; it made it impossible for women to be thought of as anything but commodities in a continuing patriarchal, patrilineal market. The new code made the authority of the patriarch absolute, whether he was a Baron or a tenant farmer.[45] *Danson johi*, that attitude of contempt for women that Meiji feminists had struggled against for three decades, was now reemphasized, with official approval.[46] The concubine system was back in favor, and women once more were to be "borrowed wombs." The difference was that they were now expected to provide sons, not only for the family, but for the Empire. Women, described by one of the authors of the code as "excelling even Japanese men in patriotism," were now to be tied to a family system designed to leave them few options other than to do the state's bidding.*

In 1899 the state initiated its most sweeping attempt to mold the lives of women through education. The government, as it instituted regulations requiring each prefecture to support at least one high school for young women, served notice that women's education would be standardized and be aimed at creating "good wives; wise mothers." An official of the Education Ministry explained to disgruntled prefectural officials the purpose of the requirement:

Girls marry, and become wives and mothers. Men and women help one another, and each carries on various duties. Since the family is the root of the nation, it is the vocation of women who become housewives to be good wives and wise mothers, and girls' high schools are necessary to provide appropriate education enabling girls from middle- and upper-middle-class families to carry out this vocation.[47]

"Good wife; wise mother" had now become part of government's accepted image of the model Japanese woman, but the meaning had been drastically changed to conform to the most backward-looking provisions of the civil code. Women were not to be educated to exercise power in the home; they were to be given practical training in childrearing and in the heavy responsibilities of being mother, wife, and daughter-in-law in a repressive family system. The "special qualities" women's education now assumed had more to do with making up any gap that might

* The description is Hozumi Nobushige's, made in a speech at an International Congress of Law meeting in St. Louis. He also disingenuously explained the position of Japanese women under the new civil code, which had "created a new legal woman" since it made "no distinction" between men and women in their exercise of rights, "so long as the woman remains single." "There is," he said, "no bar placed in the way of the women of Japan and . . . it is probable that the future will see Japan still leading the way in the recognition of the rights of women. But all such progress will be the result of the educated wish of the women themselves, not the artificial product of agitators and politicians." (Quoted in Alfred Stead, *Great Japan*, New York, 1906, pp. 382–83, 385–86.)

exist in the repressive socialization of Japanese women than with developing intellect. "Good wife; wise mother" had become a "Confucian" phrase, a slogan so changed in meaning as to be virtually unrecognizable to Meiji feminists.

It is possible to view what happened to Japanese women in the last decade of the nineteenth century as a minor theme in a larger historical drama pushing Japan toward less open and flexible attitudes toward change. But it must also be seen as a separate, significant development, constituting the patriarchy's answer to women who, for three decades, had welcomed the social change of Meiji and tried to use it to elevate their status. Having discovered the potential of women as producers of sons for Japan's expanding Empire, as teachers of patriotism and loyalty in the home, and as pillars of stability in the midst of social stress, the government set about trying to control and develop that potential and at the same time to deny women self-definition, individually or collectively.[48] The fact that, by 1900, the government had become the primary authority on acceptable women's roles in politics, the family, education, and the workplace is convincing evidence of its conscious intent to impose policies on women that were only vaguely imagined in early Meiji. It is also evidence of a major response to the activities of women during the previous two decades.

Feminists and reformers who argued, even in the most genteel voices, for a different place for women in Japanese society were answered, between 1890 and 1900, with one resounding thunderclap of patriarchal authority after another. As the century came to an end, with the prospect of another war darkening the horizon, the question was whether women would find the means to resist being used for "the sake of the nation" on someone else's terms; whether they could preserve any of the gains they had made before 1900.

6. Women Socialists

Everyone, from members of political parties to the general public, praises the Japan Women's Patriotic Association, whose activities began with the Russo-Japanese War and whose tens of thousands of members are all women without political rights under Japanese law. . . .

Are these women, whom Japanese law has already said have absolutely no power in the society, now to be appointed to carry out state functions under the very same legal system?

In the midst of the "success of the Women's Patriotic Association"—of all this glory and recognition for women—it should be remembered that women are not free. The "success" of women who are not free is the success of slaves.   *Women of the World*, 1907

Slaves? The women of the Patriotic Association? Women whose social position and dedicated work for the good of the society were respected by everyone? Only Japan's socialist women could have said so.

The Japan Women's Patriotic Association (Aikoku Fujinkai) was founded in 1901 by Okumura Ioko to console the families of the war dead and impress on women their patriotic responsibilities in the home.[1] It quickly became a major force in the government's attempt to mold women's roles ever more firmly in support of the state. Though some women in the association came to think of their roles as "instilling the responsibilities of citizenship,"[2] much like the Republican mother of postrevolutionary America, the government would have limited this to instilling loyalty and obedience in the Emperor's subjects—to encouraging mothers to give up their sons to war and consoling them when they did not come back. The association's membership, aided by wartime patriotism and direct government assistance, grew from 60,000 shortly before the Russo-Japanese War to over a million by the end of the First World War.[3] In terms of both its size and its influence on Japanese life, the association was one of the most effective political organizations in Japan's modern history. It was a "women's organization" governed by men, an organization whose functions were shaped by male definitions of women's political roles, and whose success was due largely to direct government support, including the use of facilities in areas under the jurisdiction of the Home Ministry.[4] In April 1901, a little over a year after the government had reinforced its 1890 position on political rights for women by including Article 5 in the Police Security Regulations, Okumura embarked on a nationwide speaking tour to recruit members for the Patriotic Association.[5] She spent two and a half years traveling through the country, speaking from lecture platforms denied to other women, carrying on the political work of the state at a time when women were unable to organize against Article 5 without violating it.

For those women who preferred to choose their own political goals, there were few options after 1900. The Reform Society continued to attack prostitution and the concubine system, but many of its members became members of the Patriotic Association as well, expecting, perhaps, as Hatoyama and other educators did, that ultimately that organization would bring women more important, recognized roles in Japanese society. Despite some encouraging signs that women were beginning to make a little headway in higher education,[6] there seemed to be no group that spoke to women's issues in Japanese society with any sense of continuity or outrage.

For a woman like Fukuda Hideko, it was a particularly difficult time. A living record of the struggle that had started in the popular-rights movement, Fukuda must have been stunned by what she saw after 1900. The Liberal Party, heir to the popular-rights tradition, had sold out to a new political coalition with Itō Hirobumi at its head. The country was preparing for its second war in a decade, and continuing to raise taxes and armies for that purpose. Women everywhere seemed coopted by a government that was using them to create an even more powerful and authoritarian state. The organization of the Patriotic Association and the government's orchestration of its tasks for women was an ironic conclusion to Fukuda's 1884 demand that "the great work of the nation" be shared by women who "contribute to and consider themselves part of the enterprise."[7]

1884. The year the government had closed her first school. Hideko's road since then had been extremely difficult. She had worked in Tokyo with her friend Tomii Oto, who had died when she was barely twenty; been involved in the Osaka Incident and sent to prison; lived for a time with Ōi Kentarō, and worked to support their child after she left him. The school she and her family had opened in Tokyo in 1891 for working women and their children, failed after her father and grandmother died, and she encountered financial difficulties she could not overcome. At the time, she thought about going away—to the United States. Instead, she married Fukuda Yūsaku, a man who had been there (as a student at the University of Michigan), and who was thinking of going back.[8]

Hideko became Yūsaku's wife sometime in 1892, and after bearing him two sons (in 1893 and 1894), was finally entered in the family register in 1896.* Her life with

---

* A wife who was not registered in a family's official records had no legal status in the family. Though custom varied widely throughout Japan on this point, the general assumption is that many women were not registered until they had produced at least one son or had in some way demonstrated their value to the families they had entered. Yoshioka Yayoi, one of Meiji's few woman physicians and founder of the country's first medical school for women, was apparently not registered by her husband's family until 10 years after her marriage.

Yūsaku was not idyllic, yet as she later said, his commitment to social and political change and his treatment of her made this a nearly perfect marriage. But they never managed to go to the United States as they had hoped. Yūsaku suffered from mental illness and by 1899, the year Hideko bore his third son, was in a bad state. He died in 1900, leaving Hideko with a legacy of enormous pain and very little financial support for herself or the children.[9]

In 1901 Fukuda Hideko established another private school for young women, now emphasizing vocational education.[10] At the same time, though her economic struggle was paramount, she was interested in reconnecting her life to the political battles she had been away from for a decade. The connection came fortuitously that year when Sakai Toshihiko became her neighbor.* Sakai was an important member of a small socialist community that had been struggling to survive in Japan since 1897. Like many of his colleagues, he was a journalist, and when Fukuda met him, he worked with good friends on the staff of *Yorozu chōhō* (Complete Morning Report), a newspaper strongly critical of government policy. Sakai, Kōtoku Shūsui, and other colleagues on the paper had organized a socialist association to read and discuss socialist ideas, and had tried in May 1901 to establish a socialist party grounded on parliamentary principles. Their Social Democratic Party was banned by the government just hours after they celebrated its founding.[11] Labor unions had also been effectively outlawed by the government's 1900 Police Security regulations, leaving would-be organizers like Katayama Sen to create a universal suffrage league as a long-range

---

* One of the most consistent advocates of socialism, Sakai Toshihiko worked to preserve unity in the face of both external and internal pressures. His unconventional views of the family and genuine concern about the status of women in Japanese society, expressed clearly in *Katei zasshi* (Home Magazine), which he edited after 1903, influenced many of the women who came to the socialist movement. Kondō Magara, who grew up in the Sakai family, records her memories of Fukuda in Kondō Magara and Kudsumi Fusako, "Fukuda Hideko no koto," *Rōdō undōshi kenkyū*, 29 (1962): 38–40.

alternative to the efforts they had made to organize men in heavy industry before 1900.

From May 1901 until October 1903 socialists, reformers, and critics of the government participated in Sakai's Socialist Association and published their views in newspapers, pamphlets, and books, advocating socialism as a remedy for many of Japan's ills.[12] They were an unlikely group of comrades, with very different views of Japan's problems and the best solutions to them; the fact that they were able to band together under a single ideological umbrella is testimony to the flexibility and breadth of socialism at the turn of the century—as well as its power to attract those who found nationalism an empty slogan. They came from different classes and had different aspirations. Many were disenchanted former popular-rights activists, who tried to support the Liberal Party until its demise in September 1900. Some were Christians, appalled by what they saw as the blatant exploitation of good people by capitalists who had no intention of sharing their enormous wealth. A few were labor organizers whose experience outside Japan convinced them that unions could be effective not only in changing working conditions, but in giving sufficient power to the working class to change society's priorities.[13]

What socialism offered was an ethical yet scientific critique of Japan's industrialization and foreign policy. Armed with socialist explanations, Sakai, Kōtoku, Nishikawa Kōjiro, Abe Isō, and others raised basic questions about Japan's recent experience. Why, in spite of the benefits promised by the industrial revolution, was the gap between rich and poor growing wider? Why did machines require more, rather than less, labor? Why were working conditions growing worse? Why was there so little justice and equality in a society that had supposedly made such rapid progress? And why was Japan emulating the worst traditions of Western imperialism in Asia?

The socialists were brought together by events in 1903, as war with Russia seemed more and more certain. When Kuroiwa Ruikō, the editor of the *Complete Morning Report*, reversed his stand and came out in support of war, Sakai, Uchimura Kanzō, and Kotōku resigned, attacking the newspaper Kotōku had once called "the last remaining bastion in the struggle for freedom, equality, civilization, and progress."[14] They then organized the Heiminsha (Commoners' Association) and by the fall of 1903 had begun publishing *Heimin shimbun* (Commoners' News), analyzing the government's domestic and foreign policies from both socialist and humanist perspectives.[15] From the beginning, the Commoners' Association proclaimed an allegiance to universal values and goals, cutting itself off from Japanese nationalism and its symbols. The members' commitment to international socialism was reflected in their effort to include an English-language column in the *Commoners' News* and to keep their readers abreast of developments in the socialist movement outside Japan.

The problems of women in Japanese society were never a primary concern of the men who founded the association; apart from Sakai and Kinoshita Naoe, who were wholly sympathetic to women's causes, few of them ever directly addressed women's issues.[16] And initially, except for wives and relatives of the members, there were few women around the Yurakuchō headquarters; Fukuda, whose respect for Sakai's views of women had deepened as she had gotten to know her neighbor, was one of them (and one of the fewer still with feminist experience).[17] Gradually, the antiwar stance of the newspaper, coupled with critical articles on education, employment, and family life—all issues that directly affected women—attracted other women to the Commoners and their cause. They were an extremely interesting group, though in most cases we know very little about their individual backgrounds and histories. For a time they, more than any other single group of women, pushed feminism a few steps forward by taking risks and trying to find their own niche in the socialist movement.

It was not always easy. The women of the Commoners' Association were barred from the regular political meetings of the group because of Article 5. And when they decided to meet on their own, disguising the political content of their lectures with academic language, they found themselves crowded out of their own meeting by men who came to hear the male speakers they had scheduled.[18] They eventually established a policy requiring any man who attended their meetings to be accompanied by a woman, and in November 1904, began scheduling women speakers, who almost invariably addressed audiences composed of women only. The three women who were first to discuss socialism from a woman's perspective were Sugaya Iwako, Kinoshita Naoe's younger sister; Teramoto Michiko, a young woman who had come to Tokyo to study and to try to make a living on her own; and Matsuoka Fumiko, the widow of a poet. Eventually, as the Commoners' headquarters in Yurakuchō began to operate like a commune, Matsuoka took over responsibility for "household management" there.[19]

Little by little, as women split off from the men in the association to discuss women's issues, their interest shifted to attracting other women to their cause and to organizing actions to improve the situation of women in the society as a whole. Among the women who began to come to the second floor of the Commoners' offices to listen and were led to stay, committing themselves to the struggle, were Kamikawa Matsuko and Yoshisaka Yoshiko, both students at the Aoyama Institute in Tokyo; and Imai Utako and Kawamura Haruko, two young women who had already organized a women's group in Hokkaido and were now publishing a monthly journal in Tokyo called *Nijū seiki fujin* (Twentieth-Century Woman).

Those who stayed found life in the commune both pleasant and difficult; it was a busy, intellectually exciting place with an atmosphere of camaraderie born of shared involvement in struggle.[20] But for women who insisted on playing a role more extensive than making tea, life in the group had its negative side. Many of the socialists were traditional-minded men, who could not bring themselves to think of women as political or intellectual equals. Kōtoku, who rarely discussed issues with women socialists, found the increasing number of women who frequented the association's offices irritating, or sometimes diverting. He was fond of referring to Imai and Kawamura as guest speakers, and they returned the compliment by calling him Grump.[21] Fukuda's frequent visits often produced long storytelling sessions, the experienced activist sitting in her apron, gesturing and wiping her face with a handkerchief as she described the popular-rights movement, the Osaka Incident, and her stay in prison to the younger women there. For them, it was a gift of their own political history, already beginning to be lost in the recent past.[22]

When the war with Russia began, government interference became a constant fact of life for the socialists, but as long as the prospects looked bright for a quick victory, they were relatively free to conduct their antiwar campaign, including an open letter to their Russian comrades to join them in the struggle against the "imperialistic desires" of their governments.[23] But as the war wore on, producing increasing casualties and no easy victory, the government had less and less patience with its adversaries, and began to fine and imprison those who wrote or published articles in violation of press regulations. Sakai and Nishikawa, as editors of *Commoners' News*, were the first to be fined and given jail terms; many more would spend time in prison for their views.[24] And the tiny band of socialists developed a new routine: sending off and welcoming back their comrades on the way to prison. In the photographs of these events that remain, the women stand staunchly next to the men, and the tall figure of an older woman, Fukuda Hideko, is often seen in the background. It is difficult to determine whether women writers contributed in a significant way to *Commoners' News* or other socialist publications, owing to the liberal use of pen names and the prevalence of unsigned articles.[25] But it is clear that by the time they had begun to hold their own meetings with women speakers, socialist women were doing more than packing lunches for comrades on their way to jail and tidying up the association's headquarters. In January 1905, with the war still raging, they created the beginnings of the movement to free women politically, by launching a campaign to get Article 5 of the Police Security regulations softened or deleted. Using the parliamentary tactics favored by most of the socialists at the time, and working in what may have been an uneasy alliance with Nishikawa Kōjiro's campaign for universal suffrage, they began the attack by publishing a petition demanding revision of the article in the January 15, 1905, issue of *Commoners' News*. The next step in the campaign, which was managed by Imai, Kawamura, and Matsuoka, saw women dispatched to busy areas of Tokyo to get signatures for a formal petition to the Diet. Within ten days they had gathered more than five hundred signatures and were ready to present the petition to two friendly members of the Diet, who had promised to forward it for them.[26]

One of the remarkable things about this initial step in what was to be a very long campaign to revise Article 5, a campaign that was (for a time) the Japanese woman's equivalent of the suffrage movement, was the ability of socialist women to operate in the chaotic circumstances they faced. The government had ordered the dissolution of the Socialist Association in November 1904, and Kōtoku, Nishikawa, and Sakai had been fined for violating the press laws. Kōtoku had also been sentenced to five months in prison for allegedly "inciting a change" in the Emperor system, and *Commoners' News*, with an inevitable dissolution order on the way, prepared to "voluntarily" suspend its operations as Kōtoku and Nishikawa filed an appeal. On January 29, 1905, just days after the women of the Commoners' Association had gathered the signatures on their petition to revise Article 5, *Commoners' News* went to press for the last time. Following the example of Marx and Engels when they were forced to stop publication of the *Neue rheinische Zeitung*, the editors printed the last edition in red ink, paraphrasing their predecessors: "Farewell, but not forever farewell. . . . They cannot kill the spirit."[27]

In February Kōtoku went to prison, and as the government continued its harassment of socialists, the association began to disintegrate. The pressures could be ignored while the war continued, but as socialists moved from *Commoners' News* to *Chokugen* (Plain Talk), many of the factional splits that had been papered over in the antiwar effort began to resurface. Christians were beginning to move away from materialists; those who favored parliamentary methods were discovering that some of their colleagues had begun thinking about revolution. Prison and the constant threat of imprisonment changed individual visions of present and future, and inevitably produced personal conflicts among individuals as well. By the time Kōtoku was released from prison at the end of July 1905, the war was over, but the socialist movement was too debilitated to organize and take advantage of the popular unrest over the economic dislocations of the war and the disappointing peace terms. It was in fact the government that capitalized on the situation, using the threat of unrest as a pretext to crack down on the socialists. Riots in Tokyo that followed the announcement of peace terms in September were met with martial law, and *Plain Talk* was ordered to suspend publication. In early October the Commoners' Association disbanded; the already tiny group of socialists then began to divide into even smaller ideological units. Christian socialists, led by the novelist Kinoshita Naoe and the educator Abe Isō, began publishing *Shin kigen* (The New Age), and the more militant materialists, led by Sakai, Kōtoku, and Yamaguchi Kōken, began publishing *Hikari* (Flash).

Nevertheless, the factions remained in an uneasy alliance, unified by their agreement on basic issues and commitment to parliamentary methods for achieving change. When the government changed hands in early 1906, with Saionji Kimmochi replacing the ultraconservative Katsura Tarō as premier, the unified approach seemed even more advantageous, since the government now permitted the socialists to pursue their goals "within the limits of the law." But that unity was shattered when Kōtoku, returning from a six-month stay in California, gave a speech calling for a general strike and followed it up with articles attacking suffrage campaigns and parliamentary tactics.[28] By the time *Commoners' News* reappeared in January 1907, the unity that had characterized its antiwar parent organization no longer existed. The single thread holding the socialists together as a group was their common experience of oppression.

For socialist women, the ideological splits that began to surface with the closing down of *Commoners' News* in 1905 were initially less of a concern than the practical question of finding new ways to air the women's issues they were developing. For a time, the Commoners' Association offices continued to be used for women's lecture meetings on Saturday afternoons, and provided a place for women interested in the socialist movement to make connections. The campaign to revise Article 5, more successful in its initial stages than they had anticipated, could proceed in the pages of *Plain Talk*. In fact, *Plain Talk* became a much more effective journalistic vehicle for women's issues than

Commoners' News had been, publishing a special edition on
women in April 1905.[29] At the same time, Matsuoka and
other women who were part of the association's "kitchen
crew," as they styled themselves, were signing some articles for *Plain Talk* and involving themselves with the publication of other journals, including Imai's and Kawamura's
Twentieth-Century Woman and a new socialist answer to the
prescriptive literature of the day entitled *Sweeto homu*
(Sweet Home), billed in advertisements as the magazine
"every socialist woman must read." In May 1905 Matsuoka
gave a lecture for the women's socialist group entitled
"The Mission of Today's Socialist Woman"; and with a
new arrival, Nobuoka Tameko, she instituted some language reform around the Commoners' Association offices
that reflected an increasing consciousness of class and sex
divisions.* The two women also walked the streets of Tokyo's Yoshiwara district to get a first-hand look at the lives
of prostitutes there.

For all these brave beginnings, the women of the Commoners' Association were still part of a movement that was
fragmenting. In the summer of 1905, as it became clear
that the end of the war would not bring either greater
unity to the movement or decreased government pressure, people began drifting away. And there were some
marriages in this uncertain period. Matsuoka married
Nishikawa, and Nobuoka married Sakai, whose wife had
died the previous year. By October, when the association
voluntarily dissolved, the Commoners' women were seeing
less of each other, and were finding it impossible to be
singleminded about women's issues. As they drifted into
the various ideological factions that now made up the socialist movement in Japan, they managed to keep some

---

* Nobuoka, who came to the commune in answer to Matsuoka's call for help
with cooking and managing the "household," worked with Matsuoka to get
everyone to use the same neutral form of address, eliminating distinctions of sex
and class from their language (Murata Shizuko, *Fukuda Hideko*, Tokyo, 1965, pp.
105–6).

semblance of a campaign to revise Article 5 going, but it was to be a long time before these socialist women would work together in anything like the same way again. Fukuda became involved with the Christian socialists and their publication, *The New Age*; her colleagues Matsuoka (now Nishikawa) and Nobuoka (now Sakai) went with their husbands to work on *The New Age's* ideological competitor *Flash*. Neither publication showed the kind of commitment to women's issues that *Plain Talk* had demonstrated earlier.

By the end of 1905, both journals had closed down, and women like Fukuda had time to reflect on their experience with various publications in the movement. Despite all the time and energy they had expended, women's issues in Japan and the rest of the world were never adequately covered by any of the socialist movement's important journals. Fukuda had substantial publishing and editorial experience by this time and indeed, on the basis of her autobiography, *Warawa no hanshōgai* (Half My Life), published in October 1904, had something of a national reputation as a writer and journalist.* But she had not had a regular forum in which to discuss her commitment to women's issues, by now very strong. She decided to create one of her own. The first issue of her magazine, *Sekai fujin* (Women of the World), appeared on January 1, 1907, with a front-page editorial announcing its purposes and goals:

What are our reasons for publishing *Women of The World*? In a word, to determine the real vocation of women by extracting it from the tangled web of law, custom, and morality that are a part of women's experience. Then, we hope to cultivate among all of you a desire to join a reform movement founded on what will be the true mission of women. . . .

---

* Widely read, her autobiography went through 46 printings and probably provided some economic support for a time. Kondō Magara remembers that at the time the book was published "people laughed and read 'warawa' [My in the title *Half My Life*] as 'mekake' [concubine]." (Kondō and Kudsumi, "Fukuda Hideko," p. 39.)

When I look at the conditions currently prevailing in society, I see that as far as women are concerned, virtually everything is coercive and oppressive, making it imperative that we women rise up and forcefully develop our own social movement. This truly is an endless enterprise; we have not reached our goals, but our hope is that this magazine will inspire you to become a champion of this [women's] movement.[30]

Though *Women of the World* was from the beginning an interesting blend of theory and practice, its emphasis, in keeping with Fukuda's lifelong preference, was action. She believed, as did the women who encouraged her to publish it, that the campaign to revise Article 5 would produce tangible benefits for women in their struggle to achieve more equitable status in Japanese society. The articles in the magazine were intended to get readers to think through traditional assumptions about women in Japanese society, but the movement to revise Article 5 gave them a place to take their activism and rising consciousness. The second page of the first issue reminded women of the illegality and "extreme irrationality" of the government's action by reprinting the language of the law, then offered them a movement to join—a petition campaign headed by Sakai Tameko, Kōtoku Chiyoko, and Fukuda.

The wide-ranging coverage of international feminism in *Women of the World,* important as it was in establishing links with movements outside of Japan, served the very practical purpose of showing Japanese women where they stood in relation to women elsewhere. Fukuda made a point of reporting developments in suffrage movements around the world, alongside articles in which she reminded her readers that in Japan women were not even legally able to demand the right to vote, much less run for public office. International role models were also presented for Japanese women, who from the beginning of the Meiji period interested themselves in the lives of "famous" women outside the country. The pages of *Women of the World* featured pictures and articles about well-known American and European women whose lives were marked by resistance, if not always feminism. Two women whose names had been invoked since the start of the popular-rights movement, Madame de Staël and Madame Roland, were featured in early issues. The first few issues were notable for their relative lack of discussion of socialism and their emphasis on feminism. In fact, from the second issue on, the margins of the first page bore the slogan: "This magazine is in the vanguard of the women's movement in Japan. Anyone who fails to read it is not a woman."

Commentators have often remarked that it was the various experiences Fukuda had from her youth on that made her so strongly feminist as to feel the need for a feminist journal. Certainly her life had made her acutely aware of the central issues involved in the "woman question" from the age of sixteen, when she refused a marriage proposal her family had hoped she would be willing to accept.* She learned that economic independence, or the possibility of it, was a key to woman's freedom and believed, all her life, that education was central to economic opportunity for women. Politically ambitious, she had discovered early that the only access available to women in Meiji Japan was through the men with whom they associated, and that those men, like her common-law husband Ōi Kentarō, were not often concerned about women's issues. Her marriage to Fukuda Yūsaku was marked by mutual respect and affection, but his death meant that she was once again on her own economically—this time with an aging mother

---

* At that early age she had managed to persuade her parents to reject the promising marriage proposal of a wealthy nearby family. But it was only at the cost of agreeing to turn over everything she earned from her work as a teacher's assistant to help defray family expenses. Fukuda later recalled how much it impressed her at the time. "How many unhappy women there must be," she said, "who marry a man without love because they are unable to be economically independent." (*Warawa no hanshōgai*, Tokyo, 1976, pp. 14–15.)

and more children to support in a society that still refused to admit a case such as hers could exist. Women were always cared for; always protected by the family system. By the time she met the socialists in Tokyo, she must have seen some similarities between all women and the women she had met in prison, women she called her sisters and whose fate she ascribed to the one weakness all women shared: the lack of opportunity to support themselves, or themselves and their children. What women in Japan needed was something to make them realize how similar their experiences were; something to make friends like Shimoda Utako, the director of the Peeresses' School, aware of the common experience of women, irrespective of class.*

Unfortunately, Shimoda and her associates did not join the campaign to revise Article 5, well publicized and extensive as it was. It was an effort that may have enjoyed the tacit support of the genteel women in the Reform Society and in the Women's Patriotic Association, but neither group worked actively for the change. It is a commentary on the state of the women's movement in Japan in 1907 that the petitions to revise Article 5 and proposals to end polygamy and prostitution had to compete for attention in the Diet, since there was no common effort to present all three as important and related women's issues. Fukuda and the *Women of the World* circle, despite their criticism of the Women's Patriotic Association and their chiding of the upper-class women of the Reform Society, were firmly in support of the Reform Society's efforts to end the concubine system, and said so often in the pages of the maga-

---

* Shimoda (1854–1936) was from the same part of Japan as Fukuda and shared her interest in education. But unlike Fukuda, Shimoda's interest extended only to educating the daughters of Japan's elite. Her success as an educator has often been comparerd with Fukuda's "failures." It was Shimoda who wrote the original prospectus for the Japan Women's Patriotic Association. There is a chapter on her life in Kida Jun'ichiro, *Meiji no onna*, vol. 9 of *Meiji no gunshō* (Tokyo, 1969): 79–104.

zine. But they did not make direct connections with the women in either group; nor did those women ever join them, even for symbolic purposes, as they sat through Diet sessions, awaiting the outcome of debates over Article 5 petitions. By 1907, even on issues with substantial backing among women everywhere, class and political divisions were apparently too great to permit a unified effort.

Factionalism imposed special burdens on women in the socialist movement, whose connections to husbands and lovers automatically identified them with one of the competing groups. Many of them were now geographically removed from the Tokyo area as a result of splits in the movement, and others found it more and more difficult to help Fukuda with *Women of the World* as they had promised.[31] Looking over the contributors to the journal, even taking into account the liberal use of pen names, one is struck by the small number of women who appeared in print. Except for Fukuda, who was a major contributor, the only women who wrote articles regularly were Kamikawa Matsuko, Fukuda's colleague from *The New Age*; and Nishikawa (Matsuoka) Fumiko. But socialist men were eager enough to use the journal's pages; Sakai Toshihiko and Abe Isō were major contributors over the two and a half years of the magazine's existence, along with Ishikawa Sanshirō and other well-known men in the socialist movement. There is little doubt that the magazine's emphasis changed over time as a result of the inconsistent support of the socialist women who had worked together earlier. Still, until the final few issues, it was a woman's magazine, raising important philosophical questions at the same time as it offered practical advice on cooking and sewing.

For all the emphasis that commentators have put on Fukuda's pragmatism and lack of interest in theory, what emerges in the pages of *Women of the World* is an interesting analysis of woman's condition, written principally by Fukuda Hideko. While Sakai Toshihiko pursued the reform of women's roles in the home, and Abe Isō spoke to the importance of education in raising the status of women, Fukuda offered the Article 5 campaign as a legal means of alleviating what she called the "double burden" that all women carried: oppression by the wealthy and oppression by men. It was an argument she pursued consistently in her magazine, despite obvious pressure from her male colleagues, who, since 1902, had been explaining the woman question in terms of socialist goals.[32] In 1904, Nishikawa Kojirō, commenting on the women's movement outside of Japan, had said:

Though women's groups in Euro-American countries have declared that "making women economically free" is central to the woman's movement, . . . we should consider one point. . . . If the economic structure remains as it is today . . . both men and women will find jobs difficult to get. . . . We should not be satisfied only by attaining rights for women, but realize that the answer to the women's movement lies in socialism.[33]

And in 1907, Kōtoku Shūsui, updating the argument he had first made in the pages of *Complete Morning Report* in 1902, wrote in *Women of the World*: "If I were asked what the first requirement of the women's movement is, I would reply that it is for women to learn about socialism."[34] In the same column, Kōtoku indicated that for women to use parliamentary tactics, as they were doing in the Article 5 campaign, was useless: working men in Europe and America had the vote, but were still treated like draft animals and slaves in the capitalist system; moreover, women had the vote in some parts of the United States, but that had certainly not freed them from bondage. For a few women to succeed in a society little changed from the prevailing capitalist, competitive system would simply produce a situation like the one Emma Goldman described in "The Tragedy of Women's Liberation," Kōtoku concluded. Women should realize that the liberation of all women and the complete reform of society could only come through socialism. Working for socialism *was* working for the women's movement.

Fukuda's double-burden argument, put forward in the face of the socialist line on women advocated by most of her male colleagues in the movement (both parliamentary and direct-action socialists), seems to represent an effort to accommodate socialist theory while holding to a feminist viewpoint. Changing the economic institutions of the society was important, but the liberation of women was not merely a minor theme in that struggle. What Fukuda suggested, over and over again, was that her male colleagues had their priorities mixed up. Liberating women should come first; that might make other changes the socialists wanted much simpler. She sounded that theme almost from the first issue of *Women of the World,* and she continued to sound it through the journal's final days:

There is a general call for economic liberation, which is a good thing for us to be aware of. . . . But calling for economic liberation fails to go beyond sloganeering in advocating women's liberation. As always, we must strike down today's classist, discriminatory attitudes between men and women. Without carrying out such a revolution in attitudes, is it likely that economic liberation can be accomplished?[35]

Fukuda thought that if there was no such "revolution in attitudes" beforehand, there was at least a possibility that women might be treated even worse after "economic liberation."

Of the few women who wrote for *Women of the World,* not one subscribed in every detail to the socialist position on women. Instead, all of them, like Fukuda, seemed to go to great lengths to remind their readers (and perhaps some of their male colleagues as well) that, in Meiji society, women were an oppressed group. All women were oppressed; none more than poor ones, who felt most keenly the double burdens of women. Socialist men, difficult as their situations might be, still enjoyed male privilege in

Japanese society. Socialist women did not, and neither did any other women, rich or poor. This did not mean, as Fukuda was quick to point out, that women hated men, but it did mean that the real liberation of women, along lines outlined by women themselves, would bring the society to a place where there would not be the slightest discrimination in the treatment of men and women.[36] Although Fukuda never claimed that a revision of Article 5 or, for that matter, any legal remedy would produce such a society, she did consider legal action a place for women to start—and a potential source of some basic social reform involving women. Apparently unimpressed by the ability of Reform Society women to defeat candidates for office who had mistresses, Fukuda insisted that women must first get back political power by ending the "insulting" restrictions of Article 5. Once that was done, it would be possible to make concubinage illegal; to give women equal opportunity to divorce; to get some economic rights for women in the family. These were goals that may have stopped well short of real liberation for women, but for Fukuda they were well worth the effort of women everywhere.

Not only did Fukuda differ with her male colleagues, but almost alone among the women of the Commoners' Association, she refused to recognize, even in modified form, the special roles of women as opposed to men. Some, like Kamikawa Matsuko, might admit that men and women would probably always have slightly different social roles, and others, like Kōtoku Shūsui, might want a liberated society in which women would be free to exercise their womanly virtues, but Fukuda refused to acknowledge the importance of such differences, either in theory or in practice. Without saying much about the tasks of women in their private lives, including her own,[37] Fukuda concentrated on the public woman, a woman whose right to participate and capacity for public life were unques-

tioned. This position made Fukuda's attachment to the
Article 5 campaign all the more understandable, and her
disappointment in an Upper House that consistently refused to ratify it, immeasurable. As she said on the first
occasion, after watching from the gallery of the Upper
House as the bill was voted down 300 to 4:

The Upper House could use the Women's Patriotic Association
(whose ideology is of course completely different from ours) as
an example of women who are active in society, and, using them,
would have to be in support of this revision of Article 5. . . . But
what bigoted men they are! How ignorant! They simply maintain their opposition, saying, "Observing the courts and the Diet
and reading political debate in the newspapers are acceptable,
but women may not listen to political lectures." (Even with the
government's power, it could not prevent women from reading
newspapers!) . . . The only reason they give is that a reform of
Article 5 would "contaminate womanly virtues." . . . What a
strange argument! . . . The Upper House is laughable. There
is no logic in its arguments . . . only old-fashioned sentiment
that considers women slaves.[38]

The petition campaign to reform Article 5 continued until
1910; and each petition saw bills passed by the Lower
House of the Diet, only to be rejected by the conservatives
in the Upper House.

"Beginnings," Fukuda used to say, "are easy; it's continuing that's difficult." Somehow she and her friends found
the resources and the strength to continue publishing
Women of the World for over two years, but they ran into
real difficulties in early 1907. Though Fukuda tried from
the beginning to present the magazine as a feminist publication with wide-ranging interests, one that would attract a
large enough readership to make it self-supporting, that
never happened. Between the splits among the socialists
and the inability of women to help because of other obligations, Fukuda was forced to bear the brunt of the editorial
responsibility for the magazine. She also usually financed

it. Between 1907 and 1909 she put out the paper and paid the bill for a thousand or two thousand copies at least once a month, meanwhile caring for her eighty-year-old mother and her three children. How much assistance she got from Ishikawa Sanshirō, the young socialist with whom she was now involved, is unknown.

Part of Fukuda's inability to reach a larger readership was due to the continuing harassment, official and unofficial, of all projects associated with socialism, and to some extent feminism as well. Women who took copies of the magazine to sell to students outside the gates of Japan Women's University were asked to leave by college officials. And the office frequently received letters from young women asking that their subscriptions be canceled temporarily, because school and dormitory officials were checking the mail in neighborhood post offices looking for "subversive" literature like *Women of the World*, and reporting or punishing all subscribers.[39]

In January 1908 Fukuda was forced, for economic reasons, to go to a monthly, rather than a twice-monthly, publishing schedule. In that month, too, Katsura resumed the premiership, and government pressures on the socialists were stepped up. Socialist gatherings, as during the antiwar movement, now seemed to be focused on sending off and welcoming back comrades who had been sent to prison, primarily for the violation of press laws. In June, shortly after Fukuda welcomed Ishikawa Sanshirō back from a year in prison, socialists from all over the Tokyo area gathered in Kanda to celebrate the release of Yamaguchi Kōken. The meeting was more social than political, but there was a lot of spontaneous speechmaking and singing of revolutionary songs, as well as some good-natured argument between the parliamentary socialists and the anarcho-syndicalists, who favored direct action. Members of the latter group, called the Friday Society, brought banners reading "Anarchism" and "Anarcho-Communism," which they attempted to carry into the street at the close of the meeting. The police, who had spent the evening waiting for an opportunity to move, now had a "Red Flag Incident" to justify their actions. They swept into the crowd and arrested several socialists for allegedly violating the Police Security regulations. In their trial in August these demonstrators were handed some of the severest sentences members of the movement had ever experienced. When the courts were finished, they had sentenced better than half the leaders of the socialist movement to jail terms, some for two years. Four women were among those who were picked up and jailed in the Red Flag Incident: Kamikawa Matsuko, Kanno Suga, Ōsuga Satoko, and Kokura Rei; Kamikawa and Kanno were later released.[40]

The socialist movement was now virtually without leadership, and more than ever, without a pronounced center of activity. In these circumstances, *Women of the World* came under even closer government scrutiny, and after Ishikawa decided to use it to print some translations of Kropotkin and Stendhal he had done in prison, the magazine became the target of systematic government harassment. The June 1908 issue featured nine pages devoted to Ishikawa's partial translation of the autobiography of Kropotkin, advertised as the "Author of Anarchism." This effort, applauded by Kōtoku, was criticized by many of the magazine's supporters, who wondered what was happening to the emphasis on women's issues. When Ishikawa followed the Kropotkin article with a partial translation of Stendhal's attack on the family (which Ishikawa titled "The First Enemy"), the government banned the magazine as "detrimental to good public order," and Kamisaki Jun'ichi, then listed as the editor, was given a fine of 40 yen.[41]

All of this forced Fukuda to retreat to what she thought would be a safe position for the magazine, and in 1909 it became less political and more literary. In February her mother, the woman Fukuda had said she hoped would live to be a hundred, died. For Fukuda, it was the loss of a friend, a lifelong partisan, and a woman whose life had been at least as hard as her own. She gave her mother what she could, a memorial issue of *Women of the World,* but she must have thought about the economic, if not the emotional, poverty of their lives together over the years. She cared for her mother, and had taken care of her, but their lives together had been filled with unrelenting hardship.

Meanwhile, the government continued its attack on *Women of the World,* fining Ishikawa, reprimanding Fukuda for her issue No. 37, suspending publication of No. 38, and banning No. 39. In 1909 a Tokyo court levied the heavy fine of 100 yen on the designated editors and issued a stop-publication order.[42] Ironically, at about the same time, another petition asking for a revision of Article 5 went to the Lower House. But *Women of the World* had died, and with it, some of Fukuda's hopes for legal remedies to the "woman question." Ishikawa was jailed in March 1910 as the responsible editor-publisher of the magazine, and when he was released in July, returning to Fukuda's house, the police staged a sudden search of the premises.

The Katsura government, facing strikes and various kinds of citizen protests as the economic and political instability of the postwar years persisted, continued to strike out at the tiny socialist movement, which had not been able to establish connections with any of the volatile centers of Japanese society. The socialists became symbols of government control over criticism. When Fukuda and Ishikawa retreated to his family's home away from Tokyo in August 1910, most of the socialists not already in jail were under arrest, charged with high treason—plotting the death of the Meiji Emperor. After a secret trial, conducted with great dispatch, twelve socialists, including Kōtoku Shūsui and Kanno Suga, were hanged. Japan had executed its first political prisoners in the modern period, and socialism as a movement was forced underground for nearly a decade.

7. Kanno Suga

As you must already know, since we have been sentenced, I, Kōtoku, and the others have no sense of certainty that our lives will continue as late as tomorrow. I am resigned to this fate and am satisfied. I feel fortunate that, rather than feeling uncomfortable and lonely, I have few regrets in these final moments because I have no family ties. . . .

From the depths of my heart I pray for the well-being of all of you. The execution is unlikely to be soon, so please write me again. Today there is a great deal more I would like to write, but it probably would not get past the censors, so I will leave it at this.

Good-bye.

Kanno Suga, January 21, 1911

This letter from Kanno Suga to Kōtoku Shūsui's niece was postmarked January 26, 1911, a day after Kanno died on the scaffold at Sugamo prison in Tokyo. The first woman to be executed as a political prisoner in Japan's modern history, Kanno was not to be the last to die in the custody of the state because of her political convictions.[1] A self-described anarchist as early as 1908, Kanno is supposed to have shouted from the scaffold, "We die for our principles. Banzai!"[2] Already in prison in 1910 because of her editorship of the journal *Jiyū shisō* (Free Thought), Kanno was simply moved into the government's Great Treason trial, held *in camera* from December 10 to December 29, 1910. On January 18, 1911, the 26 defendants were pronounced guilty of plotting to assassinate the Meiji Emperor, and sentenced to death. Twelve of the defendants were given life sentences, and two others lighter terms; all were eventually released at the intercession of the Emperor, but for Kanno, considered by the prosecution the instigator and coordinator of the plot, there was no reprieve.

For all her notoriety, Kanno remains one of those women about whom much has been written, and too little said. If she died for her convictions, it is ironic that we know so little about what they were or how they developed in the context of her life. What questions did anarchism answer for Kanno? What kind of a separate existence, emotionally and ideologically, could she claim, apart from her association with the men who led the socialist movement, principally Arahata Kanson and Kōtoku Shūsui? What was her life as a Meiji woman like, "unrepresentative" as she may have been? The answers to these questions are made more difficult by the fact that Kanno, like so many other women, did not provide for her own intellectual posterity. Most of what we know about her ideas is derived from newspaper articles she wrote, not so much for intellectual exercise as for a salary. And most descriptions of her personal life have come, unfortunately for Kanno, from a jilted lover, Arahata Kanson. But even the fragments we have are enough to indicate the outline of an important story, one with significant points of reference to the history of Meiji women.

Kanno was born in the Osaka area in 1881, the year women were beginning to speak out in the popular-rights movement. One of five children (three brothers and a sister), Kanno seems to have had a distant relationship with her father, a miner, but she was close to her mother, Nobu, who was determined to meet the criticism that her daughter was ugly by making her intellectually accomplished. But Nobu died in 1892, just about the time Suga was finishing the required four years of elementary school. That may have been the end of her formal education; she seems to have been on her own intellectually for the rest of her life.

The death of Kanno's mother and her father's financial problems produced drastic changes in the family. Her father remarried, bringing into the household a woman with whom Suga never got along, and the family moved from place to place as her father tried to find work. Sometime in this period, when Kanno was thirteen or fourteen, there occurred an event that changed everything about her life. According to Arahata, who recounted the story in his autobiography, her stepmother arranged to have Kanno raped by a miner who worked for her father, and then used the incident to alienate father and daughter by fastening the blame on Suga.[3] Whatever the circumstance of the rape, the assault was an indelible memory etched in the bitterness Kanno naturally felt over having been victimized, then held responsible by her family and society, while the rapist was treated as if he were innocent of all wrongdoing. At an early age, Kanno had experienced a pain and anger that she would carry with her all her life, though she refused to be a victim. She would resist.

In 1898 an opportunity to escape her family through a respectable marriage to a Tokyo merchant presented itself, and Kanno seems to have moved quickly to take advantage of it. But the marriage to a man she probably barely knew, however respectable, did not work out. After perhaps two years of marriage to Kamiya Fukutarō, Kanno pleaded that she had to return to Osaka to care for her father, who had been paralyzed by a stroke. She left Tokyo and did not return for many years; records indicate that in 1902 she was divorced from Kamiya. Kanno's experience after she returned to Osaka was perhaps not atypical of the struggle many Meiji women with little education and few connections engaged in as they tried to live independent lives. Without economic support or helpful friends, Kanno somehow survived and eventually became the mistress of Udagawa Bunkai, an Osaka novelist who wrote in late-Tokugawa style. The arrangement with Udagawa was a familiar one: some intellectual and economic assistance in return for sexual favors.[4]

Eventually, perhaps with Udagawa's help, Kanno was hired by the newspaper *Osaka chōhō* (Osaka Morning Report) as a reporter and contributor of light fiction. It was her first salaried employment, and it was related, at least peripherally, to the kind of writing she wanted to do. By the spring of 1903 Kanno was connecting her journalistic assignments with her own interests, and increasingly finding them intersecting around women's issues. In April she covered an Osaka Reform Society meeting and reported the remarks of the speaker, Shimoda Saburō, on the "need to remove the red-light district" in Osaka. Through Shimoda, Kanno met Kinoshita Naoe, who was in Osaka with Abe Isō, Kōtoku Shūsui, and Nishikawa Kōjiro, to give lectures publicizing socialism. She covered these lectures for her paper, reporting Kinoshita's criticism of the use of geisha to publicize officially sponsored events in the Osaka area, as well as a speech dealing with the legal and political implications of socialism.[5]

It is not surprising that Kanno was impressed with the group of socialists she met in Osaka that spring; they were idealistic, apparently sympathetic to some of the issues raised by the Reform Society, and committed to broadly humanistic, antigovernment goals. When she met them, they were still tied to *Complete Morning Report*, carrying on a socialist critique of government policies, and just beginning the antiwar campaign that would lead to the organization of the Commoners' Association later that year. Kanno seems to have maintained her ties with Kinoshita, perhaps through correspondence or mutual acquaintances, until the summer of 1904, when she visited the Commoners' Association offices in Tokyo. However, most of her time and energy in the year after she heard the socialists for the first time was spent on the antiprostitution campaign organized by the Osaka branch of the Reform Society.

Kanno's involvement with the Osaka Reform Society has been virtually disregarded, perhaps because of her radical political image or her reputation for promiscuity, but it is an area of her life that deserves more careful examination. Contrary to conventional wisdom, Kanno's background as she made connections with the Reform Society was consistent not only with their goals, but with her convictions as well. She had been raped, had experienced an unsuccessful marriage, and had become the mistress of an older man, before she was able to find a respectable job that paid a regular salary. She may still have been living with Udagawa when she joined forces with the Reform Society, but we should remember that Fukuda was carrying Ōi Kentarō's child when she described a Reform Society meeting she attended as a "high point"; and Yajima Kajiko, the woman who became the venerable, lifelong leader of the Reform Society, had borne a child without benefit of marriage before she helped found the organization. The life experiences of all three women produced a profound interest in the kinds of efforts the Reform Society eventually made on behalf of women.

Kanno spent most of her time between the spring of 1903 and the summer of 1904 writing in support of Reform Society activities in both the *Osaka Morning Report* and *Kirisutokyō sekai* (Christian World). Interspersed with articles she wrote condemning prostitution in the latter publication was a short antiwar novel entitled *Zekkō* (Breaking Off). *Breaking Off* was published October 8, 1903, the very day that Sakai, Kōtoku, Uchimura, and other members of *Complete Morning Report* printed their protest against the newspaper's changed position on the war. By December Kanno was presiding over meetings of the Osaka Reform Society and had become one of its officers, responsible for documents and archival materials.

All of this activity on Kanno's part suggests not only a substantial commitment to the Reform Society's priorities, but a considerable number of contacts, and even friendships, with the more "typical" women of the society. One of those women was Hayashi Utako, a respected educator and founder of the Osaka branch of the Reform Society. Hayashi, a divorcée, had made her living in Tokyo after 1885 teaching Japanese to foreign missionaries. Sometime after 1893 she moved to Osaka and founded the Hakuaisha, a charitable institution functioning as an orphanage, nursery, day school, and shelter for mothers and children. After helping to organize the Osaka Reform Society in 1899, she remained the head of the organization, pushing its antiprostitution efforts in Osaka and occasionally attending international WCTU meetings representing Japan.

Without much of a historical record to work with, we can only surmise that the friendship between Hayashi and Kanno was an important connection, perhaps more so for Kanno than for the older woman. Hayashi almost certainly helped Kanno get jobs teaching Japanese to foreign teachers (a principal source of income), and she seems to have been helpful and sympathetic when Kanno was struggling to care for her younger sister, who had tuberculosis. On Kanno's side, there is an apparent reference to Hayashi in her article "Four Mothers." The "spiritual mother" fits Hayashi well, and Kanno seems to present here a rare description of their relationship:

I have four mothers; one my biological mother; one the mother to whom I am obligated; one my compassionate mother; one my spiritual mother. . . . Sadly, my biological mother died more than a decade ago. . . . The mother to whom I am obligated, and who bore my brother, is living in Kyoto, an unusual person. . . . My compassionate mother lives in loneliness in Osaka . . . and my spiritual mother lives there as well. . . .

At a time when I had grown accustomed to tears, experiencing the sharp taste of the world's bitterness, it was my compassionate mother who consoled me. And even now, when the most inconsequential thing occurs, I confide in her, and together we cry or rejoice. . . .

My spiritual mother, with whom God has united me, is, by today's standards, a woman of unusual strength. To some she seems a little too severe and unapproachable, but each time I come in contact with her, I find my own indolence totally swept away by her intelligence, her burning faith, and her eloquence. . . .

Occasionally we argue; on occasion, she scolds me, occasionally praises me or offers an opinion; and since she is the one person to whom I can present my rational side without unpleasantness, I feel very comfortable with her, rather like being with a teacher for whom I have boundless affection and respect.[6]

Though Kanno never converted to Christianity, as Hayashi had in 1887, it seems that Christian humanism and the kind of social reform advocated by the Reform Society had a larger impact on her than has been generally assumed. In any case, her commitment to the society's work and her associations with the women in it were an important stage in her development, providing the first hints of a feminism that would surface even more clearly later.

In the summer of 1904 Kanno attended the Tokyo meeting of the Reform Society as a representative of the Osaka branch; after the meetings were over, she had an opportunity to renew associations with the antiwar socialists of the Commoners' Association and to meet one of the men who had not come to Osaka the previous year: Sakai Toshihiko. In fact Kanno seems to have gone to the association's headquarters specifically to meet Sakai, in response to his published reply to a letter *Complete Morning Report* had received from a rape victim. In it, Sakai had shown nothing but sympathy for the writer, and had emphasized the character and responsibility of the rapist in such incidents: men who victimized women in this way were little better than "rabid dogs," he said.[7] Kanno, quite naturally, was impressed; like many other women who came to the Commoners' Association, she was attracted first by the apparent sympathy for women shown by both Kinoshita and Sakai. Had Kanno stayed in Tokyo that summer, she undoubtedly would have joined Fukuda, Matsuoka, Imai, and Kawamura in their efforts to find a place for women in the socialist movement. As it was, she went back to her job in Osaka and thus played no real part in the "kitchen crew's" activities.

Still, she did try to drum up interest in the Commoners' cause on her return to Osaka, making contributions to the association herself and organizing a study group. According to Sakai, even Udagawa Bunkai, Kanno's former teacher, was now showing some interest in socialism.[8] But the next important stage in Kanno's life was to come, not in Tokyo with the socialists of the Commoners' Association, but in Wakayama, where the connection with Sakai had produced another newspaper job.[9] When Moori Kiyomasa, editor of Wakayama prefecture's progressive newspaper *Murō shimpō* (Murō News), asked Sakai to recommend a woman reporter, Sakai unhesitatingly suggested Kanno, though he barely knew her. Shortly after, articles signed Kanno Suga began appearing from time to time in the pages of *Murō News,* among them a semi-autobiographical novel entitled *Tsuyuko.* Though Moori pressed Kanno to move to Wakayama and play a more active and permanent role on the newspaper, she resisted the change. Satisfied to contribute occasional articles to the home section of the paper from a distance, Kanno also wanted to be in the Kyoto-Osaka area so she could take care of her younger sister. Her situation in this period has been described as "comfortable," meaning that for one of the few times in her life, she was probably self-supporting—with adequate money coming in from both writing and teaching jobs. But the expense, economic and psychological, of her sister's illness was another matter.

She was finally persuaded to leave Osaka after Moori made it clear that he needed someone to take over editing duties in his absence if, as he expected, he had to serve time in jail for violating press laws. She moved to Tanabe, in Wakayama prefecture, in February 1906 and within a month had brought her sister there to live with her. She took charge of the newspaper around the same time; Moori went to jail on March 12 and was not released until the end of April. The work with *Murō News* was demanding, even though some of it was shared with the young socialist Arahata Kanson, with whom Kanno had become romantically involved after coming to Wakayama.[10]

Most of the accounts of Kanno's life emphasize her relationship with Arahata at this point, but several other important things seem to have been happening simultaneously, affecting her views of herself and the world around her. She must have gained confidence in her intellectual and administrative capacities as a result of her work for *Murō News*, but it came against a backdrop of bittersweet emotions related to her sister's incurable illness and Kanno's inability to do anything about it. She indulged herself in a romantic and seemingly carefree attachment to Arahata,* but there was always a shadow on the horizon. At odd moments, in spite of brave efforts to be accepting, Kanno's bitterness spilled over, and with it, a new conviction that the kind words of the Reform Society were not adequate to deal with poverty: charity was not the answer to tuberculosis among the poor or abandoned, mistreated children; only drastic social change could make a difference.[11] Though Kanno attended (or covered for the newspaper) Reform Society meetings in Tanabe and apparently continued to correspond with Hayashi Utako,

---

* Kanno later said that she did not become involved in a sexual relationship with Arahata until he joined her in Kyoto in the fall of 1906, when they began to live together (Shioda Shōbei and Watanabe Junzō, eds., *Hiroku Daigyaku jiken,* Tokyo, 1959, 2: 156).

she was moving from reform to revolution in the spring of 1906, and socialism was increasingly attractive.

While the socialists in Tokyo were regrouping and Fukuda was concluding that the women in the movement needed a paper for themselves, Kanno was fighting her own feminist battles alone and finding, after Moori's return at the end of April, that the progressivism of *Murō News* did not include much sympathy for feminist positions. When Kanno began writing articles for the home section of the paper, she was apparently satisfied to focus her discussion on self-improvement for women, though with an interesting twist. Her article "Women and Reading," published in December 1905, sympathized with housewives, rich and poor, who found their tasks difficult and unending, but nonetheless insisted that busy women rearrange some of their priorities:

Heartless as it may seem to suggest to these women without a moment's leisure, I earnestly recommend that they do some reading. We human beings regress without fail if we are not progressive. . . . Even the woman who thinks of herself as the "good wife; wise mother" of the twentieth century, a woman who, in school, sought new knowledge and aspired to ideals, finds that her favorite books gather dust and women's magazines pile up without being opened once she marries. Finally, she does not even get around to reading the newspaper. Without new knowledge, without ideals, unable to converse about a single current event, women become "domesticated wives." They are the slaves of men. In such circumstances, how is it possible for them to cry out for freedom and rights? Are they qualified to do that? . . .

We should be women of deeds, not words, improving the lot of women in the larger framework at the same time as we fulfill the duties of housewives on a smaller scale, so that we do not become "domesticated wives," but gain new knowledge and expand our horizons. . . . Cultivate the habit of reading . . . even half an hour a day.[12]

Polite calls for self-improvement may have been what the editor of *Murō News* wanted from Kanno but now, after she had edited and managed the paper, she seemed less and less inclined to produce such work. The complications of her relationship with Arahata, anguish over her sister's illness, and the pressures of her work in Moori's absence from the newspaper brought long-held resentments bubbling to the surface. On April 15, 1906, in an article entitled "Rebuff," she attacked men's views of the world and women. Commenting that the only response men had made to discussions about improving the condition of women was totally self-interested and ignorant, Kanno suggested that it was time for women to stand their ground and rebuff men, whose words and actions betrayed both contempt and hypocrisy:

Among the many annoying things in the world, I think men are the most annoying. When I hear them carrying on interminably about female chastity, I burst out laughing. We should have some evidence of the speaker's competence to speak to such a subject before we agree to listen. I cannot contain my disgust over the fact that our society's eloquent men so brashly and brazenly speak to the issue of female chastity. . . . It is incredibly insulting to women.

And I find it exceedingly strange that we women do not rise up and stop all this male discussion of chastity. I greet with utmost cynicism and unbridled hatred the debauched male of today who rattles on about good wives and wise mothers. Where do all of these depraved men get the right to emphasize chastity? Before they begin stressing women's chastity, they ought to perfect their own male chastity, and concentrate on becoming wise fathers and good husbands! Of all the contradictions one sees in the world, this is the greatest. . . .

Though of course the root of the problem must await a socialist solution, we women must struggle not only against husbands, but against the entire self-serving world of men. . . .

Rise up, women! Wake up! As in the struggle workers are engaged in against capitalists to break down the class system, our demands for freedom and equality with men will not be won easily just because we will it; they will not be won if we do not raise our voices, if no blood is shed.[13]

Kanno's view of socialism at this point was ambivalent; she regarded socialism as perhaps an ultimate solution to many of the human tragedies she saw around her, including the unwanted children in Hayashi's orphanage, but she was impatient and felt that a socialist society could not be brought about except on the most gradual basis. Moreover, she apparently had seen nothing that encouraged her to believe socialism or socialists would provide real solutions to women's problems; women would have to shed their own blood in their own behalf. And, as she looked around at the exterior calm and satisfaction of some of the "good women" around her, she despaired of their willingness to take action, and of their hypocrisy.

There is some indication that Kanno's editor was not happy with the aggressive articles she had been writing even before he was released from jail, but Kanno persisted, and in May, two weeks after Moori returned to *Murō News,* she wrote an article that seems to have brought the conflict between them out in the open. There is at least a possibility that this article, "A Perspective on Men," was aimed at Moori and men like him. Beginning with the assumption that most men, because of their own conceit, preferred to associate with people who were weaker or less important than themselves, Kanno went on to describe men with no tolerance for women of independent views. They were "like people shut up in castles under siege whose provisions have been exhausted. On first inspection, one thinks the outer walls are strong enough, but the gate is vulnerable and easily forced, producing an immediate surrender."[14] There was only one thing that allowed such men to attach any importance to themselves, she declared: the fact that most women had learned to think of men as capable of providing security, and continued to revere them for that illusory strength.

Whether or not the article was meant to describe Moori, he reproached Kanno for writing it and three days later (May 9, 1906) printed a rebuttal (under the signature Araki Matazaemon) entitled "A Perspective on Women." Kanno seems to have diluted her anger slightly in later articles, but she was ready to leave *Murō News.* Arahata had gone to Tokyo earlier, in April, and the combination of problems with Moori and her sister's constantly worsening health certainly made leaving Wakayama attractive. Kanno moved to Kyoto with her sister at the end of May 1906; in the fall Arahata came from Tokyo to live with her and to help care for her sister. Though they both later referred to their relationship as a marriage, it was, in official terms, a common-law arrangement. In fact, though Kanno intended to marry Kōtoku at one point, her only legal marriage was to Kamiya. In December Kanno and her sister Hide moved to Tokyo, where Kanno was able to get a job writing for the society section of *Mainichi denpō* (Daily Telegraph). On January 1, 1907, coincidentally the day *Women of the World* first appeared, Kanno published "The Beginning of the Year" in *Murō News* and announced her "marriage" to Arahata.[15]

The socialists, including Arahata, were much less impressed at the time with Fukuda's publication than with the violent labor disputes then occurring at the Ashio copper mines and the plans to revive the *Commoners' News,* this time as a daily rather than a weekly. When the first issue of the *News* appeared in mid-January, a number of socialists gathered at Kanno's to celebrate,

For many of these socialists, February was an exhilarating time; the riots at Ashio seemed to bear out their faith in the revolutionary potential of workers, and their reporters on the scene were constantly hounded and harassed by police, making them feel a part of the protest.[16] But for Kanno, February was anything but exhilarating. Her sister, after suffering for more than two years from the "slow disease" Kanno hated, was dying. By Arahata's account, he returned from Ashio on February 9, to find Kanno's sister much worse, and for the next two weeks they watched helplessly (with Kanno in tears) while Hide, barely twenty-one, slipped away from them. They talked of hospitalizing her at the end, though she had not had much hospital care earlier, but between them they had little more than 40 yen to support such a last-minute effort.[17] Hide died February 21, and was cremated and buried in Tokyo's Seishunji temple the following day. Sakai reported on the funeral for *Commoners' News.* Kanno Hide was buried at six in the morning, he wrote, in a ceremony "without Buddhist or Shinto priests; without flowers or flags." It was good, he said, because it was a ceremony of "only true human feelings."[18]

Kanno took a leave of absence from her job shortly after her sister's death and went, alone, to the health resort of Ito, to rest and reflect. Her own tuberculosis had already been diagnosed, and in addition to being physically and psychologically exhausted from the demands of caring for her sister, she was very much aware of her own illness. Her life in Tokyo, even discounting the difficulties of her sister's illness, had perhaps not been what she expected. Her job with the *Daily Telegraph* probably paid less, and was certainly less attractive, than her previous two assignments in the world of journalism; she now seemed at something of a creative dead end, when it had seemed in Wakayama that she was just coming into her own.* She barely knew many of the people in the Commoners' Association, and in any case her own work and caring for her sister meant that she had not been able to spend much time with what was left of a very transient group. If she had known Fukuda or one of the other women associated with *Women of the World* better at this point in her life, she might have found some of the support she needed. But that was not to be the case. And whatever strengths there might have been in her relationship with Arahata, it is clear that he did not appreciate

---

* Her career as a published writer did not end completely when she left Osaka and Kyoto, but her output was comparatively low after she moved to Tokyo, and she published the last of the few signed articles she contributed to the *Daily Telegraph* on Feb. 15, 1907, when her sister was dying. (Itoya Toshio, *Kanno Suga*, Tokyo, 1970, p. 101.)

her intellect or consider her a serious thinker. He was, however, extremely jealous and possessive.[19]

It is likely that their relationship was cooling by the time Kanno returned to Tokyo from Ito, sometime in the early fall of 1907, though they continued to live together until spring. After her return, Kanno went back to her job with the *Daily Telegraph* because she felt she could not do without the monthly salary it brought her. Back in Tokyo, less attached to Arahata and his political activities, and without a sister to care for, Kanno spent more time with members of the socialist community, men and women. She became a friend of Sakai's second wife, Tameko, and the Sakai family, and attended most of the Commoners' Association functions.* But Kanno was not contributing her greatest strength to the movement: she was not writing for *Women of the World* or any other progressive journal in this period. She was keeping her anger and bitterness over her own situation and over her sister's death out of print and in her head. In this frame of mind, Kanno must have listened to the debate among socialists over tactics and strategy on many occasions, and may have been much more sympathetic to direct action as a tactic and anarchism as a philosophy than anyone guessed. But there is not much evidence of her changing political views until the Red Flag Incident, when she is supposed to have proclaimed herself an anarchist.[20]

The Red Flag Incident on June 22, 1908, broke the silence. After her arrest, Kanno could no longer walk a tightrope between silent respectability (to keep her job

---

* She had apparently gotten to know other women associated with the Commoners and *Women of the World* in the early part of 1907, but they were more acquaintances than friends. She seems to have been closest to the Sakai family, and Tameko has left us what is perhaps the clearest description of what Kanno looked like. She was, Tameko said, "of medium height and weight . . . with bright, clear eyes and an arresting way of looking at you. . . . She had very attractive long black eyelashes . . . and unusually thick black hair . . . so marvelous that even women were fascinated by it." (Quoted in Itoya, *Kanno Suga*, p. 211.)

with the *Daily Telegraph*) and participation in socialist activities (to preserve her political integrity). One of the four women arrested in the confusing and tragicomic events that evening, Kanno went to jail for the first time, after having experienced the standard treatment of political dissidents at the hands of undisciplined police.

Kanno, with Kamikawa Matsuko who would not let her go alone, walked from the meeting hall to the police station across the street to see what was happening to Ōsugi Sakae and Arahata, who had been arrested for waving flags bearing the words "Anarchism" and "Anarcho-Communism" outside the meeting hall. Eventually they too were detained, and when Kamikawa protested, both women were pushed and threatened by the police. Kanno, who had been standing next to Kamikawa, was knocked down, and when she tried to get up, was stopped by a police officer, who grabbed her arm and twisted it. The two women were then dragged into the headquarters and eventually reunited with Ōsuga Satoko, Kokura Rei, Sakai Toshihiko, Yamakawa Hitoshi, Ōsugi Sakae, Arahata Kanson, and the others who had been arrested.[21]

As Kanno later recalled, they were eventually put into two police carriages and taken off to the central police station, filling the cool evening air with revolutionary songs and shouts of "Long Live Anarchism!" When they arrived at the station and the high walled compounds within it, Kanno remembered thinking, "So this is where they shackle the freedom of those of us who have not committed any crime." After an emotional farewell and shouted advice on how to survive in jail from veterans who had been there before, the men and women were separated, the women to go to cells, as Kanno put it, "too narrow to turn around in without bumping your nose."[22] There are few accounts of their treatment during the two months they waited for a hearing, but a reporter for *Kumamoto hyōron* (Kumamoto Review) who visited them wrote that all of the women were "angry about the things that had been done to them" in jail, and hoped they could repay some of the people responsible after their release.[23]

By the time the courts got around to them, it was August 15, and Kanno's health was deteriorating rapidly as a result of her confinement. After hearing witnesses whose veracity was directly challenged by defendants (including Kamikawa Matsuko) and disregarding the statements of many of the accused who, like Sakai, protested that their involvement amounted to little more than an attempt to mediate between flag wavers and police, the judges began the sentencing. Even though Kanno and Kamikawa both admitted their attraction to anarchism, they were released without fines or jail terms. Others were not so fortunate. Ōsugi was sentenced to two and a half years in prison and fined 25 yen. Sakai who, with Yamakawa Hitoshi, really had done little more than try to end the incident, was sentenced to prison again, this time for two years, as was Yamakawa. Arahata was sentenced to one and a half years, and fined 15 yen. The other two women arrested, Kokura Rei and Ōsuga Satoko, were each sentenced to a year in prison.[24] Looking on at the trial and the sentencing was Kōtoku, who had been in Shikoku translating Kropotkin's *The Conquest of Bread* when the Red Flag Incident occurred.

Kanno was released on August 29, 1908, but the editors of the *Daily Telegraph*, who had until then kept her on the staff, now had no stomach for a reporter who was constantly followed by police, and fired her.[25] No one was more aware than Kanno that her freedom after August 29 was illusory. Without a salary, she was in roughly the same predicament she had faced after leaving her first husband and returning to Osaka. But now there was debilitating illness to contend with, as well as constant police surveillance and harassment. One of the few socialists out of jail, she felt (and fulfilled) obligations to those in prison, though she well appreciated that her association with former friends in the movement focused unwanted police attention on them.* It was a situation Kōtoku Shūsui could understand; he had been trying to live with it for a long time.[26]

It is not clear how Kanno lived during the first few months after her release, but by the beginning of 1909 she was gravitating to Kōtoku's camp and accepted money from him that allowed her to go to the seaside city of Kamakura for recuperation. When she returned to Tokyo, she moved into the new Commoners' Association headquarters in the Sendagaya district, to become Kōtoku's secretary and, in June, his lover.[27] Their alliance was not well received in the socialist community and left them isolated, both ideologically and personally.[28] Whether one views them as star-crossed lovers or as desperate would-be revolutionaries ready to die together for the sake of ideology, there is little question that at this point in her life, Kanno was much more prepared to act than Kōtoku was. Terminally ill and increasingly unable to restrain her rage at a government that successfully controlled her life and a society that denied her the possibility of economic independence, Kanno was determined to make the time left to her an epic story of resistance, with or without Kōtoku.

Any reservations she might have had about that course disappeared when the government made it impossible for Kōtoku and Kanno to express their views in the last journal they tried to publish, *Free Thought*. After an unsuccessful attempt to use a colleague's name, Kanno assumed the editorship of what finally became the first issue, published

* The confusion over the exact period Kanno and Arahata separated is due in part to Kanno's having registered at the prison as Arahata's common-law wife so that she would be allowed to bring things to the men in prison. Kanno later commented that Arahata understood the purpose of the ruse and knew well enough that they had agreed to separate before the Red Flag Incident. (Shioda Shōbei and Watanabe Junzō, eds., *Hiroku Daigyaku jiken*, Tokyo, 1959, 2: 226–28.)

May 25, 1909. Predictably, the government cited Kanno for violating the press laws, and repeated the charge when the second issue appeared in June, banning its distribution and adding to the fines Kanno had already accumulated. As Kōtoku said at the time, it had become impossible for socialists to publish anything in Japan, irrespective of its content. Kanno, denied the possibility of expressing herself in print, turned what strength she had left to a plan of action—an act of violence that would shake the entire nation to its symbolic foundations. Kanno would become Sofia Perovskaia, the Russian terrorist who signaled her comrades in the assassination of Tsar Alexander II; or, she would throw the bomb herself.[29] Cultivating alliances with socialists, many of whom had been on the fringes of the Japanese movement for a long time, Kanno in the fall of 1909 became part of a serious effort to manufacture explosives for terrorist activities. The ultimate goal of the group, made up of Kanno, Miyashita Takichi, Niimura Tadao, and Furukawa Rikisaku, was to assassinate the Emperor, thereby demonstrating to the country and the world that he was not a god, but a human being who would bleed and die like everyone else.[30]

By October Kanno was coughing up blood and was forced to spend a month in the hospital. As a result, little more was done toward the assassination plot until January, when the members of the group began to meet sporadically in the Commoners' Association headquarters in the Sendagaya district. By then Kōtoku had decided he had heard enough; he withdrew from the plot and thereafter was openly disapproving of what he considered a disastrous course that could not, as he said, "help our ideology."[31] According to Kanno's later testimony, the group continued to meet that spring at their house when Kōtoku was around, but they did not discuss plans in his presence because it would simply have produced a disapproving lecture. Knowing how ill Kanno was, and so ill himself that he expected his own death in a matter of months, Kōtoku was being persuaded to retreat from his battle with the government by his old friend Koizumi Sakutaro. Koizumi thought that if Kōtoku would confine himself to writing history for a while, the government might give both him and Kanno some breathing space. Exhausted by his struggle against the state and his failing health, feeling, as he said, that he was "fighting the whole of Japan," Kōtoku simply wanted to go the countryside with Kanno, perhaps even to his native village in Kochi, to die in peace.[32]

Kanno, though, was ready to die in battle. She compromised by agreeing to go with Kōtoku to Yugawara on the Izu peninsula at the end of March, but returned to Tokyo in May to begin a prison term in lieu of the heavy fines the government had imposed in the *Free Thought* case.[33] She did not go directly to prison but met first with her revolutionary comrades in Sendagaya. She was disturbed to find that the group's lack of discipline, particularly on the part of Miyashita, had made them all vulnerable, and when she entered prison on May 18, Kanno must have had grave misgivings about the future of the group and its plans, though they had agreed to take no action of any kind until she could join them after her release from prison.[34] Within a week, the government began making arrests in what was to be called the Great Treason Incident. Kōtoku was arrested in Yugawara on June 1, 1910, as he was waiting to catch the train for Tokyo, where he hoped to find a publisher for his most recent book.[35] In all, the government arrested 26 persons, two of whom were later released.[36]

The secret trial began on December 10, 1910. The prosecution ran through reams of testimony and evidence with all the deliberation of a "galloping horse," and by December 25 they were ready to ask the death sentence for all the defendants.[37] The defense lawyers were given three days, December 27–29, to present a case for all the defendants. On January 18, all were pronounced guilty, and 24 were sentenced to death. The reduced sentences that saved the lives of half of the defendants came only after extensive discussion of the case in the international press and well-publicized protests from groups and individuals around the world.[38]

The most obvious target of the trial was Kōtoku Shūsui, the ideologist with the vitriolic pen, who was found guilty largely because others were demonstrably influenced by his ideas. Many others were executed or imprisoned after only the flimsiest demonstration of guilt by association. Ideologists like Ōsugi Sakae were saved by the bitter irony of an earlier fate: they were still in prison as participants in the Red Flag Incident.[39] The others in the Great Treason trial, Kanno Suga and her three co-conspirators, Miyashita, Furukawa, and Niimura, were of course tried as if they had successfully carried out their plans, though from the beginning they had been no match for the Japanese police.[40]

Kanno testified, both at the preliminary hearings and at the trial itself, that Kōtoku was only initially interested in their plans and then withdrew. Kōtoku, she said, sound as he was ideologically, was a man of words, rather than deeds, a man not as capable of acting to carry out revolutionary violence as others were.[41] At the same time, she left little doubt that, given time and opportunity, she herself was willing to act. In testimony reminiscent of the famous trial statement of the Russian terrorist Vera Figner, she ascribed her actions to a government that made anything short of violence an ineffective mechanism of change. She had concluded, as Figner had, that unusual measures were required to dismantle social institutions and topple the corrupt and powerful personalities who oppressed the entire society.[42] Much as Kanno admired the goals of socialism, she thought that ordinary measures in a society like Japan's were too slow and ponderous. She could not afford to wait, but neither could Japan, she thought. Her testimony reveals that the Emperor was for her a symbol of state power, but that she held the men who actually ran the government, like former Prime Minister Yamagata Aritomo, personally responsible for much that had gone wrong with the country's political system.

PROSECUTOR: You belong to the most radical faction of the socialists; is that correct?

KANNO: That is correct.

PROSECUTOR: What are the goals and tactics of the radical faction?

KANNO: Revolution, to begin with. To accomplish something like the French Revolution. I previously told the prosecutor that we would cause rioting, but it is more than that. No, rioting is an inappropriate description. Retract that. Revolution is more correct.

PROSECUTOR: Concretely, what kinds of things would you do?

KANNO: We would carry out assassinations. Disrupt transportation systems. Set fires that would burn down buildings. All with the aim of taking back institutions from the exploiters.

PROSECUTOR: For about how long have you entertained such radical ideas?

KANNO: Since I was put in jail in the Red Flag Incident. Though it was not a major incident, socialists were given severe sentences; Sakai Toshihiko was sentenced to two years for no reason. From these experiences, my anger grew, and I came to realize that ordinary methods could never be successful against such a government. . . .

PROSECUTOR: Did you plan to bomb the Imperial procession as the Emperor made his way to the military review in Aoyama?

KANNO: Taking the life of the sovereign was of course necessary. For Miyashita, it seems to have been the only goal, but my feeling was that, since there is little difference between killing one person and killing many people, we should make more extensive plans.

PROSECUTOR: What do you mean more extensive?

KANNO: Burning down the prisons and freeing the inmates, for example; divide up the responsibilities, and include the courts and police stations; include business concerns like Iwasaki. I thought that though we might not be able to start a full-scale revolution, we should at least begin on a small scale. I think the Emperor as an individual may be deserving of sympathy, but he heads the system that oppresses us and . . . is politically responsible. That is, it is unavoidable because he is chief of the exploiters. . . . The person I consider most abominable as an individual is Yamagata. I think, given the opportunity, I would try to throw a bomb at him.

PROSECUTOR: For what reason?

KANNO: Among the genro, Yamagata's ideas are the most antiquated. He has consistently persecuted us for our proletarian ideology.[43]

After the testimony was over, the private Kanno Suga emerged in a diary she kept (only half of which was recovered) and in letters written to friends.[44] What these sources reveal is that, though anger may have sustained her in public moments, lifelong pride in her own integrity and sense of her own capacities strengthened her as she sat alone in her cell. Aware that her life had not been what she intended, taking responsibility for the parts of that failure that were most important to her, Kanno, facing death, could find more than enough meaning in her life. Characteristically, she spent her last days reading and writing, exercising a kind of self-discipline that she reminded herself she should pursue, even though she was going to the gallows. And she systematically distributed the few possessions she had accumulated in her 31 years of life. In a postcard to Sakai's daughter Magara, Kanno willed her several of the most important reminders of her own fragile continuity.[45]

Dear Maa-san,   January 24, 1911
    Thank you for the beautiful postcard. I can see you have studied well; your characters are very good. I was very impressed!
    Please have your mother make the short coat I gave you into a jacket you can wear over your kimono. And I want you to have the doll, and the pretty box, and the box with the nice little drawers that are packed in my belongings. Please have your mother and father get them out for you.
    I would like to be able to see your cute face sometime.
    Good-bye.

Though she shouted a brave "banzai!" from the gallows, Kanno was not eager to give up her life. After her death, Sakai Toshihiko, one of the men she said she loved, and who loved her in return, transferred a poem she had written in prison to the back of her koto.[46] In 1971 the poem was inscribed on a memorial marker placed on her grave. Part of a letter to Koizumi Sakutaro, the friend who hoped both she and Kōtoku would be able to escape violent death at the hands of the state, it read:[47]

> Watching the sun's shadows
> Filtering through
>   the barred windows,
> Living
>   one more day.

8. The Bluestockings

In the beginning, woman was the sun.
   An authentic person.
Today, she is the moon.
   Living through others.
   Reflecting the brilliance of others. . . .
And now, *Bluestocking*, a journal created for
   the first time with the brains and hands
   of today's Japanese women, raises its
   voice.
               Hiratsuka Raichō, September 1, 1911

In the wintry intellectual climate that followed the Japanese government's execution of Kanno Suga and other political prisoners, these brave words announced the birth of *Seitō* (Bluestocking), a literary magazine created by women alone as an outlet for their art. To some who feared for the nation's intellectual life in the aftermath of the Great Treason trial, the event may have seemed irrelevant. To women who saw in Raichō's powerful imagery a call to feminism, the publication of *Bluestocking* may have offered new hope. But Hiratsuka Raichō, a prime mover in what became more than a literary effort, had little sense in September 1911 of the importance of the Bluestocking Society's mission, and even less feminist consciousness. As she later commented, she had only a vague awareness of international women's issues carried over from the nineteenth century and did not "at that point feel it was my own personal problem. . . . I was, however, conscious of the need to rebel against irrationality, . . . the external pressures repressing the talents of women."[1] The choice of the name was particularly telling, verifying the lack of connection between the aims of the Bluestocking women and the struggles of Japanese feminists who had so recently preceded them.* Unaware of, or unappreciative of, their own heritage, the Bluestockings looked outside the country for women with whom they could identify. With Raichō and her group, it seemed the slender thread of Japanese feminist history that began with the popular-rights movement had been broken. But the discontinuity between the Bluestockings and the earlier women's movement is often overstated.[2] There was continuity, after all, in the social conditions that had created the women's movement in the first place, and the Bluestockings' innocence of political and economic issues involving women began to disappear as they confronted them.

Initially, as Raichō pointed out, *Bluestocking* magazine was not a vehicle for advocating the economic and political liberation of women; it was designed to encourage and advertise the creative talents of women, many of whom were relatively unknown in Japanese literary circles. Creative freedom and the development of women's genius were the major issues; everything else was peripheral. Thus: "The power to fully develop . . . great hidden ability and genius makes it necessary to first remove all obstacles to women's development, . . . including outside pressures . . . and a general lack of knowledge. . . . However, the most significant barriers lie within ourselves."[3] That everything else was *not* peripheral, but that politics and art were intimately connected was a painful lesson the Bluestockings began to learn as they watched the reaction to their efforts. As Raichō put it, "That our literary activities would put us in direct opposition to the ideology of 'good wife; wise mother' was not totally unexpected. What

* The choice of a name identified with militant international feminism seems to have been guided as much by the founders' interest in adopting a European name that would identify them with a larger cultural context as by a conscious wish to convey an image of independence and a willingness to challenge social convention.

we did not expect was to have to stand and fight immediately all of the traditions of feudalism in the society."[4]

Though the decision to stand and fight was not clear-cut for the Bluestockings, to the extent that they did struggle against their critics and the social institutions that inhibited them, they seemed to replicate the experience of earlier feminists. The Bluestockings owed a greater debt to the earlier Meiji feminists than they may have realized, but they were nonetheless symbols of a new stage, if not a second wave, of Japanese feminism—one that was to have considerable impact on the future. To the struggle for political expression, social reform, economic independence, and educational opportunity waged by the women who preceded them, the Bluestockings added very significant demands for the recognition of self and of female sexuality.

One of the obvious explanations for the apparent discontinuity between the Bluestockings and the Meiji women who had earlier engaged in the struggle for women's rights was class. Hiratsuka Haruko (Raichō) was only a few years younger than Kanno Suga and the socialist women who had worked to reform Article 5. The enormous differences between them were not generational; they derived from Raichō's social position and the insulation that was a part of it. The daughter of a respected Tokyo family, whose economic circumstances were more than comfortable, Raichō, had she been a less complex personality, might easily have spent her life uneventfully, secure and studiously unaware of the issues confronting women in her society. Instead, perhaps partly thanks to the influence and support of her mother, Tsuya, Raichō early developed a consciousness of herself and a dissatisfaction at finding obstacles thrown in her path. After graduating from the Ochanomizu Girls' High School in Tokyo, Raichō enrolled in Naruse Jinzō's Japan Women's University in 1903. The school, later described as little more than a finishing school for upper-class women, seemed a natural place for a woman with her background and prospects; but the course in "domestic science" had unexpected results. Raichō had entered the university partly out of respect for Naruse, whose commitment to incorporating traditional values in the education of women was well publicized. But after hearing his conservative views, being called on to prepare and serve meals whenever a guest came to campus, and noting the display of cordiality he reserved for outside visitors, she had less and less respect for this pillar of the Japanese educational community.[5]

More important, Raichō was dissatisfied with the quality of her education, and, as soon as she was graduated in 1906, she embarked on a series of activities that seem to have been designed to compensate for the lack of substantive content in the work she had done at the university. She continued the study of Zen at a Tokyo temple, and studied English at Tsuda Umeko's college for women and Seibi English Academy for Women. She also joined a literary group led by Ikuta Chōkō, a writer and student of German philosophy who exercised enormous influence on her, encouraging her intellectual development and creative impulse. It was Ikuta who suggested the idea of a literary magazine exclusively for women to Raichō (and others), and who encouraged her to develop the interest in Nietzschean philosophy and Zen that may have informed the language and point of view in her now famous essay launching *Bluestocking*.[6]

The literary group itself was an important stepping-stone for Raichō, putting her in personal touch with the personalities then shaping Japan's literary community. Yosano Akiko, the celebrated and controversial Meiji poet, who was to be a continuing presence in Raichō's life, came to speak to the group. So did Morita Sōhei, a young writer with whom Raichō had an impulsive affair that ended in a highly publicized failed double suicide, referred to later as the *Baien* Incident.[7] Newspaper coverage of the event was extensive, and for the next year or more, Raichō found herself the object of thinly veiled contempt and laughter; she had been presented to the world as a spoiled, impetuous young woman, not to be taken seriously. It was an experience not easily lived through or forgotten, and it sharpened her consciousness of her vulnerability as a woman. As she said in 1911, "Things that women do invite only ridicule and laughter. . . . This I know well enough . . . and consequently have not the slightest dread of it."[8] Though some women in similar circumstances might have been celebrated in Japanese society, Raichō's attempted suicide with her lover was not seen as heroic; Japan Women's University was so unimpressed that officials struck her name from its list of graduates.[9]

By 1911, with the support of her mother, Ikuta Chōkō, and other friends, Raichō was ready to assume major responsibility for the publication of *Bluestocking*. With the help of Yasumochi Yoshiko, Mozume Kazuko, Kiuchi Teiko, and Nakano Hatsuko, all founding members of the society, she gathered support from the literary community and handled the administrative tasks associated with publishing a literary journal in a thousand to three thousand copies.[10] The first edition was paid for with money intended for Raichō's wedding expenses, one of a series of "endowments" her mother, Tsuya, managed to funnel to the magazine in support of her daughter's effort.[11] The first edition, published on September 1, 1911, was impressive, from the striking cover designed by Naganuma Chieko to the literary work it contained. Yosano provided a long poem, "Verses in Idle Moments," very much in keeping with her own life and with what she perceived as *Bluestocking*'s goals in the first nine pages.[12] That was followed by "House of Death," a short story by Mori Shigeko, and

"Life Blood," an erotic account by Tamura Toshiko of a woman's feelings after spending the night with a man at an inn.

Though many of the Bluestockings were unpublished writers whose social and academic backgrounds paralleled Raichō's, the magazine won important support from the kinds of established writers who appeared in the first issue—Yosano Akiko and Tamura Toshiko. The society also included many women tied to the mainstream of Japan's literary community by kinship and marriage. Mori Shigeko, the wife of novelist Mori Ōgai, has already been mentioned; his younger sister, Koganei Kimiko, belonged as well. Other novelists' wives were Kunikida Haruko (Kunikida Doppo), Iwano Kiyoko (Iwano Hōmei), and Oguri Kazuko (Oguri Fuyo). Chino Masako, who was married to the German literary scholar Chino Shōshō, and Okada Yachiyo, the younger sister of the playwright Osanai Kaoru, were also members. Nogami Yaeko, an important writer, was a contributor to the magazine, though she was often in basic disagreement with many of its policies.[13]

The roster of supporters and contributors is, in its own way, a significant statement about the state of women and the literary arts in 1911, and certainly could be seen as justification for the creation of a women's literary journal. To some degree, Raichō's insistence that women reclaim their creative heritage, become the sun again, was a quite specific reference to the Japanese context, whether the imagery was inspired by the Sun Goddess or Nietzsche. After the brilliance of Heian Japan and the achievements of Murasaki Shikibu and other women writers, the participation of women in the world of Japanese literature diminished, paralleling their own declining status in the historical periods that followed.[14]

By the time Tokugawa ended and Meiji began, in fact, Japanese literature was itself in an uncertain state, and the future of women in the world of Meiji letters was not at all clear. Except for Higuchi Ichiyo, a writer in the traditional style who died in 1896 at the age of twenty-five, few women had managed to achieve critical recognition in the literary world by the time *Bluestocking* appeared in 1911. Yosano Akiko (the poet of whom Kanno Suga had said "Of all Japan's women, more than Murasaki, or even Ichiyo, I like Yosano best"),[15] was grudgingly conceded to be an important literary figure by 1911. But her early reputation was based in part on her connection with her husband, Yosano Tekkan, a well-known poet and editor of the controversial literary magazine *Myōjō* (Morning Star); Akiko was probably never given the critical acclaim she deserved in the Meiji period.[16] From 1901, when she published her stunning collection of poems, *Midaregami* (Tangled Hair), celebrating the passion and sensuality of love from a woman's point of view, to 1904, when her well-publicized antiwar poem appeared, Yosano was treated by her critics, artistic and political, as a rather notorious Meiji woman whose poetry was secondary to her unconventional behavior. Politicians called for her conviction as a traitor during the Russo-Japanese War, and literary critics described her first collection of poetry as the work of a precocious and glib girl.[17] It may have been easier to deal with Yosano's supposed lack of respect for convention than her talent, but by 1911 her art and her prolific output of poetry, essays, and literary scholarship had secured her place on the Meiji literary scene.[18] Yosano's contributions to *Bluestocking*, along with those of Tamura Toshiko, brought it a measure of literary credibility and critical attention, but not enough to guarantee serious consideration of the journal and its young, unpublished writers by Japan's literary establishment. The first issue of *Bluestocking* was less a literary than a news event; Tokyo newspapers spent more time discussing the new "women's journal" than the literary establishment did, a harbinger of a public more interested in the journal's ideas and personalities than in its art.[19]

Bluestocking carried, from the beginning, a burden too large for any brave new literary magazine. Expected to open doors to women who had been denied access to the literary world on their own merits, the journal was also expected to carry on the feminist struggle in the absence of other standard bearers. It was a difficult, if not untenable position, and few of the women of the Bluestocking Society, including Raichō, were equipped to deal with it. Splits within the group began to develop as soon as reaction to the journal began to surface; women like Yosano already knew what many of the Bluestockings were now learning: reaction to women expressing their views about sexuality and with a developing sense of self would not be favorable—no matter how creatively it was expressed. Male writers, the naturalists in particular, had already encountered substantial public hostility around these same issues, but where they might use rejection to validate their art, the Bluestockings found it more and more difficult to focus solely on art, rejecting politics.[20]

The Bluestockings did not make a decision to deal with women's issues directly in the pages of their journal until 1913, and then primarily as a result of the need to answer attacks that had been made on them in the previous year and a half. Much of their creative energy before that time was spent criticizing and evaluating new currents in Japanese theater, particularly the work of Ibsen being presented in university drama circles and in Tokyo's new theater. *Bluestocking* devoted one entire issue to Ibsen's *A Doll's House*; without much consciousness of where it might lead, Raichō and others quickly became involved in many of the implicit questions Ibsen's work raised about women—a debate that was already worldwide in scope. Raichō's response, expressed in an open letter to Ibsen's character Nora, illustrates some of her views in 1912.

Dear Nora,

    Japanese women cannot quite believe that a woman like you, a woman so innately instinctive, not a young girl of fourteen or fifteen, but the mother of three children, exists. . . . The slamming of the door behind you was a powerful act. But once outside, you found yourself in total darkness, . . . your steps so uncertain that one wanted to follow after you.[21]

As Raichō later recalled, she was concerned for Nora's future primarily because she had demonstrated such a low level of self-awareness before she left home; because her decision was based not on the discovery of her true self, but on an incomplete self-knowledge that could not lead to real freedom and independence. Other members of the *Bluestocking* staff—perhaps, as she said, "because of their youth"—were even less charitably inclined toward Ibsen's character, "pouring scorn on Nora's head" in the pages of the journal.[22]

    Though the Bluestockings tried to retain their concentration on creative, rather than political, issues, their experience led them inevitably to a stronger feminist consciousness. The mail they received from women all over Japan was an education and a reminder, for many of them, of the universality of women's experience. They also attracted some members whose interest in literature was joined by a desire to stir feminist discussion within the society and among the journal's readers. The two most important names in this connection are Kamichika Ichiko and Itō Noe.

    Kamichika, a student at Tsuda's college for women, spoke forcefully at Bluestocking meetings of the problems women faced and the need for continuing public discussion of them. Kamichika, however, left the group after a year, fearful of not being allowed to graduate from the college.* The fiery Itō Noe was still in her teens when she presented herself at the *Bluestocking* offices looking, as Raichō said, much too young to have already graduated from high school.[23] But she already had an interesting history. Her fierce desire to be a "free woman" had involved her in what were essentially feminist struggles, revolving around experiences common to many of Japan's women. Growing up in northern Kyushu in economic and intellectual circumstances far different from those of most of the Bluestockings, she had settled into what was considered a good job for a woman; she worked in the local post office. But Itō, who after only six years of compulsory education, liked to read and to think, was unwilling to accept the future her life seemed to present in Kyushu, and made her way to Tokyo, to enroll in Ueno Girls' High School.

The relative freedom she found in Tokyo was short-lived; her family began making arrangements for her marriage even before she was graduated, and she returned to Kyushu immediately after graduation to marry in accordance with her family's wishes. The man she was married to had emigrated to the United States and had achieved some economic success; it was considered a good match in part because of the expectation that Itō would return there with him. But just days after the ceremony, she left Kyushu for Tokyo, to live with Tsuji Jun, her former high school teacher, a man who eventually lost his

* Though she was later criticized by Raichō for her faintheartedness, Kamichika was an important 20th-century feminist, who worked for women's suffrage and was elected to the House of Representatives from Tokyo's Fifth District after the Pacific War. That her concern about graduating from Tsuda if she did not break with the Bluestockings was well founded is made clear by Yamakawa Kikue in her autobiography. According to Yamakawa, Tsuda thought of the Bluestockings as agents of the devil and prayed that her students would not be misled by them; on one occasion, a teacher in Kamichika's classroom offered a prayer for her after she returned from a meeting of the society. (Hiratsuka Raichō, *Genshi, josei wa taiyō de atta,* 4 vols. Tokyo, 1971, 2: 399; Yamakawa Kikue, *Onna nidai no ki,* Tokyo, 1955, pp. 157–59.) Kamichika did lose a job in Aomori prefecture when her connection with the Bluestockings was discovered.

job because of his relationship with her. Still legally married and with a long, complicated list of issues to settle with her family, Itō found her way to the offices of *Bluestocking* in July 1912, where she talked with Raichō. In September, having returned to Kyushu to get a divorce, Itō wrote to Raichō asking for help; Raichō responded by sending five yen, enough to enable the young woman to get through the difficulties with her family and return to Tokyo.[24]

By the time Itō joined the group, the Bluestockings had begun to feel as if they were under siege, both for their supposed lifestyles and for the content of their journal. The Japanese government banned the April 1912 issue because of an article censors defined as "disruptive of public morality" and the family system. Tokyo newspapers were having a field day with the group, printing stories about their lives that were often based solely on a misreading of the content of their magazine. In July, for example, the Tokyo newspaper *Kokumin shimbun* (Citizen's News) printed a story about Raichō implying that she had seduced a "beautiful young boy of fifteen or sixteen" and kept him with her for amusement.[25] That story was apparently based on the reporter's reading of Odake Kazue's account of "five-colored sake" in that month's issue of *Bluestocking*. Odake, one of the newer members of the society, formerly of Osaka, had written a story about a "beautiful young boy" (*bishōnen*) who drank *goshoku sake* (a strong, rainbow-colored drink then popular in Tokyo's French restaurants) before making a visit to Raichō. The beautiful young boy was Odake's rather fanciful and unconventional description of herself, something the reporter might have found even more titillating, had he figured it out.[26]

The public image of Raichō and other Bluestockings, symbols of Japan's New Woman, was further embellished by stories of their visits to the Yoshiwara in the summer of 1912. The Yoshiwara, the old licensed pleasure quarter of

Tokyo, had been visited by "respectable women" before; but such visits since Meiji had usually carried an implicit message of social criticism. Raichō, Odake, and Nakano Hatsue went to the Yoshiwara that summer out of curiosity; they were able to stay overnight through arrangements made by a relative of Odake's, who was a regular patron of the quarter. Their visit to that "mysterious" world, closed to ordinary women, was eagerly exploited by Tokyo newspapers, which lengthened the visit to four days, increased the number of visits, and added appropriate details to satisfy their readers through the remainder of the summer. Public criticism was harsh and produced rock-throwing crowds at Raichō's home.[27]

Though members of the Bluestocking Society knew that their three colleagues had done little more than visit the Yoshiwara overnight and were angered by the response of the press and the public, they were also critical of the visit. The Yoshiwara excursion prompted one of the first serious debates within the group; it was long overdue, and as it progressed, a sharpened sense of the issues that united and divided the members began to emerge. Though there was general agreement that it was time for *Bluestocking* to answer its critics, it was more difficult to get unanimity on the specific issues to be addressed. Many of the most important questions had less to do with newspaper gossip than with the relevance of the Yoshiwara excursion to the goals and purposes of the magazine. Though some members were appalled by the bad taste the three women showed in visiting a part of the city off limits to all women except prostitutes, others, like Yasumochi Yoshiko, were upset for different reasons. Raichō had made it clear that her visit to the Yoshiwara was made out of curiosity, not social conscience;[28] Yasumochi thought that anyone connected with the magazine should have paid more attention to the implications of such a visit. Such a frivolous excursion to a place that degraded the value of women was, she thought, typical of the lack of seriousness displayed in the magazine after the initial issue. Their visit was "a very bold, and cruel, thing. I am unaware of the profound reasons you might have had for going there, but I was saddened and felt personally insulted by it. . . . There seems to be a tinge of frivolousness and pedantry about *Bluestocking* these days. . . . The seriousness of the first issue is lacking; there is little sincerity."[29]

Some dismissed Yasumochi's anger as related to her connections with Christianity and with the Reform Society's antiprostitution campaigns, but the charge that the magazine had lost its seriousness of purpose seems to have struck home. To the delight of Itō Noe, the Bluestockings decided to provide a serious forum for women's issues, a policy to be initiated with the January 1913 issue of the magazine. They later reinforced this effort, sponsoring a series of lectures on women's issues in February, and covering the debates in successive editions of the magazine. In spring and summer two of the country's most important journals, *Taiyō* (The Sun) and *Chūō kōron* (Central Review), published special issues on "women's problems," in part as a result of the interest sparked by *Bluestocking's* three-month coverage.

A number of the Bluestockings were asked to write articles for the *Central Review* issue, including Raichō, who pronounced herself, for the first time, one of the New Women, trying at the same time to extricate the definition of the term from the gossip and innuendo that then surrounded it. To the public and the press, the term meant an indulgent and irresponsible young Japanese woman, who used her overdeveloped sexuality to undermine the family and to manipulate others for her own selfish ends. The literary establishment had its own definitions, based on a reading of Ibsen, which emphasized the uniqueness and heroic proportions of the New Woman. For many feminists, neither definition was useful; they preferred to emphasize the New Woman's legitimate struggle for autonomy and equality, and linked her emergence to international feminism, particularly to suffrage movements and social reform.[30] Raichō's own definition in *Central Review* not only underlined the importance of developing individual strengths, but also emphasized, more than anything she had written to this point the reality of male oppression.

> The new woman; I am a new woman.
> I seek, I strive each day to be that truly new woman I want to be.
> In truth, that eternally new being is the sun.
> I am the sun.
> I seek; I strive each day to be the sun I want to be.
>   . . .
> The new woman curses yesterday. . . .
> The new woman is not satisfied with the life of the kind of woman who is made ignorant, made a slave, made a piece of meat by male selfishness.
> The new woman seeks to destroy the old morality and laws created for male advantage. . . .
> The new woman does not merely destroy the old morality and laws constructed out of male selfishness, but day by day attempts to create a new kingdom, where a new religion, a new morality, and new laws are carried out, based on the spiritual values and surpassing brilliance of the sun.
> Truly, the creation of this new kingdom is the mission of women. . . .
> The new woman is not simply covetous of power for its own sake. She seeks power to complete her mission, to be able to endure the exertion and agony of learning about and cultivating issues now unknown to her. . . .
> The new woman today seeks neither beauty nor virtue. She is simply crying out for strength, the strength to create this still unknown kingdom, the strength to fulfill her own hallowed mission.[31]

While others spoke of more tangible issues involving the New Woman in *Bluestocking's* first feminist-oriented issues, Raichō disclosed the source of much of her recent thinking, translating parts of Ellen Key's *Love and Marriage* (1911) in the January and February editions. Key was a Swedish thinker in whom some Japanese began to be interested about the same time as they took up Ibsen; Raichō had heard about her ideas and read something of them in Japanese journals but only became firmly attracted to them after acquiring an English translation of *Love and Marriage*.[32] In Key, Raichō had found a woman who spoke to the art and spirituality so important to her, a woman whose views seemed to express a new version of the biological superiority of women, and whose priorities were very much like those of Raichō herself.

As the Bluestockings looked around for outside contributors to their special editions on women, they made contact with the socialist women who had spoken for feminism in the previous decade. The January issue contained a sardonic essay by Ōsugi Sakae's wife, Hori Yasuko, commenting on the rush of the Bluestockings to identify themselves as New Women, pointing out the impossibility of such a development so long as the society operated in the "old," feudal ways.[33] In February Fukuda Hideko's essay "A Solution to the Woman's Problem" appeared, presenting a socialist feminist view that upset both the government and many members of the Bluestocking Society. Moving from an earlier position (expressed in *Women of the World*), that women's liberation from the double burden of economic and male repression should take priority, Fukuda now spoke for human liberation, to be achieved through socialism. In her typically self-effacing style, Fukuda began by saying that she knew the Bluestockings had their own, new views of the problem, and that she hoped they would not see her opinions as the sarcastic comments of an older woman proud of earlier days in the movement. The forty-six-year-old Fukuda found the contrast between those "proud early days" and the appearance of the Bluestockings intensely interesting, not least because "as you might expect, I have changed."[34]

Dividing women's liberation into relative and absolute states, Fukuda described the recent history of the woman's movement in Japan, from the popular-rights movement through the campaign to revise Article 5, as a struggle for equality with men, allowing little progress beyond that point. The achievement of absolute liberation required such initiatives on the part of women, she said but equality with men should be recognized as a means, not an end. Women might construe absolute liberation differently than men, as freeing them from loveless, economically determined marriages and from the lack of opportunity to develop themselves as free women. But both men and women would be free in absolute liberation, freed from the tyranny of artificial, irrational economic and social systems created by self-interested elites. Women, Fukuda reminded her readers, were at the moment part of those elites; in the future, class struggle among women should be expected, as it was for men.

It would be wonderful if all women could see themselves as Raichō did when she said, "I am the sun." But this is not just woman's perception; it must be man's as well. . . . No matter what arguments are offered to refute it, it cannot be doubted that carrying out the communist system is the ultimate key to women's liberation. When this system prevails, scientific knowledge and technology will be applied for everyone's benefit. . . . The prosaic household tasks of today will be done simply. . . . There will no longer be a need for family servants, and women will find themselves with a surplus of time and energy. For the first time, women's liberation will have been realized. But unless the system is carried out, the achievement of voting rights, of opportunities for women in universities, courts, and the government bureaucracy, will benefit a few elite women. The majority will be rejected and continue to operate without access to such opportunity. As there is class struggle among men, so there will be class struggle among women.[35]

Fukuda's essay was a characteristically strong statement, made at a time when people were fearful of whispering the words socialism or communism in Japan.[36] Fukuda (and the Bluestockings who agreed to publish it) showed great courage in presenting such a view of feminism to the world in 1913, but the essay, and the government's reaction to it (the issue was banned because of Fukuda's article) reinforced the growing divisions among the group.

Itō Noe was particularly incensed by the predictable concern voiced by "patriots" over the dangerous thoughts being presented in *Bluestocking* and hoped the magazine would take an even stronger position on women's issues in the future.[37] But many of the society's members, still believing that their art could be divorced from the politics and culture around them, wanted the magazine to return to a purely literary format. Raichō, in the meantime, was busy with her critics, and notably with her old nemesis Naruse Jinzō, of Japan Women's University. In a newspaper interview, Naruse had claimed Japan's education for women was superior to that in other countries because of its emphasis on producing "good wives and wise mothers," and had described the "new woman" as little more than a "flapper." In April Raichō challenged Naruse's estimate of higher education for women, calling it "pitiful" rather than glorious, and reminded him that, as a respected member of Japan's intellectual community, he should be able to arrive at a more balanced view of the New Woman than the man in the street.[38]

In the same article Raichō challenged female defenders of the status quo like Hatoyama Haruko and Shimoda Utako to shed their fears and engage in the search for real answers to women's problems. But she made it clear that, for her own part, she would not respect social conventions and institutions that continued to be based on male privilege alone. Above all, she said, she would not submit to marriage as it currently existed in Japanese society. No woman should submit to a system that made her yield to power, not love; that treated her as a legal incompetent; that gave her no right to her own children, much less property; that punished adultery only when she practiced it. Though Raichō had little in common with Fukuda, she agreed that sexual fulfillment could be realized only in relationships based on love, and that Japanese social institutions mitigated against the development of such natural feelings in marriage. Many Japanese wives, she noted, had married without love and resigned themselves to the sexual demands of their husbands as the price of security. "Worst of all," she said, were the cases of "women who, obeying convention requiring obedience to a husband's sexual demands, no matter how immoderate," had been physically harmed by successive pregnancies.[39]

The Home Ministry, which to the surprise of some of the Bluestockings seemed to consider this article just as offensive as Fukuda's, summoned Nakano Hatsuko and Yasumochi Yoshiko to police headquarters, where they were told that the Metropolitan Police, "looking at *Bluestocking*, noticed several things that seemed corruptive of the virtues traditionally associated with Japanese women."[40] At first they had considered banning the April issue, but they had decided on a warning instead. The message Nakano and Yasumochi were to convey to their group, the police said, was that there would be careful police scrutiny of the magazine in the future, and contributors should be especially careful of any content that might be considered disruptive of national custom and social order.[41]

Bluestocking, through the discussion it provoked, the literature it produced, and the lectures it sponsored, had revived the women's movement, and the government had now begun a series of moves designed to counteract that. In April the Ministry of Education attempted to establish its own policies for "controlling the publication of articles in women's magazines opposed to the concept of good wife; wise mother." And a month later the Home Ministry banned a long list of women's magazines, serving notice that the government considered the women's movement dangerous again.[42]

In such a context, it was impossible for *Bluestocking* to revert to a purely literary format; but by this time, in any case, more women realized that literature, if it was used to express unpopular or unorthodox views, did not represent a safe or comfortable haven from politics. In the fall of 1913, without convincing unanimity, the group decided to remove from its founding statements any language that appeared to limit the magazine's mission to literature, thereby making it officially the kind of journal it had become when the year began: one that concentrated on social and political issues important to women. To make this change work required the cooperation of most of the long-term members of the Bluestockings, but there was very little consensus among the group. Many women remained members because the journal offered them a potential outlet for their literary work, others because of loyalty to Raichō or friends, and still others because they did not want to quit while the magazine was under attack. Though the press had hoped that other literary women would criticize the Bluestockings, very few of them yielded to that temptation, even though they privately disagreed with the direction in which the magazine seemed to be moving. Unfortunately for *Bluestocking,* such passive support was the most its sponsors could expect from many women at a time when they needed the active participation of everyone.

From September through December the struggling journal showed a clear shift of emphasis that reflected, among other things, an increasing reliance on Itō Noe as both contributor and administrator. Itō had begun reading Emma Goldman at the suggestion of Tsuji Jun, and in the September issue she published Tsuji's partial translation of "The Tragedy of Women's Liberation" under her own name.[43] The November and December issues included more of Goldman and two works by the South

African activist Olive Schreiner, translated by Yamada Waka.[44] Itō, who was approaching her twentieth year and who had gone through several stages of intellectual growth after joining the Bluestockings, was now becoming committed to the anarchist views she was to hold until her death in 1923. Those views, and the publication of Goldman in the pages of *Bluestocking,* did not endear her to many of the women in the group, whose political consciousness, such as it was, rejected most of the assumptions of anarchism. Others asked, as socialists had asked when *Women of the World* was used for Ishikawa's translations of Kropotkin in 1908, what relevance all of this had for the women's issues they had been discussing.

Though Goldman and Schreiner were not difficult to justify from that standpoint, women began to dissociate themselves from *Bluestocking* in increasing numbers, compounding the economic and editorial problems of the journal. When, in January 1915, a tired and somewhat dispirited Raichō turned over the editing and publishing responsibilities to Itō, the defections increased.* For many women, what was left of *Bluestocking* bore so little resemblance to the journal they had proclaimed with such exuberance in September 1911 that staying on was a useless exercise. And the journal, which for a year had relied on the efforts of a smaller and smaller nucleus of women, now was placed firmly on the shoulders of one woman, twenty-year-old Itō Noe. Itō, who had a year-old son, very little economic support, and a rapidly changing emotional and political life of her own to contend with, edited *Blue-*

---

* Hiratsuka, *Genshi,* 2: 545–53. The year before, Raichō had moved out of her parents' house and into a relationship with Okumura Hiroshi; she became a neighbor of both Itō Noe and Nogami Yaeko, and often relied on Itō for help with kitchen chores unfamiliar to her. In fact, after Okumura and Raichō took turns cooking, and she still managed to burn everything, they ate at Itō's house. Raichō refused to marry for reasons she had outlined in "To the Women of the World," and the press continued to harass her for her lifestyle. For a sympathetic view of this period of her life, see Ide Fumiko, *Seitō no onnatachi* (Tokyo, 1975), pp. 182–88.

stocking out of her own home until 1916, when she too was exhausted by the effort.

During the year she edited the magazine, she introduced a number of interesting debates on women's questions. Stating that, in the absence of firm new bylaws, she meant to make *Bluestocking* a journal for all women, operating without regulations, without direction, and without ideology, Itō opened the pages to extended discussions of abortion, prostitution, and motherhood.[45] The debates continued long after *Bluestocking* was gone; in 1918 Raichō and Yosano Akiko were still engaged in long and heated discussions of the desirability of state protection for mothers and children;[46] and prostitution and abortion continued to be divisive issues among Japanese women.

The debates over prostitution and aboriton were a natural corollary of feminist discussions of sexuality, but they were also an implicit challenge to society's power to determine how, and in what contexts, women's bodies would be used. Itō, whose own reading of Goldman had sharpened many of her perceptions of these issues, must have read with interest Nishizaki Hanayo's comments on chastity in *Hankyō* (Reflections), published in the fall of 1913. Nishizaki's claim that female chastity was relatively unimportant, in fact was a luxury that women in straitened economic circumstances could not afford, was answered in the December issue of *Bluestocking* by Yasuda Satsuki, who urged women to guard their chastity jealously, no matter what hardships life offered.[47] Itō's reaction to this was very much what Kanno's had been earlier; any discussion of chastity that did not include male habits and assumptions was laughable. Women who wanted to proclaim their chastity, sweetly accepting the double standard, should be prepared for Itō's anger.

The abortion debate produced another article by Yasuda, published in the June 1915 issue of *Bluestocking*. Arguing from a position very radical at the time (maintaining, for example, that the fetus was a part of the woman's body, and whether she chose to carry it or not was purely her own decision), Yasuda counseled women to have abortions if motherhood was going to be difficult. Ignoring the fact that safe abortions were unavailable, Yasuda told her readers that they should follow their own dictates, even in violation of the law.[48] Attractive as Itō found any injunction to follow one's own instincts, she could not agree with Yasuda. Using a letter to Nogami to answer Yasuda, Itō said that Yasuda's mistake lay in her assumption that the fetus was only a part of the woman's body: the child was carried in the mother's body, to be sure, but it had a life of its own, and that life was precious.[49] Behind everything Itō (who was then pregnant, as was Yasuda) said was an instinctive distaste for anything she perceived as unnatural. Predictably, the government banned the June issue of *Bluestocking* because of Yasuda's article, but it had no objection in August, when Yamada Waka wrote an article branding both abortion and birth control as "sinful."[50]

The debates over the issue of prostitution brought Itō into a confrontation with Yamakawa Kikue, who argued against it from a Marxist perspective.* Itō's impassioned arguments were no match in debate for the cool logic of Yamakawa, but both shared the view that well-intentioned efforts on the part of Christian reformers would not eliminate prostitution; only drastic social change would do away with "the traffic in women." Itō's arguments owed much to Goldman. She stressed the hypocrisy of antiprostitution campaigns in the absence of efforts to make nec-

---

* Yamakawa is another graduate of the Tsuda College who illustrates that, conservative as Tsuda's curriculum and view of feminism supposedly were, it was an institution that produced a striking number of women with radical views. Kikue was a theorist who worked closely with her socialist husband, Yamakawa Hitoshi, one of those jailed in the Red Flag Incident, and was a fervent feminist all her life. She was the first head of what has become a powerful branch of the Ministry of Labor—the Women and Minors Bureau.

essary social change, and expressed doubt that the drastic changes needed could ever be legislated. Itō also showed characteristic sympathy for the "despised" women who had no choice but to become prostitutes, and who were, by definition, victims of the reformers' scorn. Prostitution, she said, was just another occupation for a woman; for Itō, as for Goldman, it was "merely a question of degree whether she sells herself to one man, in or out of marriage, or to many men."[51]

Itō managed to carry most of the responsibility for *Bluestocking* until, in February 1916, less as a result of a conscious decision than because of her own exhaustion, what proved to be the last issue appeared. Itō had run the magazine for a very long time without benefit of consultation or assistance, editing and carrying on administrative routines while she was pregnant and carrying her first child on her back. Giving up her solitary effort and letting the journal slide, she began to make some changes in her own life in the spring of 1916. According to Nogami, Itō visited her in April to tell her she was leaving Tsuji and planned to live with Ōsugi Sakae.[52] Nogami reminded Itō that Ōsugi was still married to Hori Yasuko, and that he was also having an affair with an old colleague of Itō's, Kamichika Ichiko. Unimpressed by these arguments, and expressing a profound love for Ōsugi, Itō turned aside Nogami's offers of help, and after leaving Tsuji, went to Chiba on the outskirts of Tokyo. She became Ōsugi's common-law wife in September and eventually settled into a relationship that ended only with their deaths seven years later, but the initial stages were difficult and well publicized. For one thing, Kamichika, rejected by Ōsugi, attempted to kill him at an inn where he was living with Itō in November 1916.[53] More important, Ōsugi's political life was as stressful for Itō as it was for him.

Ōsugi was under constant police surveillance, and the government's interest in him grew with the social upheavals that shook the country at the end of the First World War and not least, with the shock over the success of the Russian Revolution. Itō's life with him was a constant round of police harassment, economic hardship, and childbearing combined with intellectual and emotional passion.* There is little that could be identified as distinctively hers in Ōsugi's works, though she certainly assisted with two of them, *Bummei hihyō* (Critique of Civilization; 1918) and *Rōdō undō* (The Labor Movement; 1919). The picture of Itō that comes down to us from this period of her life is a mixed one: the arresting image of a young woman, just past twenty, demanding that the police who trailed her carry diaper bags, or sending her husband to the well at her home in Kyushu to wash diapers;[54] and the tragic portrait of a woman whose last years were filled with anxiety over Ōsugi's impending imprisonment or death, and perhaps her own as well. On September 16, 1923, just days after Tokyo's Great Earthquake, Ōsugi, Itō, and a young nephew were picked up for questioning and later strangled in their cells by a police officer who considered them "enemies of the state."†

* Itō had 2 children while she was working on *Bluestocking*; these children, both boys, she left with Tsuji when she became Ōsugi's common-law wife. She had 5 children (between 1917 and 1923) by Ōsugi including a daughter (one of two named Emma) who was adopted by relatives. None of the remaining children was registered in any family's records, but Itō's relatives took care of them after her death. See Iwasaki Kureo, *Honō no onna* (Tokyo, 1963); Itō Noe, *Itō Noe zenshū* (Tokyo, 1970), vol. 2; and Ide Fumiko, *Jiyū, sore wa watakushi jishin* (Tokyo, 1979), for documents and descriptions about Itō's relationship with Ōsugi.

† The day before, Itō and Ōsugi, after assuring that their friends' children were all right, had gone to check on Itō's son, Makoto, who was living with Tsuji; Itō was disappointed to find that he had been sent to stay with relatives, and Ōsugi suggested that they visit his relatives in the Tokyo area instead. They were followed by an officer in the special police, Amakasu Masahiko, as they returned home from this visit, bringing Ōsugi's seven-year-old nephew, Tachibana Munekazu, with them. The next day, while Ōsugi, Itō, and Tachibana were on another outing, they were arrested by Amakasu. A little more than 3 hours later, Amakasu murdered Ōsugi in his cell, and an hour after, Itō and Tachibana. Perhaps only because Itō's influential uncle pursued the matter, Amakasu was given a 10-year prison sentence. He was released early, and was sent to Europe and then to Manchuria, where he did public relations work for the army. (Ide Fumiko, "Itō Noe koden," in *Itō Noe zenshu*, vol. 1; Kondo Tomie, "Itō Noe," in Enchi Fumiko, ed., *Jimbutsu Nihon no josei shi*, Tokyo, 1978, 11: 115–20.)

Itō Noe's death profoundly shocked and saddened the women who had worked with her and knew her passion for life. But the women's movement she had helped to revive had been moving forward, even as her own life was taking her away from it. In 1918, as Yosano and Raichō debated state support for mothers, and women workers were beginning to achieve some recognition within the union movement, there was a growing desire among women of very different political persuasions to unite in an effort to improve women's status. One tangible result was the formation, in January 1920, of the Shinfujinkyōkai (New Woman's Society), put together by Raichō, Ichikawa Fusae, Oku Mumeo, and others interested in achieving political power for women. With the creation of the magazine *Josei dōmei* (Women's League) later the same year, the suffrage movement began. It seemed that at last the connection between Meiji feminism with its stress on equality and political rights, and Taishō feminism, with its emphasis on the spiritual and creative strengths of women, had been made. Ichikawa's summary of the goals of women involved in the suffrage movement shows clearly the combined impact of Meiji and Taishō experience:

When we were involved in the movement to obtain the right to vote for women, we said there were four reasons why women desired the right to vote. [First,] to change and improve the bad legal system and to increase welfare. Second, to bring together people's lives and politics; those who run the kitchens, namely the women, should also participate in politics. Third, we wanted to clean up politics. Last was the pursuit of peace. Because women are the most badly affected by the throes of war, we wanted women around the world to join . . . to preserve the peace of the world.[55]

The Bluestockings were not Japan's first feminists, or probably even Japan's first literary feminists, but they became, almost in spite of themselves, the shapers of Taishō feminism. Though they began with little consciousness of connections with the Meiji feminists who preceded them, they did manage to break through barriers of class and government control to claim a continuity that stretched back to the 1870's. They were not unique in the Taishō context, but the women of the Bluestocking Society added important new ideas and demands to the feminist legacy of Meiji. They discussed sexuality openly and related it to the politics of women's condition. They added to the Meiji feminists' demand for economic independence a call for psychological and emotional independence—from men and from the family system. For all of this, they paid a heavy price. But their willingness to accept responsibility for themselves and other women, even though it was often grudging, pushed the feminist movement in Japan to a new level.[56]

9. A Retrospective View

Many of the efforts of Meiji women were not obvious on the surface. . . . Compared with contemporary women, Meiji women were very strong.
                                              Ichikawa Fusae, July 1978

Meiji was the beginning, not the end, of the women's movement in modern Japan. The resistance of Meiji women to male definitions of their proper social roles and their attachment to other dreams and visions were part of a feminist legacy that, in spite of formidable obstacles, they managed to leave for later generations. The sense of continuity that seemed so tenuous, that link from Kishida Toshiko and the popular-rights movement to the *Bluestockings*, was, finally, strong enough, flexible enough, to connect women in an expanding movement that is still developing.

Though Japanese feminists were unable to achieve their goals until after the Pacific War, their struggle to improve women's status was an important and continuing one. After the First World War, women finally began to make important inroads in the male-dominated union movement, winning the right to seat women delegates at conventions and to send women as union representatives to international gatherings.[1] In the 1920's and 1930's, working women continued to go out on strike, with or without union assistance. The 1927 Toyo Muslin strike is still remembered as representative of the labor struggles of the period.[2]

The New Woman's Society pushed for women's political rights, but even though universal male suffrage was passed by the Diet in 1925, the best women were able to do was to win a revision of Article 5 in 1922, allowing them to attend and participate in political gatherings.[3] Various women's groups continued to demand all rights of political participation and suffrage, but until 1946, Japanese women were legally prohibited from joining political parties, organizing political groups, and, of course, voting. Women routinely violated such laws in the 1920's and 1930's, joining groups of every political shade, from tenant unions in the countryside to left-wing organizations in the cities. But their struggle was made increasingly difficult by the xenophobic and repressive atmosphere of Japanese society after the Manchurian Incident (1931) and various failed right-wing revolutionary efforts (1931–36). The left wing, a target even in the seemingly liberal 1920's, was savagely attacked in the 1930's, when the government imprisoned anyone described as dangerous to good public order and sought the resignations of dissident college professors. Members of the Diet, not surprisingly, found time in the 1930's to remind Japanese women of their roles as "good wives; wise mothers" and gave speeches praising Japanese women for their superiority over their Western counterparts, who selfishly interested themselves in "women's liberation."[4]

As the country mobilized in the years following the invasion of China proper in 1937, women found themselves asked to redouble their patriotism and, marching under the common banner of the Greater Japan Women's Association, to support the war effort by bearing more children, accepting assigned jobs in war-related industries, providing volunteers for civil defense, and working in neighborhood associations. Japanese women have been particularly acute observers of the war, leaving us, in their diaries and journals, important firsthand descriptions of the human costs of a conflict that saw the firebombing of

Japan's major cities, and, finally, the destruction of Hiroshima and Nagasaki.[5] Though Japanese women were active in international peace groups before the Pacific War, the anti-nuclear peace movement in Japan has been a major focus of women's political activities nationwide in the postwar period.

The American occupation that began after Japan's surrender in 1945 saw the initiation of broad programs designed to demilitarize and democratize the country—programs that naturally included major changes for Japanese women. In regulations dealing with election laws, the occupation authorities announced, on December 17, 1945, that all Japanese women over the age of twenty would have the right to vote. In the following year, at the urging of Japanese suffragists, the authorities made it possible for women over the age of twenty-five to stand for office.[6] Sixty-eight years after Kusunose Kita had demanded the right to vote, Japanese women had finally won full political rights.

Women were also substantially benefited by the enactment of a new constitution, which became operative in 1947 and gave them important protections under the law; by a revised civil code emphasizing equality and the importance of the individual; and by the Women and Minors Bureau's encouragement of women's full participation in the union movement.[7]

When the occupation ended in 1952, Japan, thanks largely to its role as supplier to forces in the Korean War, was on its way to economic recovery and on the brink of previously unimagined economic growth. And Japanese women were ready to initiate the "second wave" of their own feminist movement.

From the standpoint of comparative women's history, the crucial issues raised by the experience of Meiji women focus on the connections between work and family and on the ability of the state (particularly in late-developing societies) to redirect the energies of women to its own ends, often shaping ideologies based on rather subtle combinations of traditional sentiment and modern authoritarian methods. The Meiji experience lends support to the growing body of research suggesting that modernization, rather than bringing women into more independent, visible roles in society, often artificially perpetuates traditional roles and denigrates the value of their contributions.

In Japan, the roles women were assigned in the effort to build a unified, stable, and independent state ranged from working 16-hour shifts in textile mills to communicating ideas of patriotism and national unity in their homes and in political organizations tailored for them. That these are not the roles women would have chosen for themselves is obvious from their history. But the struggle between Meiji women and the state over this issue, though not of epic proportions, is nonetheless an important part of Meiji history that has been virtually ignored. Policies affecting women in Meiji were not the product of some vague accumulated social inertia;[8] they were the government's response to women who attempted to define their own roles in a rapidly changing society that seemed to invite such redefinition.

The government denied this right to women, inhibiting their early use of the popular-rights movement as a forum and disapproving, later, the emergence of a female perspective of self and sexuality that carried significant political implications. In a reactive, two-stage development, the Meiji government first began the direct control of women in 1890 by denying them access to politics and then, in 1898, enacted a civil code that made them prisoners of an anachronistic family system. The program for women continued with changes in education and other institutions designed to socialize women to become the stable core of family and society, mediating the clash between tradition and modernity, between loyalty to the family and loyalty to the state, encouraging some kinds of social change and discouraging others not thought to be in the state's interest. By 1900 the original meaning of "good wife; wise mother" had been drowned in a flood of government rhetoric, and the education of women everywhere was increasingly standardized to meet the state's requirements.

Women who disagreed with this had few options. They could openly resist and pay the price of that resistance. Or they could quietly build new institutions and roles for women under cover of cooperation with government policy. In either case, they faced enormous difficulties, operating in an environment that often seemed to make women with shared goals enemies of each other.

Not only was the Japanese government immensely successful in disrupting the networks of its critics—replicating and refining after 1890 the methods used against the popular-rights movement earlier. The society itself was changing; the emergence of a new urban aristocracy signaled the development of a modern, capitalist social structure full of the divisions that affected women everywhere. It is a commentary on the impact of these two developments that there were no political gatherings for women in Meiji after 1883 that matched the success of Kishida's Kyoto meeting with its 2,000 participants. Lecture platforms after 1890 were reserved for women like Okumura Ioko, who carried out state policy. The Reform Society, which might have taken the lead, found its efforts blunted not only by Okumura's Japan Women's Patriotic Association and its access to networks unavailable to everyone else, but by the inability to bridge class (and ideological) differences among women even though their program touched the lives of women at every level of society and in every region. By the time socialist women had begun their struggle to reform Article 5, they found themselves isolated, not only out of touch with Reform Society members, but out of touch with working women as well. It is more than just an irony of women's history in modern Japan that women in the textile mills may have had more contact with the local affiliates of the Women's Patriotic Association than with any other women's group in Meiji. The association was the only women's organization given unlimited resources to develop networks linking city and countryside, elites and farm women throughout the country.

Still, the failure to incorporate diverse groups of women into the feminist movement, paralleling the experience of women's movements elsewhere, had more than institutional roots. Feminists in the popular-rights movement missed important connections with working women, although they did have access to women from farm families in the impoverished countryside. The Reform Society had an unfortunate tendency to treat working women as social problems or potential converts, mirroring differences imposed by class and Christianity. Working women were also ignored by labor organizers and socialists, even though they continued to go on strike, maintaining a volatile center of protest in Japan's industrial work force. By the end of the Meiji period, there was not even a pretended connection between working women and the women's movement. When women wage earners and factory workers finally became part of the movement after the First World War, it was largely the result of their own initiatives and their desire to be a part of organized feminism. The apparent inability to bring working women into women's organizations and networks at an early stage has been a hallmark of twentieth-century feminism. In the Japanese case, it may have been even more costly than in other countries, given the numbers of women involved and their overriding importance to the economy.

The universals in the Japanese experience are obvious, though some, the total denial of access to political structures, for example, seem extreme. The importance of the lack of economic independence, the devaluation of women's work, the treatment of women as property and their lack of legal identity in the family, the pervasive double standard, and the state's assumption of the right to determine the use of both women's bodies and their minds are part of the common experience of women that seems to differ only in degree, not substance, in the Japanese case.[9] There are also confirming feminist patterns in the Meiji experience, among them the effort to make connections with international feminism and the strength of the mother-daughter relationship among well-known feminists. The supportive relationships between Kishida, Fukuda, and Raichō and their mothers will certainly come as no surprise to anyone working in women's history today, whether in the United States or China.

After 1900 feminism in Japan was carried on the shoulders of individuals and small groups of women who refused to give up the struggle, but who understandably had great difficulty organizing the power of women in their own behalf. Their inability to create strong organizations and maintain the fragmenting networks of the women's movement is testimony to the effectiveness of class division and government interference in Japan, but their resilience meant that the feminist program developed before 1900 was not lost; it was heard and refined by the women who came later. Very few of the demands made by outspoken Meiji feminists were met in their lifetimes; many of the issues they raised are still unresolved. But the willingness of Meiji women to make the fight for social change they thought would be beneficial not only to them, but to their society, has made significant differences in the lives of all Japanese women.

Notes

Notes

Unless otherwise stated, the place of publication for the works cited in these Notes is Tokyo. The ten-volume collection *Nihon fujin mondai shiryō shūsei* (1976–80) is cited by the abbreviation *NFM*.

Chapter One

EPIGRAPH: Quoted in Miyoshi Masao, *As We Saw Them* (Berkeley, Calif., 1979), p. 76. See also Yanagawa Masakiyo, *The First Japanese Mission to America*, tr. Junichi Fukuyama and Roderick H. Jackson (New York, 1938), p. 56.

1. Miyoshi, pp. 73–74. Other writers have commented that the mission members were even more surprised by the apparent power of women in the Perry household in Belmont, N.Y.

2. *Ibid.*, p. 76.

3. On the "true woman" and the implications of her accession to that role in America and Europe, see Nancy Cott, *The Bonds of Womanhood* (New Haven, Conn., 1977); Gerda Lerner, "The Lady and the Mill Girl," in Lerner, *The Majority Finds Its Past* (New York, N.Y., 1979), pp. 15–31; Kathryn Kish Sklar, *Catherine Beecher* (New Haven, Conn., 1973); and Erna Olafson Hellerstein, Leslie Parker Hume, and Karen M. Offen, eds., *Victorian Women* (Stanford, Calif., 1981).

4. Cited in Leonore Davidoff, *The Best Circles* (Totowa, N.J., 1973), p. 95.

5. The first use of the term borrowed womb (*hara wa karimono*) to describe women in Japan is ascribed to a literary work—Ishida Mitoku's *Gogin Wagashu*, which was written sometime between 1661 and 1672 (Joyce Ackroyd, "Women in Feudal Japan," *Transactions of the Asiatic Society of Japan*, series 3, 30.7, Nov. 1959, p. 62).

6. Unlike aristocratic women elsewhere, whose difficulties in the

family might be cushioned by economic privilege, many samurai women in 1860 lived in more impoverished conditions than the women in some farming and merchant families. See *ibid.,* pp. 56–58, for a discussion of specific demands made on samurai women.

7. *Mikudari han,* or the three and one-half lines that became customary for letters of divorce, were sent home with the offending bride. Ackroyd, p. 65, quotes a typical example: "I received your daughter to wife, but since she does not please me, I now divorce her. Hereafter, there is no objection to her marrying anyone else. For this reason, I make this declaration."

8. Tokugawa law declared that it was no crime for a husband to kill an adulterous wife and recommended that offending wives be put to death, preferably with the man involved. How harsh this could be is graphically illustrated by the kabuki play "The Drum of the Waves of Horikawa," first performed in 1706 (and, in 1958, made into a powerful film, *Night Drum,* by Tadashi Imai). It shows the disintegration of a family when the suspicion of adultery touches a young samurai's wife. She is forced to kill herself, and the rest of the family spends itself in a vendetta, ending with the death of the itinerant drum teacher who was involved.

9. See, for example, the arguments of John C. Pelzel, "Japanese Kinship: A Comparison," in Maurice Freedman, ed., *Family and Kinship in Chinese Society* (Stanford, Calif., 1970), pp. 227–48.

10. Translation from Ackroyd, pp. 53–54.

11. Matsudaira Sadanobu (1758–1829), quoted in *ibid.,* p. 56.

12. See R. P. Dore, *Education in Tokugawa Japan* (Berkeley, Calif., 1965), pp. 317–22. Dore estimates that, on the basis of school attendance, male literacy in Japan was roughly 50%, and female literacy 10% in the middle of the 19th century.

13. For an introductory discussion of these differences, see Takamure Itsue, *Takamure Itsue zenshū,* 10 vols. (1966–67), vols. 4 and 5.

14. There are many Japanese novels, implicitly or explicitly critical of the family system, that explore this destructive tendency at length. See, for example, Ariyoshi Sawako, *The Doctor's Wife,* tr. Wakako Hironaka and Ann Siller Konstant (1978).

15. The successful merchant houses of the Tokugawa period developed detailed "constitutions" that often mirrored the practices of the samurai *ie* (house/family) in matters of succession to and transfer of property, approval of marriages, and the general conduct of the house. Women in these merchant houses were, legally, only a little better off than samurai women.

Chapter Two

EPIGRAPH: Quoted in Alice Rossi, *The Feminist Papers* (New York, 1973), p. 469.

1. Baron Suematsu's comments, published in 1904, are typical of the period: "The position of woman in Japan has always been different, to a significant extent, from that of the same sex in other Asiatic countries. Looking back to the history of Japan over thousands of years, we see many renowned figures of the fair sex." ("Woman's Education," in Alfred Stead, ed., *Japan by the Japanese*, New York, 1904, p. 255.) Alfred Stead, the great British champion of Japan, commented that "Japan's greatness as a nation is an effective contradiction of the widely held opinion that one-half her race occupies an inferior position intellectually to the others" (*Great Japan*, New York, 1906, p. 360).

2. For an interesting discussion of "geisha society," see Takamure Itsue, *Takamure Itsue zenshū* (1977), 5: 490–512. Takamure points out that several government leaders, among them Kido Takayoshi, Yamagata Aritomo, and Itō Hirobumi, were married to former geisha.

3. Murray, an American educator from Rutgers, spoke and published widely in support of the idea that Japanese women must be included in educational reform for the sake of Japan's future generations (Mitsui Reiko, ed., *Gendai fujin undō shi nempyō*, 1976, p. 9).

4. For long periods in early and mid-Meiji, the percentage of girls attending school under the compulsory system was 20% or less of those eligible, compared with 50% and more of the eligible boys (Tanaka Sumiko, ed., *Josei kaihō no shisō to kōdō*, 1975, 1: 123–24).

5. Kuroda's comments are paraphrased in Charles Lanman, ed., *The Japanese in America* (New York, 1872), p. 46.

6. See Tsunoda Fusako, "Tsuda Umeko," in Enchi Fumiko, ed., *Jimbutsu Nihon no josei shi* (1978), 12: 22–26; and Takamizawa Junko, *Nijūnin no fujintachi* (1969), pp. 62–63.

7. Mitsui, p. 7.

8. Fukuda Hideko, *Warawa no hanshōgai* (1976), pp. 13–14.

9. Hanna Papanek, "Development Planning for Women," in Wellesley Editorial Committee, *Women and National Development: The Complexities of Change* (Chicago, 1977), p. 15.

10. The 1877 version of Spencer's *Social Statics* was the first translation of a Western work bearing on the question of women's rights. In 1881, a separate translation of his chapter on women was published as *Joken shinron* (New Essay on Women's Rights), and a complete translation of the work appeared in the same year. The British feminist Millicent Fawcett's work was also translated in 1881 and published as *Fujin sansei no ken o ronzu* (Making a Case for Women's Political Rights). (Tanaka, 1: 48–49.)

11. The best work in English on the Meirokusha is William Braisted, trans., *Meiroku Zasshi* (Cambridge, Mass., 1976). His introductory essay gives a history of the society and a complete description of its members.

12. But its circulation was not negligible. *Nichi Nichi Shimbun*, one of Tokyo's leading newspapers, for example, had only an 8,000 circulation in that period (*ibid.*, p. xx).

13. Mori Arinori, "On Wives and Concubines," part 2, *Meiroku zasshi*, 11 (June 1874), translated in *ibid.*, pp. 143–45.

14. Fukuzawa Yukichi, *An Encouragement of Learning*, tr. David Dilworth and Umeyo Hirano (1969), p. 53.

15. *Ibid.*, pp. 52-53.

16. *Ibid.*, p. 55.

17. Mori, part 5, 27 (Feb. 1875), translated in Braisted, pp. 331–33.

18. *Meiroku zasshi*, 32 (March 1875), translated in *ibid.*, p. 399.

19. See Katō Hiroyuki, "Abuses of Equal Rights for Men and Women," *Meiroku zasshi*, 31 (March 1875), translated in *ibid.*, pp. 376–79.

20. Fukuzawa, "The Equal Numbers of Men and Women," *Meiroku zasshi*, 31 (March 1875) translated in *ibid.*, pp. 385–86.

21. Fukuzawa Yukichi, *Gakumon no susume*, in Ishida Takeshi, ed., *Fukuzawa Yukichi shū*, vol. 2 of *Kindai Nihon shisō taikei* (1975), p. 4.

22. Mori, part 4 (Nov. 1874), translated in Braisted, pp. 252–53.

23. Mitsukuri Shūhei, "On Education," *Meiroku zasshi*, 8 (May 1874), translated in *ibid.*, p. 108.

24. Nakamura Masanao, "Creating Good Mothers," *Meiroku zasshi*, 33 (March 1875), translated in *ibid.*, p. 402.

25. *Ibid.*, p. 403.

26. Braisted, pp. xli–xliii.

27. Ienaga Saburo credits Fukuzawa with advocating reforms in the family that were possible only after Japan's defeat in the Pacific War. Though he feels Fukuzawa compromised with feudal custom more than Ueki Emori, an organizer of the popular-rights movement, Ienaga believes Fukuzawa's work, especially *Nihon fujinron* (An Essay on Japanese Women; 1885) and *Onna Daigaku hyōron; Shin Onna Daigaku* (A Critique of the Greater Learning for Women; A New Greater Learning for Women; 1899) should be valued as an important pioneering effort. (*Fukuzawa Yukichi*, 1963, pp. 37–38.)

Chapter Three

EPIGRAPH: Fukuda Hideko, *Warawa no hanshōgai* (1976), p. 16. A *kappa* is a mythical animal said to frequent riverbanks in Japan, and to resemble an otter except for its strange expression, its dish-shaped head (which must be filled with water at all times), its fondness for cucumbers, and of course, its ability to comprehend human language. The day after Fukuda's participation in these political activities, prefectural officials closed ("pending further investigation") the private school she and her mother had opened the previous year to provide basic education for women. The school never reopened, although Fukuda and her family established other private schools in later years patterned after this initial effort in Okayama. (Murata Shizuko, *Fukuda Hideko*, 1965, pp. 24–27.)

1. That debate, stimulated by the Western threat to Japan, had initi-

ated the reevaluation of native and Chinese traditions and the exploration of European political theory; and had been brought up to date, in the 1870's, by would-be Social Darwinists, who stipulated that voting, an acquired right, should not go to "women, minors and criminals." See Sotozaki Mitsuhiro, *Kōchi ken fujin undō shi* (1975), pp. 21–24.

2. On the 1874 memorial of Itagaki and his followers demanding representative political institutions, and on their early activities in Shikoku, see Nobutaka Ike, *The Beginnings of Political Democracy in Japan* (Baltimore, Md., 1950), pp. 56–71.

3. For a discussion of the exclusion of women from the liberal revolution fostered by the ideas of John Locke and Jean Jacques Rousseau, see Zillah Eisenstein, *The Radical Future of Liberal Feminism* (New York, 1981), Chaps. 3 and 4.

4. Sotozaki, pp. 24–25.

5. The early leadership's commitment to natural-rights theory in a general sense was always open to question in any case. Itagaki's speech "On Liberty," delivered in Kochi in 1882, is often used as an example of his conception of "upper-class democracy" (Roger W. Bowen, *Rebellion and Democracy in Meiji Japan*, Berkeley, Calif., 1980, p. 110).

6. For a discussion and documentation of this change, see *ibid.*, Chap. 3.

7. For an abbreviated account of the debate on the motion, which was put forward by Hirayama Yasuhiko, see *NFM*, 2: 83–84; and for earlier debates, *NFM*, 3: 86.

8. Quoted in *NFM*, 8: 102–3. On Kusunose Kita's (1833–1920) political role in Shikoku, see Sotozaki, pp. 30–32.

9. On Ueki and his ideas, see Ienaga Saburō, *Ueki Emori kenkyū* (1960) or Ienaga Saburō, *Ueki Emori senshū* (1974). For an account of his friendships with women in the political movement and his support of women's rights, see Sotozaki Mitsuhiro, *Ueki Emori to onnatachi* (1976). For a more critical view of Ueki's feminism, see Tanaka Sumiko, ed., *Josei kaihō no shisō to kōdō* (1975), 1: 53–61.

10. His "Danjo dōken ni tsuite koto" (Equality Between the Sexes), published June 13, 1879, is thought to be the first published essay advocating equal rights for men and women (Sotozaki, *Ueki Emori*, p. 49).

11. Sotozaki, *Kōchi ken*, p. 30, characterizes accounts describing Kusunose's role as speaker and activist for the popular-rights movement after 1881 as *tsukuribanashi* (made-up stories).

12. Ike, *Beginnings of Political Democracy*, p. 102.

13. See Bowen, *Rebellion and Democracy*.

14. See, for example, the descriptions in Irokawa Daikichi, *Shimpen Meiji seishin shi* (1973).

15. Lois Banner comments on Jacksonian America's reinforcement of "traditional definitions of separate masculine and feminine spheres of behavior, particularly after the women's rights movement challenged it. The average politician, patterning himself after Andrew

Jackson, strove to be forceful and aggressive. Martin Van Buren was ridiculed for his elegant manners. The political world was masculine, its competitiveness symbolized by party battles and . . . elections, in which heavy drinking and fist fights were the order of the day." (*Elizabeth Cady Stanton*, Boston, 1980, pp. 42–43.)

16. Tanaka, 1: 45–46.

17. Kishida's itinerary is listed in Sōma Kokkō, *Meiji shoki no san josei* (1940), but the most detailed description of her speaking tours is contained in Murata Shizuko, "Kishida Toshiko no yūzei to sono eikyō," *Rekishi hyōron*, 4 (1960): 5–7.

18. Sumiya Etsuji, "Jiyū minken no bijin tōshi," *Bungei shunjū*, 43 (1965): 236–44.

19. Takamure Itsue, *Takamure Itsue zenshū* (1977), 5: 679.

20. Sōma, pp. 40–41.

21. Morosawa Yōko, *Onna no rekishi*, 2 vols. (1970), 2: 71–73.

22. Fukuda, *Warawa no hanshōgai*, pp. 15–16.

23. *Ibid.* Murata Shizuko, *Fukuda Hideko* (1965), is one of the best treatments of this important Meiji personality. It is also one of the best biographies written on a Meiji-period figure. The only source on Fukuda in English is Sharlie Conroy Ushioda, "Women and War in Meiji Japan: The Case of Fukuda Hideko (1865–1927)," *Peace and Change: A Journal of Peace Research*, 4 (Fall 1977): 9–12.

24. Murata, "Kishida Toshiko," pp. 6–7.

25. Showa joshidai kindai bungaku kenkyūshitsu, *Kindai bungaku kenkyū sōsho* (1957), 6: 42.

26. "Dōhō shimai ni tsugu" (To My Brothers and Sisters) is reprinted in *NFM*, 8: 103–13. This article, the first written by a woman advocating equality between the sexes, was originally published in *Jiyū no tomoshibi*, May 18–June 22, 1884. "Haikoiri musume" (Daughters Confined in Boxes) was reprinted by *Jiyū shimbun* in 1883 (411; Nov. 20), but a more accessible version is provided in Itoya Toshio, *Josei kaihō no senkusha tachi* (1975), pp. 37–46.

27. Kishida expressed her admiration for the work of Millicent Fawcett and the women who had joined together to present a petition to Parliament asking for equal rights for women in England. She expected women in the West to win their struggle, because it was just. ("Dōhō shimai," p. 113.)

28. *Ibid.*, p. 103.   29. *Ibid.*, pp. 105, 112.

30. *Ibid.*, p. 104.   31. *Ibid.*, pp. 104–5.

32. For school attendance summaries, see Mitsui Reiko, ed., *Gendai fujin undō shi nempyō* (1976), *passim*.

33. Kishida, "Hakoiri musume," p. 41.

34. Kishida, "Dōhō shimai," p. 105.

35. Kishida, "Hakoiri musume," p. 43.

36. *Ibid.*, pp. 38–45.

37. Sumiya, "Jiyū minken," pp. 240–41.

38. Sotozaki, *Kōchi ken*, pp. 34–35.

39. Ike, *Beginnings of Political Democracy*, pp. 156–57.

40. See Bowen, *Rebellion and Democracy*, for a description and analysis of these events.
41. Ike, p. 165.
42. From an article by a woman published in *Taiyō shimbun*, July 17, 1884, cited in Sotozaki, *Kōchi ken*, p. 37.
43. Itoya, *Josei kaihō*, pp. 45–46, points to a newspaper account describing the crowd's reaction to Kishida's speech as the reason for her arrest; in this context, the "box" of "Hakoiri musume" becomes a metaphor for government repression of the popular-rights movement, and the speech itself an attack on government, rather than the family system. Sumiya, p. 240, likewise feels that the titles of Kishida's speeches may not have matched their "political" content.
44. In an article in the May 24, 1884, edition of *Taiyō shimbun*, the writer expressed the hope that "in the days to come . . . all of the women in this area will organize in friendship so that, in unity, we can acquaint one another with political ideas and cultivate freedom" (cited in Sotozaki, *Kōchi ken*, pp. 36–37).
45. Newspapers, including those in Shikoku, published articles critical of women's education in this vein from 1883 through the 1890's (*ibid*, p. 36).
46. *Ibid.*, p. 39.
47. *Ibid.*, p. 36.
48. This article is apparently the first work on women's rights published by a woman; though it has been given much less notice by historians than Fukuzawa Yukichi's *Nihon fujinron* (An Essay on Japanese Women) and Ueki Emori's *Tōyō no onna* (Eastern Women) it preceded both (published, respectively, in 1885 and 1889).
49. Sōma, *Meiji shoki*, pp. 57–58.
50. Murata, *Fukuda*, pp. 24–27.
51. Fukuda, *Warawa no hanshōgai*, pp. 16–17.
52. Murata, *Fukuda*, p. 44; Fukuda, p. 28.
53. Murata, *Fukuda*, p. 46.
54. *Ibid.*, pp. 31–49.
55. Fukuda was supposed to have read an account of Joan of Arc that impressed her greatly; the description of her as Japan's Joan of Arc in a work on her life published after her arrest was picked up by the newspapers and often used in later accounts.
56. *NFM*, 3: 377–85.
57. Yoshimi Kaneko, "Yajima Kajiko," in Enchi Fumiko, ed., *Jimbutsu Nihon no josei shi* (1978), 11: 174–76.
58. Improving living and working conditions for women was an implicit, if not explicit, goal of the Reform Society, but the society was particularly concerned about the sexual abuse of women factory workers, an issue referred to in several textile disputes of the period.
59. Yoshimi, pp. 175–76.
60. *Chōya shimbun*, June 20, 1889, p. 1.
61. *Jogaku zasshi*, 170 (July 13, 1889).
62. *NFM*, 3: 377–86.

63. A copy of the revised law appears in *NFM*, 2: 131–34. Maruoka Hideo comments that these severe political restrictions on women came against the background of Kishida's advocacy, Fukuda's involvement in the Osaka Incident, and Japan's first strike in 1886. "There is," she says, "a clear relationship between these events and the revised law, particularly between the labor strikes and the new restrictions." (*Fujin shisō keisei shi*, 2 vols., 1975, 1 41–42.)

64. See *NFM*, 2: 35–36.

65. *Ibid.*, p. 35.

Chapter Four

EPIGRAPH: Cited in Yamamoto Shigemi, *Āa Nomugi Tōge* (1977), pp. 15–16. This work, based largely on oral histories, has become a classic source on working women. A film based on the book was produced in Japan in 1979.

1. *Ibid.*, p. 19.

2. *Ibid.*, p. 49.

3. *Ibid.*, pp. 29–30.

4. Selling daughters into prostitution was one of many drastic measures destitute families used to survive difficult times, including the depression of the late 1920's and early 1930's. Other ways of trading daughters for cash included selling them to a geisha for training and apprenticeship and sending them off to live with wealthy families, where they were often not only family servants, but concubines as well.

5. The figures in the following table are not complete, but they convey a sense of the involvement of women in Japan's industrial revolution.

Women in the Factory Labor Force of Japan, 1894–1911
(Establishments with 10 or more operatives)

Year	Factories	Women workers	Total workers	Percent women
1894	5,985	239,000	381,000	62.7%
1898	—	235,000	412,000	57.0
1899	6,699	264,378	423,171	62.5
1903	8,274	301,435	483,839	62.3
1905	10,361	369,233	612,177	60.3
1907	11,390	400,925	649,676	61.7
1911	—	476,497	793,885	60.0

SOURCES: *Teikoku nenkan*, vols. 13–15 (1893–96); Yokoyama Gennosuke, *Nihon no kasō shakai* (1945 reprint; originally published 1899), pp. 145–50, 203–13; Ministry of Agriculture and Commerce, *Menshi boseki shokkō jijō* (1903); Ministry of Agriculture and Commerce, *Kōjō chosa yoryō* (1904), p. 7; International Labour Office, *Industrial Labour in Japan*, Studies and Reports, Series A, No. 37 (London, 1933); Sanpei Kōko, "Meiji zenki ni okeru fujin oyobi yōnen rōdōsha no jōtai," *Rekishi kagaku*, 5 (1936).

6. The importance of light industry to the whole economy and the government's appreciation of that fact are made clear in Sanpei Koko, "Meiji zenki ni okeru fujin oyobi yōnen rōdōsha no jōtai," *Rekishi kagaku*, 5 (1936). See also Thomas C. Smith, *Political Change and Industrial Development in Japan: Government Enterprise, 1868–1880* (Stanford, Calif., 1955), p. 58.

7. Mori Arinori, acting as a Japanese consular official in the United States, wrote at length about American textile mills in 1872. "A leading American writer," he commented, "said that the patron saint of Lowell was Work; that the factory girls might be counted by the acre; that the motto over the gateways should be 'Work or Die'; and that fifty factories in the city were each larger and more imposing than the temples of worship in Japan and China." Impressed by what he had learned, he speculated: "If something like this enterprise can be transported to Japan, what may we not expect, in the future, from that Empire?" (Charles Lanman, ed., *The Japanese in America*, New York, 1872, pp. 250, 256.)

8. Yamamoto, pp. 25–26. For a description of Japan's early difficulties with the silk market, see Smith, pp. 54–60.

9. Akamatsu Yoshiko comments, in a foreword to the third volume of *NFM*, p. 1: "At the time Japan was . . . taking the initial steps toward industrialization, women were just making their appearance as wage laborers. From that time to this [1978], throngs of women have gone to work as 'women workers,' 'women factory workers' and/or 'employed women.' . . . Sometimes flattered, sometimes held in contempt . . . though society could not have existed without them, women workers were never able to rise above the lowest wage-earning levels."

10. Hugh Patrick's comments, first reported in the Social Science Research Council's *Items*, 28 (June 1978): 33, are worth noting in this context: "One has been tempted in the past to dismiss female industrial workers as an unimportant category, only temporarily employed, with no distinctive life style, analytically uninteresting. An unexpected feature of the [SSRC] conference was the rehabilitation, as it were, of analysis of the role of women in Japan's industrialization." See also Hugh Patrick, ed., *Japanese Industrialization and Its Social Consequences* (Berkeley, Calif., 1976), p. 11.

11. Many of these works are now classics of Japanese labor history. They include Yokoyama Gennosuke, *Nihon no kasō shakai* (1899); *Shokkō jijō* (1903); Hosoi Wakizō, *Jokō aishi* (1925); Yamamoto Shigemi, *Āa Nomugi Tōge* (1968): and Wada Ei, *Tomioka nikki* (1976). Yasue Aoki Kidd, "Women Workers in the Japanese Cotton Mills: 1880–1920," Cornell University East Asia Papers No. 20 (1978), is based largely on Hosoi's *Jokō aishi* and contains the best analysis of it in English.

12. Many different commentators have pointed out that, in spite of the Confucian description of women's work as "inner" as opposed to the man's "outer" tasks, Japanese farm women not only reared children, but also managed the household, worked in the fields, spun

thread, made clothes, and did piecework. Merchant women worked beside their husbands, and often, like farm women, did piecework at home for cash as well. Samurai women, as we have already seen, also often did piecework at home for cash. See, for example, Tsumura Setsuko, "Jokō aishi," in Enchi Fumiko, ed., *Jimbutsu Nihon no josei shi* (1978), 11: 215.

13. *NFM,* 3: 55–57.

14. Women in contemporary Japan have struggled against this pattern established in Meiji, but have had great difficulty in the face of management policies encouraging their "retirement" and marriage at age 24 or 25, and their consequent lack of access to seniority systems that are at the heart of upward mobility in all Japanese companies. The number of married women who work is increasing in Japan. A large number of the working women, however, are classified as part-time by their employers, a characteristic they share with American working women. In Japan, recent studies show that women who work part-time average 7 hours a day on the job, and that in some companies full-time women work 9:00 to 5:00, whereas part-time women work 8:00 to 4:00. See Alice H. Cook and Hiroko Hayashi, Working Women in Japan, Cornell International Industrial and Labor Relations Report No. 10 (1980); and Fujin hakusho, ed., *Nihon fujin dantai rengokai* (1970), pp. 80–82.

15. In announcing the opening of the Tomioka mill, the first of three modern silk-reeling mills established before 1880, the government noted the declining reputation of Japanese silk in foreign markets, the need for change, and its willingness to initiate that change: "When the reputation of our most important product was about to be destroyed, how were we to overcome this evil? The government, wishing to recover from this decline, . . . has built a large silk reeling mill at Tomioka . . . at great expense to the public treasury. Reelers and instructors have been summoned from France. . . . Four hundred women will be employed and will be instructed solely in silk reeling. . . . The women employed by the government, after they have been given instruction, . . . will be transferred to the various districts, where they may be used to teach." (Quoted in Smith, *Political Change,* p. 59.)

16. Wada Ei, *Tomioka nikki* (1976), pp. 167–68.

17. Before the dining room was completed, meals were brought to workers' rooms; such unusual treatment must have produced the same reaction in some Tomioka workers as it did in at least one New England worker. "One Manchester mill girl was overcome by the unfamiliar luxury of her 'very pleasant front room.' . . . 'It seems funny enough to be boarding. I don't even have my bed to make. Quite a lady, to be sure.'" (Quoted in Benita Eisler, ed., *The Lowell Offering,* New York, 1977, p. 26.)

18. For Tomioka regulations and instructions to students, see *NFM,* 3: 172.

19. Wada, p. 20.

20. Some observers of the Tomioka operation were able, with less than 5% of the capital the government had invested there, to establish their own mills with 50 workers. The emphasis was always on technology, though many foreign advisers pointed out the link between working conditions and productivity. When night work was established, mill owners ignored the warnings of French advisers that such long hours would ultimately lessen productivity. (Yamamoto, *Āa Nomugi Toge*, pp. 42–44; Murakami Nobuhiko, *Meiji josei shi*, 4 vols., 1969–72, 3: 162.)

21. *NFM*, 3: 378–79.

22. Lanman, *Japanese in America*, pp. 249–51. Mori added, in an amusing afterthought: "But these immigrants, as they grow in intelligence, . . . demand higher wages, shorter hours for work, and more freedom. They have learned the European lesson of fighting employers by combinations. . . . The problem has become so confused that manufacturers are beginning to look for relief to the Chinese."

23. *Shokkō jijō*, ed. Tsuchiya Takeo (1947), 1: 65. *Shokkō jijō* was originally published by the Ministry of Agriculture and Commerce in 1903, but was allowed only limited circulation by the government because of its clear and detailed descriptions of the abuse of workers in the textile industry. It is thought that the government commissioned the study primarily because tuberculosis was spreading through Japanese society, and the mills seemed to be a major source of the problem (Murakami, 3: 124).

24. *Shokkō jijō*, 1: 53; 3: 326–28.

25. Indeed, several writers have made the point that signing contracts with textile mills was not terribly different from selling a daughter into prostitution. See, for example, Takamure Itsue, *Takamure Itsue zenshū* (1977), 5: 368–71; and Tsumura, 11: 221.

26. Yamamoto, pp. 14–15.

27. *Ibid.*, p. 17: "There were mothers like those of Nabari Tsuya and Tada Ei who could not leave; they followed all the way to Okatani and worked in the mill there."

28. Kidd, "Women Workers," p. 12.

29. Yokoyama, *Nihon no kasō shakai*, pp. 70, 107–12. A single spinning company reported 2,800 desertions among women living in company dormitories in 1899; joint-stock company reports for the year 1898 indicated that nearly 50% of all females employed in the factories stayed less than a year, and a very large percentage of that group remained for less than 6 months. See also Kidd, pp. 16–19.

30. Gary R. Saxonhouse reports that the apparent (and well-publicized) efforts of the Kanebō mill in Hyōgo to institute more humane treatment of workers had little or no effect: in 1897, 44% of its workers left within 6 months; by 1914 the figure had risen to more than 55%. He also expresses skepticism that "the mill dormitories . . . were the

prisons they were made out to be" because of the high percentage of successful escapes. It is an argument Yasue Aoki Kidd describes as "curious," for "the fact that one can escape from prison . . . does not negate the reality of the prison. Workers were . . . treated like prisoners as long as they were . . . in the employ of the mills." (See Saxonhouse, "Country Girls and Communication Among Competitors in the Japanese Cotton Spinning Industry," in Hugh Patrick, ed., *Japanese Industrialization and Its Social Consequences,* Berkeley, Calif., 1976, pp. 103–4; and Kidd, pp. 64–65.) Though I agree that the number of successful escapes does not negate the prisonlike conditions in the mills, and that it is logical to assume the harshness of those conditions provided the strongest kind of motivation for potential escapees, it should be remembered that employers could benefit too (e.g., by confiscating back pay or a savings account left behind). The conflicting evidence of relatively easy escape in some mills, and harsh, unrelenting punishments for those who attempted it in others does not, on its face, seem so contradictory, given the diversity of the industry and its conditions. However, it is clear that more research is needed comparing conditions in various kinds of mills and changes over time.

31. Yamamoto, p. 22.

32. Yokoyama, pp. 205–6.

33. *Shokkō jijō,* 1: 26–27. See also pp. 19–22 of the same work. The Japanese thus managed to follow the West in producing, at least in some cases, the 36-hour shift that Marx had found so shocking.

34. It is interesting that in spite of the evidence of harassment by male supervisory personnel reported in *Shokkō jijō* and elsewhere, women workers are described in the literature less as victims (except of circumstance) than as aggressors. "Life in the textile industry has been criticized as approximating that of a desert, which drove female factory workers to satisfy their hunger and their sexual desires by having trysts with men" (Hazama Hiroshi, "Historical Changes in the Life Style of Industrial Workers," in Hugh Patrick, ed., *Japanese Industrialization and Its Social Consequences,* Berkeley, Calif., 1976, p. 32). The source Hazama uses (Yokoyama's *Nihon no kasō shakai*) does describe the worker's environment as a desert, but the conclusion that they were driven to satisfy their sexual desires in this way is the author's, and it is typical of such descriptions of women workers. What Meiji textile workers were driven to do, we may not be able to prove. But the reality of the environment in which women were recruited and worked made them extremely vulnerable to harassment and sexual violence of various kinds. According to Hosoi, *Jokō aishi,* p. 58 (cited in Kidd, p. 12), recruiters routinely raped or compromised the young women they were escorting to the mills. *Shokkō jijō,* vol. 1, has numerous references attesting to the fact that male floor supervisors had absolute control over the women working on their shifts, and that during night work they often treated these women as a private harem. In larger companies, the floor super-

visors recommended bonuses, reported tardiness, docked workers' pay for various infractions, and ultimately decided how long the shift would be. It was extremely important for women working with these men not to displease them.

35. For a detailed description of these conditions, see Kidd.

36. Yamamoto, p. 22.

37. Another universal is the differential between men's and women's wages. In Japan and the United States today, women make roughly 60% of what men make. In the early textile mills, even in the first days of Lowell, when owners boasted the highest wage paid to women anywhere, women made about 50% of men's wages. In Japan the average was probably about 75% at that time, but men were paid a fixed amount, whereas women's basic wages were figured on a quota; if a worker did not make the quota, she could lose her wages for the day. (Eisler, *Lowell Offering*, pp. 15–19; *Shokkō jijō*, 1: 37–38.)

38. Kidd, pp. 24–30; Hosoi, pp. 152–53.

39. According to descriptions in both Hosoi, pp. 134–37, and Yamamoto, pp. 23–25, it was impossible to earn a substantial bonus in this factory system without risking serious health problems. The 100-yen worker described in Yamamoto, for example, dies as she is being carried home from the factory by her brother.

40. See Hosoi, pp. 182–85. See also, for various examples, Yamamoto, Chaps. 1 and 2.

41. Kidd, pp. 32–36. In fact, the spread of tuberculosis from textile workers to the general population remained a major social problem well into the modern period. At one point, the medical staff of the Japanese army became concerned that tuberculosis from the mills in various areas of Japan was affecting the health of the local draftees. See Ishihara Osamu, *Eiseigaku jō yori mitaru jokō no genkyō*, 1913; and Ishihara Osamu, *Jokō no genkyō*, 1928, pp. 175–97.

42. Spinning associations, which kept fairly careful statistical records, seem to have spared themselves the burden of both suicides and many of the deaths due to tuberculosis that occurred away from company grounds.

43. Yamamoto, *Āa Nomugi Tōge*, pp. 55, 133–41.

44. This is the general description given in such standard labor histories as Ōkochi Kazuo, *Reimei-ki no Nihon rōdō undō shi* (1952); and Kishimoto Eitarō, *Nihon rōdō undō shi* (1950).

45. The association was organized by Takano Fusatarō and Katayama Sen. For an account of some of their activities, see Hyman Kublin, *Asian Revolutionary: The Life of Sen Katayama* (Princeton, N.J., 1964).

46. For a discussion of women textile workers as pioneers of Japan's labor movement, see Akamatsu, *NFM*, 3: 27–28.

47. Male unionists were objecting, as late as 1920, to being represented at meetings of the International Labor Organization in Geneva by women "with no consciousness" (Kosho Yukiko, *Bungo no onna dokō*,

1979, p. 100). On the difficulties encountered by women workers in Japan's labor movement, see Yamanouchi Mina, *Yamanouchi Mina jiden* (1975), *passim*.

48. Thus standard explanations for the slow start of the union movement in Japan focus as much on the predominance of "unorganizable" female textile workers in the industrial work force as on the government's suppression of union activities. See, for example, Ōkochi; Kishimoto; and Akamatsu Katsumaro, *Nihon rōdō undō hattatsu shi* (1925).

49. Except where otherwise noted, the details on these early strikes, and specifically on the Amamiya and other Kōfu strikes discussed below, are drawn from *NFM*, 3: 377–89.

50. See *ibid.*, p. 27; and Ōkochi, pp. 23–28.

51. This strike came closest to winning major demands, and workers continued to stay off the job in the face of harassment by management. In that sense, it was more successful than other textile strikes, both in Japan and in the United States.

52. It is interesting to compare this situation with Sarah Bagley's Female Labor Reform Association in New England and its efforts, in the 1840's, to educate and organize textile workers throughout the region in "turnouts" protesting worsening conditions of work. The Reform Association seems to have relied heavily on free access to and circulation of newspapers and journals, as well as the connections its leaders made as they traveled from place to place. It is difficult to imagine that any of this could have been possible in the Japanese textile industry in the 1880's.

53. Reliable comparative statistics are not widely available, but Saxonhouse, "Country Girls," p. 99, provides the following data on the percentage of women in the factory work forces of various countries:

1900		1901		1911	
Belgium	23.9%	France	31.5%	India	17.4%
U.S.	32.6	Italy	37.4	Italy	46.2
Japan	61.6	Japan	61.3	Japan	59.9

54. According to Murata Shizuko, Shimizu gave speeches in many areas, including at least one speech for women factory workers (*Fukuda Hideko*, 1965, p. 64).

55. Early British and American suffrage movements communicated little, if at all, with women workers. There were workers at the American women's rights convention in Seneca Falls, N.Y., in 1848, and Elizabeth Cady Stanton included them in the Declaration of Sentiments, but none of the feminists made connections with the Female Labor Reform Association, which was coming apart in 1848 (Carol Hymowitz and Michaele Weissman, *A History of Women in America*, New York, 1978, p. 136).

56. On the creation of the new aristocracy, see Ienega Saburō, *Nihon kindai shisō shi kenkyū* (1967).

57. The lady and the mill girl image is borrowed from Gerda Lerner's now classic essay "The Lady and the Mill Girl," in Lerner, *The Majority Finds Its Past* (New York, 1979).

Chapter Five

EPIGRAPH: The bylaws are printed in *NFM*, 1: 206–7, citing *Jogaku zasshi*, 44 (Dec. 15, 1886); the quote is from Asai Saku, "Kyōfūkai no mokuteki," *Tokyo fujin kyōfū zasshi*, 1 (April 1888), cited in the same source, pp. 211–13.

1. There was virtually no opposition to the Sino-Japanese War from those who would later oppose the Russo-Japanese War. Kitamura Tōkoku, one of the earliest and most consistent advocates of peace and the individual's right to reject government demands for acquiescence in its policies, died just a few months before the war began in 1894. On popular support of the war, see Donald Keene, "The Sino-Japanese War of 1894–95 and Its Cultural Effects in Japan," in Donald H. Shively, ed., *Tradition and Modernization in Japanese Culture* (Princeton, N.J., 1971), pp. 121–75; and Nobuya Bamba and John Howes, eds., *Pacifism in Japan* (Vancouver, B.C., 1978).

2. After the Sino-Japanese War, Russia, France, and Germany, forced Japan to retrocede Port Arthur on the Liaotung peninsula. Port Arthur, a warm water port, was critical to the Russians' Far Eastern policy, and after forcing the Japanese to give it up, they leased it from the Chinese in 1898. The end of the war with China could thus be seen by government and military leaders as a prelude to war with Russia. See Roger Hackett, *Yamagata Aritomo in the Rise of Modern Japan, 1828–1922* (Cambridge, Mass., 1971), pp. 166–71.

3. Leavitt's tour of Japan was sponsored by *Jogaku zasshi*.

4. Yoshimi Kaneko, "Yajima Kajiko," in Enchi Fumiko, ed., *Jimbutsu Nihon no josei shi* (1978), 11: 174–75.

5. Takamizawa Junko, *Nijūnin no fujintachi* (1969), pp. 6–14.

6. Tokutomi Iichirō, *Nihon meijoden* (1928), pp. 126–28. Tokutomi Iichirō (Sohō) was the editor of *Kokumin no tomo* (The Nation's Friend), an influential mid-Meiji journal; his brother, Tokutomi Kenjirō (Roka), was a writer. Both were critical of their aunt throughout their lives, though Sohō consistently claimed a reluctant admiration for her.

7. Yoshimi, pp. 162–63.

8. *Ibid.*, p. 164.

9. Kubushiro Ochimi, ed., *Yajima Kajiko den* (1935), pp. 196–99; Takamizawa, p. 16.

10. The parallels with Nancy Cott's description of the New England Female Moral Reform Society are interesting. "The moral reformers' aim took them outside the family. . . . Since they believed that men practiced licentiousness, and women suffered it, they were sensitive to prevailing sexual injustice. They opposed the double standard . . . as much as they opposed licentiousness." (*The Bonds of Womanhood*, New

Haven, Conn., 1977, pp. 152–53.) Since none of the Reform Society women were likely to have read Engels' *Origin of the Family* or Emma Goldman's "The Traffic in Women," they were undoubtedly not aware of some of the potential arguments they were creating, but they certainly experienced the interconnectedness of sexuality, politics, and economics in their work on behalf of women. For an interesting contemporary discussion of that interconnectedness, see Gayle M. Rubin, "The Traffic in Women: Notes on the 'Political Economy' of Sex," in Rayna Rapp Reiter, ed., *Toward an Anthropology of Women* (New York, N.Y., 1975), pp. 157–210.

11. For a description of the Rokumeikan and its social events, see Donald H. Shively, "The Japanization of the Middle Meiji," in Shively, ed., *Tradition and Modernization in Japanese Culture* (Princeton, N.J., 1971), pp. 93–96.

12. These were advantages that neither women in the popular-rights movement nor women workers were able to manage. Consequently, by 1890 the Reform Society was *the* women's organization in the country.

13. An example from *Tokyo fujin kyōfūkai zasshi*, 29 (Sept. 20, 1890): 8: "Succumbing to the easier life of prostitution . . . they brazenly walk the streets in broad daylight. . . . There is no way to stop them other than to shame them into reforming!"

14. There is an interesting contemporary connection to these early efforts in the protests Japanese women have made of company-sponsored *kisaeng* tours to Korea, offering Japanese men the services of Korean prostitutes. Organizers of the protests, many of whom are members of Japan's WCTU, have emphasized the connections between the tours and Japan's sexist, racist, imperialist history.

15. The plight of the *karayuki san* was publicized in *Sandakan No. 8*, an internationally acclaimed film based on Yamasaki Tomoko, *Sandakan hachiban shōkan* (Tokyo, 1972).

16. *Tokyo fujin kyōfūkai zasshi*, 18 (Aug. 16, 1890): 7. Letter to the magazine from Kawaguchi Masuye.

17. *Ibid.*, 29 (Sept. 20, 1890): 8. For a discussion of Japanese prostitutes sent to America, see Yuji Ichioka, "Ameyuki-san: Japanese Prostitutes in Nineteenth Century America," *Amerasia Journal*, 4.1 (1977): 1–23.

18. *Tokyo fujin kyōfūkai zasshi*, 32 (Dec. 20, 1890): 2–3.

19. This position was reinforced by petitions to the government requesting that children of concubines be listed as illegitimate, and that adultery be added to the criminal code as an offense applying to men as well as women.

20. Nakajima Toshiko, "Nihon shakai no kūki," *Jogaku zasshi*, 153 (March 16, 1889): 10.

21. Asai Saku, "Giin senkyo ni tsuite," *Tokyo fujin kyōfū zasshi*, 27 (July 19, 1890): 3.

22. Shimizu Toyoko's article protesting the regulations reads curiously like Kishida's earlier essay "Dōhō shimai ni tsugu" in its reiteration of woman's qualifications for intellectual and public life: "Naniyue ni joshi wa seidan shūkai ni sanchō suru to o yurusarezaruka?" *Jogaku zasshi*, 228 (Aug. 30, 1890): 61–64.

23. *NFM*, 2: 126.

24. Shimizu Toyoko, "Naite aisuru shimai ni tsugu," *Jogaku zasshi*, 234 (supplement, Oct. 11, 1890): 2.

25. *Ibid.*

26. *NFM*, 2: 87–88. A number of incidents were recorded in the early part of the decade involving women in various parts of Japan who were fined or arrested after they tried to hold or attend meetings that local authorities interpreted as political. See Mitsui Reiko, ed., *Gendai fujin undō shi nempyō* (1976); and *NFM*, 10: 38–44.

27. After 1895, especially, the society was heavily engaged in organizing relief efforts for victims of industrial pollution, earthquakes, and other man-made and natural disasters.

28. *NFM*, 1: 233–34. The society's shelters were also intended to provide a home for young women who, after escaping the mills, migrated to the cities and were easily recruited as prostitutes. One of the goals was to teach women the kinds of skills they needed to support themselves and help them find employment.

29. Mitsui, pp. 61–62.

30. Donald Shively makes the point that as early as 1884, after Itō's return from Germany, the government began an ambitious program to perpetuate authoritarianism within the coming constitutional system by blending Confucian language with Prussian institutions; a notable example was the creation of the peerage in that year ("Japanization of Middle Meiji," pp. 84–89).

31. Nagai Michio, "Westernization and Japanization," in Donald H. Shively, *Tradition and Modernization in Japanese Culture* (Princeton, N.J., 1971), pp. 69–76.

32. Komano Yoko, "Ie shisō no kakuritsu," in Tanaka Sumiko, ed., *Josei kaihō no shisō to kōdō* (1975), 1: 131–32.

33. In 1887, for example, there were 40 mission schools, many of which offered a high school curriculum (Sugaya Naoko, "Kirisutokyo to sono shūhen no joseikan," in *ibid.*, pp. 64–65).

34. Komano, pp. 127–28.

35. Nagai, p. 45.

36. On Catherine Beecher and the education of American women, see Kathryn Kish Sklar, *Catherine Beecher, A Study in American Domesticity* (New York, 1976).

37. Quoted in Komano, p. 124.

38. Sōma Kokkō, *Mokui* (1977), and Shimazaki Tōson, *Sakura no mi no juku suru toki* (1919), are both autobiographical novels that bear out the special relationships between teachers and students, as well as the

intellectually exciting and romantic atmosphere of *Meiji jogakkō*. Noguchi Takehiko has described the mission school as "first and foremost" a place where young men and women could meet freely. The "emotions of romantic love welling up within young Meiji intellectuals were those awakened by the singing of hymns to the accompaniment of the organ." ("Love and Death in the Early Modern Novel: America and Japan," in Albert M. Craig, ed., *Japan: A Comparative View*, Princeton, N.J., 1979, pp. 161–69.)

39. See Fukuda (Kageyama) Hideko's comments in *Joken*, 1 (Sept. 1891), for an example of this tendency.

40. Shimizu Toyoko, "Tōkon jogakusei no gakugo ikaga," *Jogaku zasshi*, 239 (Nov. 15, 1890): 364–66.

41. For a discussion of Hatoyama and her ideas, see Takamure, *Zenshū*, 5: 538, 547–54.

42. Hatoyama insisted, after 1900, that women should not involve themselves in politics, a position incomprehensible to Fukuda and others who later initiated a campaign to rescind Article 5, but also puzzling to many other women, including some members of the Japan Women's Patriotic Association (discussed in Chap. 6, below). See, for example, editorial comments in *Aikoku fujin*, 11 (Aug. 25, 1902), supporting the political actions of the Reform Society.

43. The French legal scholar Gustave Emile Boissonade (1825–1910) was appointed by the Ministry of Justice to draft Japan's criminal code in 1873, and was then assigned the task of drafting a new civil code. The criminal code, based on combined elements of Japanese feudal law and the Code Napoléon of 1804, was put into effect in 1882. The civil code was sent back for revision twice, in 1878 and again in 1890. In 1891 Hozumi Yatsuka, a leading Meiji jurist and supporter of absolute monarchy, fiercely attacked the civil code as conceived by Boissonade. This attack, which appeared in the legal journal *Hōgaku shimpō* in Aug. 1891, initiated a conservative push to redraft the code. The revision emphasized the authority of the father as head of the family (as the Meiji Emperor was head of the Japanese family state), and the authority of the family over the individual. Much of the work on the revised draft was done by Hozumi Nobushige (the elder brother of Yatsuka) and his conservative colleagues in the legal establishment. (See *NFM*, 5: 151–276.) The final version that was accepted in 1898 contained very few of Boissonade's original recommendations. For a summary of the provisions of the Japanese civil code before and after the Pacific War, see Watanabe Yōzō, "The Family and the Law: The Individualistic Premise and Modern Japanese Family Law," in Arthur Taylor von Mehren, *Law in Japan* (Cambridge, Mass., 1963), pp. 364–98.

44. Takamure, *Zenshū*, 5: Chap. 3.

45. Or, as Komano, "Ie shisō," p. 129, puts it: "The greatest casualties in the distortion of the modernization process . . . were women. In order to strengthen patriarchal authority under the civil code, it was

necessary to strengthen the basis of discrimination between men and women in education, and emphasize the lovely feminine virtues of subordination and submission."

46. See Chūbu katei eigyōgaku kenkyū kai, eds., *Meiji ki katei seikatsu no kenkyū* (1972), pp. 37–49.

47. Komano, p. 136.

48. As colleagues have pointed out to me, there are some interesting parallels between the political roles assigned to Japanese women by the patriarchy and the "Republican mother" who, denied a real political role after having been politicized by the experience of the American Revolution, was kept on the periphery of the political community. Her "political" role was in the home: "To the mother's traditional responsibility for maintainance of the household economy, and to the expectation that she be a person of religious faith, were added the obligation that she also be an informed and virtuous citizen. . . . She was to guide her husband and children. . . . She was to be a teacher as well as a mother." (Linda K. Kerber, *Women of the Republic,* Chapel Hill, N.C., 1980, p. 235.) In the Japanese case, what Hozumi and other architects of the new female role sought was the narrowest definition of education and patriotism, one that demanded, not rationality, but submissiveness from mothers and their children. The denial of political rights to women in Japan seems to have gone further than anything on paper in American history, though it had the character of the disenfranchisement of women and free Blacks by white American males bent on maintaining a monopoly over political power. But it *is* clear, in both cases, that men made conscious decisions about "proper" political roles for women, and that those roles were thought to be domestic and private.

Chapter Six

EPIGRAPH: *Sekai fujin,* 2 (Jan. 15, 1907): 1.

1. Okumura Ioko (1845–1907), described in the *Biographical Dictionary of Japanese History* as a "Meiji period leader in women's social work," was an interesting personality whose earliest political interests stemmed from her family's close connections to the *sonnō jōi* (revere the Emperor, throw out the barbarians) faction in late Tokugawa. Married and widowed, Ioko remarried in 1872 and then was divorced in 1887. At that point she began to devote much of her energy to Japan's interests in Korea and China. When Japanese troops were sent to North China during the Boxer Rebellion, she recognized that the wounded would need proper care and their families would require assistance, and with the backing of Konoe Atsumaro, president of the Upper House of the Diet, founded the Aikoku Fujinkai. (Iwao Seiichi, ed., *Biographical Dictionary of Japanese History,* 1978, p. 443.)

2. *Aikoku fujin,* Feb. 10, 1904.

3. Mitsui Reiko, ed., *Gendai fujin undō shi nenpyō* (1976), p. 55.
4. Kindai joseishi kenkyūkai, eds., *Onnatachi no kindai* (1978), pp. 121–22.
5. *Ibid.*
6. In 1900, for example, Yoshioka Yayoi, who had once expressed a desire to "become a woman like Kageyama Hideko," was given a room in Shisei Hospital for her new Tokyo Women's Medical School. The same year Tsuda Umeko (1864–1929), having graduated from Bryn Mawr, fulfilled a dream she had discussed with her friend Alice Bacon a decade earlier, establishing the Academy of English Studies for Women, a college-level institution, in Tokyo. (Morosawa Yōko, *Shinno no onna,* 1974, 1: 272.) Tsuda was the youngest of the group of girls who accompanied the Iwakura Mission to the United States in 1871. Her school, known later as Tsuda College, was recognized in the Meiji period as a superior institution of higher learning for young women. The college still exists, but the curriculum is now devoted almost exclusively to vocational training.
7. Quoted in Murata Shizuko, *Fukuda Hideko* (1965), pp. 26–27.
8. *Ibid.*, pp. 66–70. The school was typical of the efforts Fukuda and her mother tried to make for working women and their children; it was open to women of all ages and emphasized practical education. Boys were admitted only up to the age of 13.
9. *Ibid.*, pp. 81–86.
10. *Ibid.*, pp. 88–89.
11. The party platform called for an end to the Police Security regulations, the reduction of armaments, the abolition of the Upper House, universal suffrage, and public ownership of major land and capital resources (Kishimoto Eitarō, ed., *Shiryō Nihon shakai undō shisō shi, 1955,* 11: 155–59).
12. They published a number of interesting works, including Kōtoku Shūsui's "Nijū seiki no kaibutsu teikokushugi" (Imperialism, the 20th-Century Monster; 1901) and "Shakaishugi shinzui" (The Essence of Socialism; 1903), as well as translations of the writings of Saint-Simon, Lassalle, and Henry George.
13. In 1901 the former popular-rights faction was led by Kōtoku Shūsui, the Christian Socialists by Abe Isō, and the unionists by Katayama Sen.
14. Kōtoku Shūsui, *Hyōron to zuisō* (1949), p. 154.
15. The declaration issued at the founding of the Heiminsha illustrates the breadth of the organizers' ideology at this point: "The three great principles of all humanity are freedom, equality, and benevolence. . . . We want to strike down class, to eradicate oppression . . . completely. . . . It is necessary that there be common ownership of production, and that both production and distribution be controlled by the entire society. . . . We hope to join hands with the world in ridding ourselves of armaments and halting war, without reference to political or racial differences . . . but we completely repudiate such temporary

measures as the resort to violence to gain our ends." (*Heimin shimbun*, 1, Nov. 15, 1903: 1.)

16. Kinoshita and Sakai both wrote extensively about women's issues, particularly in the pages of *Katei zasshi*. But their colleagues interested themselves in the subject only peripherally, addressing questions they had read about in literature from the international movement or considering the narrow question of Japanese women and their support of the war. Kōtoku Shūsui, who described himself as "in love with love, but not with marriage" ("Fujin shokan," *Sekai fujin*, 2, Jan. 15, 1907: 2), was well known for his chauvinist attitudes toward women, but his views probably differed only in degree from those of many other men in the socialist movement.

17. The diary kept at the Heiminsha headquarters records Fukuda as a frequent visitor (Ōta Masao, ed., *Heiminsha nikki: Yo wa ikani shite shakaishugisha to narishika*, 1972).

18. Murata, *Fukuda Hideko*, p. 100.

19. *Chokugen*, 2.4 (Feb. 26, 1905); *Heimin shimbun*, 60 (Jan. 1, 1905): 6.

20. Murata, p. 102.

21. *Ibid.* They called him Shibugaki (lit., "sour persimmon"), usually only after he had been drinking.

22. *Ibid.*, p. 103.

23. *Heimin shimbun*, 19 (March 20, 1904): 1.

24. Sakai spent two months in jail after the newspaper published an article criticizing the higher taxes resulting from the war, and the government began to harass dealers and subscribers of the newspaper in June 1904 (Shirayanagi Shūko, *Saionji Kimmochi den*, 1929, pp. 486–88.)

25. An examination of socialist newspapers published from November 1903 through June 1909 (excluding Fukuda's *Sekai fujin;* Women of the World) reveals, in each case, fewer than five women contributors over the entire period. The papers I checked are *Chokugen, Heimin shimbun* (weekly), *Hikari, Osaka Heimin shimbun, Shakai shimbun,* and *Shin kigen,* most of which have been reprinted in the *Meiji shakaishugi shiryō shi* series.

26. The Diet members were Ebara Sōroku and Nemoto Sei (*Sekai fujin*, 3, Feb. 1, 1907: 2).

27. *Heimin shimbun*, 64 (Jan. 29, 1905): 1.

28. The text of Kōtoku's speech was printed in *Hikari*, July 5, 1906: 1.

29. *Chokugen*, 2.12 (April 23, 1905).

30. *Sekai fujin*, 1 (Jan. 1, 1907): 1.

31. Murata, *Fukuda Hideko*, p. 125.

32. Fukuda bent only so far as to make the argument in slightly modified form (to emphasize the plight of poor women). But she clung to her basic position through issue 37, one of the last she published. Kōtoku Shūsui published the first article advising women to pursue

socialism as a means to their own liberation in the Oct. 15, 1902, issue of *Yorozu chōhō*. (Mitsui, *Gendai fujin undō shi nenpyō*, pp. 58–59.)

33. *Heimin shimbun*, May 22, 1904.
34. *Sekai fujin*, 16 (Sept. 1, 1907): 1.
35. *Ibid.*, 37 (June 5, 1909): 1.
36. *Ibid.*
37. On the burdens of housework, child care, economic support, and editing that Fukuda carried, see Joseishi kenkyūkai, eds., *Fukuda Hideko kenkyū* (Nagoya, 1962), pp. 2–6.
38. *Sekai fujin*, 7 (April 1, 1907): 2.
39. Murata, pp. 147–48.
40. For a detailed description of the Red Flag Incident, see Sakai Toshihiko, *Nihon shakaishugi undō shi* (1954), pp. 193–96.
41. Murata, pp. 148–50.
42. *Ibid.*

Chapter Seven

EPIGRAPH: From Maeda Toshiko, *Nyonin no sho* (1974), pp. 250–51. Kanno also said, in this letter: "I appreciate your concern over Shūsui; however, I ask that you remind people that this too is fate, and one should resign oneself to it. Now it seems his mother's death was, for her and for Kōtoku as well, a blessing. . . . I was very disappointed that I was unable to see the two of them, even briefly, when they came to Tokyo; I was very resentful for a time of what seemed to me unkind. . . . Now I think it was not unreasonable, and all I have are fond memories of the past."

1. As we will see later, in Chap. 8, Itō Noe, the common-law wife of Ōsugi Sakae, was jailed and strangled by a policeman in 1923.
2. Maeda, p. 24.
3. Arahata Kanson, *Kanson jiden* (1961), p. 126.
4. Itoya Toshio, *Kanno Suga* (1970), p. 16. Udagawa was in his 50's at the time; Kanno was about 22. It is possible that Kanno was supporting her father and brothers as well as herself at this point.
5. *Ibid.*, pp. 22–24.
6. Kanno Suga (pen name Yūgetsujo), "Yonin no haha ue," *Murō shimpō*, 576 (April 3, 1906), reprinted in Sekiyama Naotarō, ed., *Shoki shakaishugi shiryō* (1959), pp. 147–48
7. Itoya, pp. 41–42; Ota Masao, ed., *Heiminsha nikki* (1972), p. 38.
8. Reported in *Heimin shimbun*, 49 (Oct. 16, 1904): 3.
9. See *Murō shimpō*, 561 (Feb. 15, 1906), reprinted in Sekiyama, pp. 141–42.
10. See Arahata, p. 125.
11. After attending a charity event for the Hakuaisha in April 1906 with her sister, Kanno remarked that society should be held responsible for the suffering of orphaned children, and that socialism would address the root of the problem (Itoya, p. 64).

12. Kanno Suga (pen name Sugako), "Fujin to dokusho," *Murō shimpō*, 540 (Dec. 9, 1905), reprinted in Sekiyama, pp. 119–20.

13. Kanno Suga (pen name Yūgetsujo), "Hiji deppō," *Murō shimpō*, 580 (April 15, 1906), reprinted in Sekiyama, pp. 162–63.

14. Kanno Suga, "Danshi sokumenkan," *Murō shimpō*, 587 (May 6, 1906), reprinted in Sekiyama, p. 183.

15. Kanno Suga (pen name Yūgetsu), "Toshi no hajime," *Murō shimpō*, 664 (Jan. 1, 1907), reprinted in Sekiyama, p. 207.

16. *Heimin shimbun* reporters were arrested regularly trying to cover the Ashio riots; on one occasion, Arahata had to fill in for Nishikawa Kōjiro when he was arrested (Itoya, *Kanno Suga*, p. 94).

17. Arahata Kanson, *Hitosuji no michi* (1954), p. 153.

18. *Ibid.*, p. 154; *Heimin shimbun*, 30 (Feb. 24, 1907).

19. Arahata's descriptions of Kanno are striking in their failure to discuss, even superficially, her intelligence or her ideas. On the other hand, he is the primary source on her reputation for promiscuity, claiming that she had or tried to have a sexual relationship with nearly every man she encountered before and after she met him. Those claims, whether accurate or relevant, have been rather uncritically accepted by many of the people who have written about her, and indeed made the focal point of discussion about her. That many of Arahata's descriptions of colleagues, including Kanno, are self-serving and somewhat distorted seems obvious enough; why in Kanno's case they continue to be accepted is puzzling. In one often-quoted description of their relationship, Arahata portrays himself as an innocent and naïve young man, and Kanno as a not particularly beautiful woman, but one so fully versed in attracting men that "it must have been as easy as twisting a baby's arm" for her to seduce him. In another passage, he describes Kanno's work for *Osaka chōhō* as "mediocre," explaining that she was doing as well as she could with the little talent and education she had. (*Kanson jiden*, pp. 123–27.)

20. Kōtoku later claimed that she was the only woman arrested in the Red Flag Incident to proclaim her anarchism openly, but the record shows only that she expressed sympathy with anarchist views, as Kamikawa Matsuko did (*Jiyū shisō*, 1, May 25, 1909: 1, reprinted in Rōdō undōshi kenkyūkai, eds., *Kumamoto hyōron*, 1962, p. 275).

21. See Itoya, pp. 108–12.

22. *Jiyū shisō*, 2 (June 10, 1909), reprinted in Rōdō undōshi kenkyūkai, eds., p. 277.

23. *Kumamoto hyōron*, 27 (July 20, 1908): 1, reprinted in *ibid.*, p. 223.

24. Sakai Toshihiko, *Nihon shakaishugi undō shi* (1954), pp. 193–96.

25. Itoya, p. 137.

26. Katayama Sen, commenting on the routine surveillance of Kōtoku after the Red Flag Incident, notes that "his house was guarded by four policemen, two in front and two in back. Everyone who visited him was forced to give his name, and then this person was also followed by a detective." (*The Labor Movement in Japan*, Chicago, 1918, pp. 132–35.)

27. This chronology is Kanno's; see her trial testimony in Shidoda Shōbei and Watanabe Junzō, eds., *Hiroku Daigyaku jiken* (1959), 2: 106, 219.

28. Criticism of Kōtoku was often expressed in other terms (e.g., he was not providing sufficient leadership), but a major issue in the community then, and after his execution in 1911, was his apparent betrayal of Arahata, still in prison. Arahata did little to dispel that notion after his release from prison, letting it be known that he and Kanno had been married while he was in prison. (Shioda Shōbei, ed., *Kōtoku Shūsui no nikki to shōken* 1965, p. 288; Itoya, *Kanno Suga*, pp. 138–39.)

29. That Kanno might play the same role as Sofia Perovskaia played in the nihilists' assassination of the Tsar in 1881 was the suggestion of Niimura Tadeo. Kanno's response was that she would do more than give signals in such a case. Since her execution, Kanno has often been compared with both Sofia Perovskaia and Catherine Breshovsky, the so-called grandmother of the Russian Revolution, but the comparison is a superficial one at best: women were heavily involved in terrorist activities in 19th- and 20th-century Russia. They also, as Gail Lapidus points out, paid heavily for it; besides Perovskaia herself, who was executed, 21 women were among the 43 terrorists who received life sentences at hard labor in the years 1880–90 (*Women in Soviet Society*, Berkeley, Calif., 1978, p. 38).

30. The growing mystery shrouding the Japanese Emperor was a political fact of the Meiji period not lost on socialists like Kōtoku, who had warned of its danger much earlier. The tendency to withdraw the Emperor from public life, then speak in his behalf, using his enormous symbolic power as a political weapon, grew more pronounced in the Taishō period.

31. Itoya Toshio, *Kōtoku Shūsui kenkyu* (1967), p. 277.

32. *Ibid.*, pp. 279–81.

33. She expected to be in jail for at least 100 days; the fines the government had imposed on Kanno and Kōtoku were well over 400 yen.

34. Miyashita's efforts to construct and test bombs were particularly easy to trace since he made little effort to keep them secret.

35. At the suggestion of Koizumi, Kōtoku had begun work on an account of the civil war period in Japan; but when he went to Yugawara, he decided instead to write a refutation of Christianity that he had always been interested in. It was this book, *Kirisuto massatsuron*, that was taking him to Tokyo.

36. It is widely believed that the government, as it had in the Red Flag Incident, used events in 1910 opportunistically, to rid itself of the few socialists who were not already in prison. Police were well aware that, at most, 5 people were directly involved in the discussions of the assassination: Kanno, Kōtoku, Miyashita, Niimura, and Furukawa. See commentary in *Daigyaku jiken arubamu*, comp. Kōtoku Shūsui zenshū henshu iinkai (1972), pp. 130–33.

37. The description is that of the defense lawyers, quoted in Itoya, *Kōtoku,* p. 314.

38. Samples of that protest are reproduced in *Daigyaku jiken arubamu,* pp. 106–9.

39. Ōsugi, Kōtoku's intellectual heir, composed the following poem in the spring after the executions: "Spring has come and now / In April / I, left unhanged, / Dance in the blossoms." (Translated in Tsuzuki Chushichi, "Kōtoku, Ōsugi and Japanese Anarchism," *Hitotsubashi Journal of Social Studies,* 3, 1966: 38.)

40. The police had been trailing most members of the group for a long time before they actually arrested anyone; the pretrial interrogation and trial testimony contained in Shioda and Watanabe, *Daigyaku jiken,* make it clear that the government could have moved much earlier but hoped to incriminate as many people as possible by delaying the arrests.

41. Describing him as *bumptisu no hito* (a man of letters), she was nonetheless careful to delineate his responsibilities; she referred to him often as one of the five who had discussed terrorist revolutionary methods, but was firm on the point of his withdrawal and disapproval of their plans in January (*ibid.,* 1:106, 219–51).

42. Figner, one of the participants in the assassination of Alexander II, said at her trial in 1884: "All my experience had convinced me that the regime could only be changed by violence. Without liberty of the press the dissemination of ideas through the written word is impossible. If some social institution had shown me some other way of achieving Russia's liberty perhaps I would have adopted it. I would certainly have tried it. But I saw that there could be no solution except by violence." (Ronald Seth, *The Russian Terrorists,* London, 1966, pp. 156–57.) Figner was sentenced to death, but her sentence was later commuted to imprisonment. After 20 years in prison, she was first exiled and then allowed to go abroad. She returned to Russia as a heroine after the 1917 revolution.

43. Shioda and Watanabe, 1: 220–21.

44. The fragment of the diary that remains begins at Jan. 17; Jan. 1–16 was never found. For a reprint of the fragment, see Kanzaki Kiyoshi, *Daigyaku jiken* (1964), pp. 63–64.

45. Morosawa Yōko, *Onna no rekishi,* 2 vols. (1970), 2: 154.

46. Itoya, *Kanno Suga,* pp. 210–12, 226.

47. Shioda and Watanabe, 1: 238. Dated Dec. 1, 1910.

Chapter Eight

EPIGRAPH: Hiratsuka Raichō, *Genshi, josei wa taiyō de atta,* 4 vols. (1971–72), 1: 328–32, reprint of *Seitō,* 1.1 (Sept. 1, 1911).

1. *Ibid.,* pp. 332–33.

2. It was perhaps logical, given class differences and the lack of good information about socialist women interested in feminist issues or

about Kanno Suga's history as a woman, not just an ideologue, that women at the end of Meiji would have had difficulty making connections. But the difficulties late-Meiji women had have been compounded for postwar women by less easily explained tendencies in recent years to describe the Seitōsha as "Japan's first feminists," and their founding statement as Japan's "first declaration of women's rights."

3. Hiratsuka, 1: 330–31.

4. *Ibid.*, p. 338.

5. *Ibid.*, pp. 149–55.

6. It is widely assumed that Raichō's inspiration was from Shintō, since the image of the sun goddess Amaterasu, the original ancestor of the Japanese, comes from Shintō mythology. Raichō credits the image to no special circumstance or inspiration, but she did say, in answer to those who see in it some link with Nietzsche's heroic figures, that Zen had a much greater influence. (*Ibid.*, pp. 334–35.)

7. The incident takes its name from the title of a novel Sōhei later wrote containing a description of his well-publicized relationship with Raichō (Ide Fumiko, *Seitō no onnatachi*, 1975, pp. 24–25).

8. Hiratsuka, 1: 328.

9. Ide, p. 22.

10. In an effort to make sure the magazine was not a financial disaster, the Seitōsha sent out 1,000 postcards pre-announcing the new publication to potential subscribers (Hiratsuka, *Genshi*, 1: 323).

11. *Ibid.*, p. 295.

12. Yosano's poem, "Sozorogoto," uses the metaphor of a rumbling volcano, long dormant in a mountain, for the power of women. Ide Fumiko describes it as reflective both of Yosano's own life and the aspirations of the Seitōsha. The poem, the first few lines of which have been translated under the title "Mountain-Moving Day," has become a hallmark of international feminism, though few people who see it know much about its author. Most of the poem is printed in Ide's *Seitō no onnatachi*, pp. 12–16.

13. Among the other women who joined the magazine after the first issue were Okamoto Kanoko, Kamichika Ichiko, Hara Asao, Mikashima Yoshiko, Senuma Kayō, and Nishizaki Hanayo. The three youngest members of the staff, Itō Noe, Kobayashi Katsu, and Odake Kazue, joined when they were still in their teens.

14. Murasaki Shikibu, whose celebrated work *The Tale of Genji* is generally accepted as the world's first novel, was a part of a society that not only produced other important female authors, but apparently offered many options to women that were not available later. At the moment, the question of the status of women in Heian is the subject of intense research and debate in Japan.

15. Maeda Toshiko, *Nyonin no sho* (1974), p. 253.

16. The only full-length work in English on Yosano is Sanford Goldstein and Shinoda Seishi, *Tangled Hair* (Lafayette, Ind., 1971).

17. Morosawa Yōko, *Onna no rekishi*, 2 vols. (1970), 2: 134–35.

18. Yosano's attitudes toward convention and custom, including sexuality, were both individual and complex. Though the erotic content of her early poetry and her involvement in a celebrated triangle with her future husband Tekkan and her friend Yamakawa Tomiko suggest a willingness to flout social custom, Akiko spent the rest of her life in a very settled monogamous relationship with Tekkan, bearing 13 children (11 of whom lived) and providing most of the economic support for the household. In addition to all of the poetry she produced, Yosano Akiko was a superb essayist. She also produced one of the major translations of *The Tale of Genji* into modern Japanese.

19. Ide, *Seitō no onnatachi*, pp. 50–51.

20. See Noriko Mizuta Lippit, *Reality and Fiction in Modern Japanese Literature* (White Plains, N.Y., 1980), chap. 1.

21. Hiratsuka, *Genshi*, 2: 352.   22. *Ibid.*

23. *Ibid.*, p. 404.   24. *Ibid.*, pp. 403–6.

25. *Ibid.*, p. 374.

26. *Ibid.*, 2: 371–72. Odake, who later married a well-known potter, Tomimoto Kenkichi, was a free spirit and a very creative young woman, whose relationship with Raichō has often been described as lesbian-like. Raichō, while admitting her affection for the woman who called herself Kōkichi (Kazue), later said that she "had always tried to maintain some distance and made an effort to control the situation." "It seemed," she wrote, "that though Kōkichi had many interesting male friends" and "was familiar with many poets and artists, . . . she was not attracted to the opposite sex." (*Ibid.*, p. 368.) Individual and social attitudes toward lesbians in Japan are questions that could and should occupy a separate volume. In this context, two issues are important: (1) the extent to which lesbianism was a spoken or unspoken source of the social criticism the Seitōsha (and earlier feminists) faced and (2) the implications of Raichō's own attitude (revealed in her comments about Kōkichi). There is no question that in Meiji Japan, as everywhere else, feminists (irrespective of their sexual identification) were often dismissed as lesbians or "man-haters," or both. Fukuda Hideko, suspected of lesbianism in prison and later castigated as an immoral woman for her relationship with Ōi Kentarō, was busy explaining, in her *Sekai fujin* days, that she was not a "man-hater." In Raichō's case (though one could hardly expect a proclamation of "political lesbianism" on the order of Ti Grace Atkinson's in the second wave of American feminism), the comments about Kōkichi and her own recollections of their relationship raise questions about her identification with women of the sort Blanche Cook discusses in "Lesbianism and the Cultural Tradition," *Signs*, 4.4 (Summer 1979): 718–39.

27. Hiratsuka, *Genshi*, 2: 376–77.

28. *Ibid.*, p. 375.

29. *Ibid.*, p. 377.

30. Ide, *Seitō no onnatachi*, pp. 119–24.

31. *Ibid.*, pp. 129–32.

32. Hiratsuka, 2: 424–26. Ellen Key (1849–1926) argued for the creative and biological superiority of women, as well as their importance in "improving and preserving" the race. The price women paid for this superiority in her view was relinquishing the outside world in favor of woman's mission, the ultimate source of her creativity: motherhood. Key, who remained single all her life, expressed some understanding of women who preferred the "life of the soul" to that of the family but decried the loss of the "most valuable . . . from the standpoint of generation. When these are content with one child or none . . . then it is their work, not the race, which receives the richness of their blood, the fire of their creative joy . . . the beauty of their feelings. . . . But it may be . . . that there are annually produced by the women of the world a hundred thousand novels and works of art, which might better have been girls and boys!" (*Love and Marriage*, tr. Arthur G. Chater, New York, N.Y., 1979, pp. 216–17.) Key also was a commentator on Ibsen and may have first been noticed by the Japanese in this context. Explaining what she thought Ibsen's appeal for women was, she wrote, that "Ibsen frequently makes the masculine soul inorganic, definitive, finished, determined; the feminine soul, on the other hand, he often makes organic, growing, in evolution" (*The Torpedo Under the Ark: Ibsen and Women*, tr. Mamah Borthwick, Chicago, 1912, p. 14).

33. The essay was widely believed to have been written by Osugi and submitted in his wife's name, but this is no more certain than that Ishikawa Sanshirō wrote Fukuda's socialist feminist essay that appeared later. Japan's socialist women were no doubt influenced by the ideas of the men they lived with, but like women in socialist traditions elsewhere, they found it difficult to establish their own intellectual credentials apart from husbands and lovers.

34. Fukuda Hideko, "Fujin mondai no kaisetsu," *Seitō*, 3.2 (Feb. 1913): 1–2.

35. *Ibid.*, pp. 3–4.

36. Murata Shizuko, *Fukuda Hideko* (1965), pp. 177–82. Though Fukuda showed little fear about raising the issue of socialism in 1913, she does seem to have been uneasy about writing for the Bluestockings, women from whom she felt great social distance. And her discomfort was no doubt justified: Raichō's distaste for Fukuda is obvious in her recollections of the great Meiji feminist.

37. Miyamoto Ken, "Itō Noe and the Bluestockings," *Japan Interpreter*, 10.2 (Autumn 1975): 195, offers the following example of the reaction to Fukuda's article: "If this kind of thinking spreads, the disruptive influence it will have upon the family and society in general will be immeasurable. Such thinking bespeaks a deep despair and resentment toward the male sex—feelings born out of a failure to win husbands and settle down as young brides. As women of Imperial Japan, we would hope that you will not forget your patriotic love for your country."

38. Raichō, "Yō no fujintachi ni," *Seitō,* 3.4 (April 1913). Translated in Pauline C. Reich and Atsuko Fukuda, "Japan's Literary Feminists: The *Seitō* Group," *Signs,* 2.1 (Autumn 1976): 280–91.

39. *Seitō,* 3.4 (April 1913), p. 33.

40. Hiratsuka, *Genshi,* 2: 458. This is one of many examples of the government's ongoing "management" of issues related to the family system and the place of women in it. In the preceding years Kawada Shirō's *Fujin mondai* (The Woman Problem) had been taken out of circulation by the government (in 1910); and Okamura Tsukasa, a professor of civil law at Kyoto University, had been reprimanded for delivering a lecture critical of the family system and the civil code (1911). For details, see Bernard S. Silberman and H. D. Harootunian, eds., *Japan in Crisis* (Princeton, N.J., 1974), pp. 24–25; and Chūbu katei eigyōgaku kenkyū kai, eds., *Meiji ki katei seikatsu no kenkyū* (1972), pp. 42–43.

41. Hiratsuka, *Genshi,* 2: 458–59.

42. *Ibid.,* p. 459; Mitsui Reiko, ed., *Gendai fujin undō shi nempyō* (1976), p. 76.

43. Several authors have noted that one of Itō's greatest frustrations was her lack of foreign-language skills, forcing her to ask others to translate foreign works for her into Japanese. See *Itō Noe zenshu,* 2 vols. (1970), 1: 417–54; and Hiratsuka, *Genshi,* 2: 497.

44. Yuji Ichioka, "Ame-yuki-san: Japanese Prostitutes in Nineteenth-Century America," *Amerasia Journal,* 4.1 (1977): 8, describes Yamada Waka, "a noted writer in Japan before World War II," as follows: "A native of Kurigahama, a small fishing village near Yokohama, she . . . was beckoned to come to America by a man who had been here. Believing his exaggerated tales of riches in this country, she accompanied him to Seattle in 1902. Upon landing, he compelled her to become a prostitute in a Seattle brothel under the nickname Oyae of Arabia. In 1903, befriended by the Seattle correspondent of *Shin Sekai,* an immigrant newspaper of San Francisco, she fled with him . . . only to be forced into prostitution again in a Chinatown brothel. . . . She managed to escape and gained refuge in the Chinese Mission Home, . . . and through eventual self-education became a writer-critic upon her return to Japan. Although Yamada Waka arrived after the turn of the century, her initial fate illustrates the case of women brought by men who personally returned to Japan to secure them."

45. Ide, pp. 204–5.

46. Raichō, then the mother of 2 children, wanted to see both mothers and children protected by the state, a position very similar to Key's. Yosano, the mother of 11, not only thought that this policy would be degrading, but saw such state support as meaning less, not more, independence for both women and their children. (Yosano Akiko, "Hiratsuka san to watakushi no ronsō," in Morosawa Yōko, ed., *Yosano Akiko, Gekidō no naka o iku* (1970), pp. 173–84.

47. Hiratsuka, *Genshi,* 2: 530–35.

48. Yasuda Satsuki, "Gokuchū no onna yori otoko ni," *Seitō*, 5.6 (June 1915): 33–45.

49. Hiratsuka, *Genshi*, 2: 558; Ide, pp. 228–30.

50. Yamada's views of abortion and prostitution in the debates initiated by *Seitō* were very much informed by her conversion to Christianity after her rescue in San Francisco, though she showed more tolerance of individual decisions not to have children than had many others. Yamada remained in the women's movement after *Seitō* stopped publishing, working for suffrage.

51. Emma Goldman, *Anarchism and Other Essays* (New York, N.Y., 1969), p. 179.

52. From an account in Miyamoto, "Itō Noe," pp. 199–200.

53. Kamichika wounded Ōsugi, and he spent some time in the hospital; in the meantime, the press had another celebrated incident among the (former) Bluestockings to discuss (Kondo Tomie, "Itō Noe," in Enchi Fumiko, ed., *Jimbutsu Nihon no josei shi*, 1978, 11: 144–46).

54. Reported by Itō's sister. Ide Fumiko, "Itō Noe koden," in *Itō Noe zenshū*, 1: 430–31.

55. Quoted in Haruko Watanabe and Yoko Nuita, "Fusae Ichikawa: Japanese Woman Suffragist," *Frontiers*, 3.3 (1978): 61.

56. Or, in Noriko Lippit's words: "The Seitō women reflected the consciousness of the Japanese elite; their eyes were turned to the feminism in Europe and America, and they discussed issues in the context of world feminist movements. The Seitō movement represents the Japanese counterpart to the Western development of feminism, the achievement of which, in terms of intellectual endeavor, it matches or surpasses." ("Seitō and the Literary Roots of Japanese Feminism," *International Journal of Women's Studies*, 2.2, March-April 1979, p. 162.

Chapter Nine

EPIGRAPH: Author's interview with Ichikawa Fusae, Tokyo, July 12, 1978.

1. See Yamanouchi Mina, *Yamanouchi Mina jiden* (1975), for an account of women's activities in the Japanese union movement, particularly in the labor federation Yuaikai (Friendly Society).

2. On the continuing efforts of women involved in strikes like the very large and potentially violent Toyo Muslin strike, see Makise Kikue, *Hitamuki no onnatachi* (1976).

3. The New Woman's Society was later replaced by the Women's League and several other organizations pressing for women's political rights, but all of them continued to call for other basic changes as well, from laws barring men with syphilis from marrying to rights and greater protection for working women. See Ichikawa Fusae, *Ichikawa Fusae jiden* (1974), chaps. 3, 5.

4. An example of such rhetoric can be found in the speech given by Kinoshita Seitarō in the 67th session of the Diet, March 20, 1935.

5. For several interesting accounts of the war as it was experienced by women, see Tsurumi Kazuko, *Social Change and the Individual* (Princeton, N.J., 1970); in Japanese, see Kurashi no teicho, eds., *Sensōchū no kurashi no kiroku* (1979).

6. Ichikawa Fusae, commentary in *NFM*, 2: 3–4.

7. See Gail Mieko Nomura, "The Allied Occupation of Japan: Reform of Japanese Government Labor Policy on Women," Ph.D. dissertation, University of Hawaii, 1978.

8. One is reminded, looking at traditional treatments of women in history, of Barrington Moore's wry comment on the treatment of social and cultural continuity in the social sciences. "To maintain and transmit a value system, human beings are punched, bullied, sent to jail, thrown into concentration camps, cajoled, bribed, made into heroes, encouraged to read newspapers, stood up against a wall and shot, and sometimes even taught sociology" (*The Social Origins of Dictatorship and Democracy*, Boston, 1966, p. 486).

9. This fact of women's experience is not such a distant memory, as the following quote suggests: "In the U.S., in principle, abortion is a personal liberty upon which laws cannot infringe. The Japanese legislation does not view abortion as a personal liberty but, rather, as a procedure which is presently legal under most circumstances. Japanese women are vulnerable to changes in abortion law which may make abortion more restrictive. U.S. women are not, in principle, so vulnerable, since it is unlikely that the Supreme Court decision recognizing abortion as a personal liberty would be reversed. And, although a constitutional amendment prohibiting abortion is a possibility, it seems unlikely." (Margaret-Mary Franz and Motoko Chiba, "Abortion, Contraception, and Motherhood in Post-War Japan and the United States," *International Journal of Women's Studies*, 3.1 [Jan.-Feb. 1980]: 67.)

Index

Index